This is not just a Bill. It is a people's charter – a people's charter for the open air, for the hikers and the ramblers, for everyone who lives to get out into the open air and enjoy the countryside. Without it they are fettered, deprived of their powers of access and facilities needed to make holidays enjoyable. With it the countryside is theirs to preserve, to cherish, to enjoy and to make their own.

Rt. Hon. Lewis Silkin M.P.   *Hansard* 31 March 1949

A People's Charter?

Forty years of the *National Parks and Access to the Countryside Act 1949*

Written and edited by John Blunden and
Nigel Curry, with contributions from
Theo Burrell, Gerald Smart, Roger Smith
and Richard Steele.

LONDON HER MAJESTY'S STATIONERY OFFICE

© Crown Copyright 1989

First published 1990

ISBN 0 11 701439 7

British Library Cataloguing in Publication Data.

A CIP catalogue record for this book is available from the British Library.

HMSO publications are available from:

HMSO Publications Centre
(Mail and telephone orders only)
PO Box 276, London, SW8 5DT
Telephone orders 01-873 9090
General enquiries 01-873 0011
(queuing system in operation for both numbers)

HMSO Bookshops
49 High Holborn, London, WC1V 6HB   01-873 0011 (Counter service only)
258 Broad Street, Birmingham, B1 2HE   021-643 3740
Southey House, 33 Wine Street, Bristol, BS1 2BQ   (0272) 264306
9-21 Princess Street, Manchester, M60 8AS   061-834 7201
80 Chichester Street, Belfast, BT1 4JY   (0232) 238451
71 Lothian Road, Edinburgh, EH3 9AZ   031-228 4181

HMSO's Accredited Agents
(see Yellow Pages)

And through good booksellers

Contents

Lord Hunt of Llanfair Waterdine KG, CBE, DSO
Past-President, the Council for National Parks

Foreword

The 40th anniversary of the National Parks and Access to the Countryside Act 1949 occurs at a uniquely opportune and crucially important time. Never before has there been such general public concern about our open spaces, threatened as they are by man's technological progress and ever-growing material demands.

The source of this concern lies very deep in human nature. It has to do with the relationship between man and his native soil; it has to do with a need, however dimly perceived, to preserve spiritual values alongside economic growth. It has to do with the future of life on earth.

The importance of safeguarding our national parks and other areas of coast and countryside must be seen in this context of meeting fundamental human needs. The value of marking this milestone in the conservation movement is that it will serve to strengthen public awareness of, and caring for, our natural environment, and will thus enlighten and influence public policy.

As one who first walked, camped and climbed in some of the areas later designated as national parks as a result of the 1949 Act, I welcome this book, the purpose of which is to ensure that those opportunities are available for future generations.

September 1989

John Hunt

Acknowledgements

The editors would like to express their very warm thanks to:

Liz Savory for her tireless efforts in tracking down many of the pictures that appear in this book; *Paul Smith*, liaison librarian to the Faculty of Social Sciences in The Open University, for his careful checking of our *Further Reading;* and to our respective secretaries *Doreen Warwick* and *Lesley Upton* who word-processed the text in its various drafts with speed and efficiency.

Introduction

The National Parks and Access to the Countryside Act 1949 was the
first comprehensive piece of legislation concerned with the protection
and enjoyment of our countryside for the public at large. It laid the
foundation of many of the statutory conservation and recreation
powers that exist in the countryside today. This volume marks 40
years of the passing of the Act. It was commissioned by the
Countryside Commission, jointly with HMSO, to record and
evaluate progress made since the legislation. Its publication comes
at a time when the future role of national parks, set up as a result of
this Act, is under review.

In Part I, it considers the way in which the main factors that led
to the passing of the Act came together from a number of different
origins. This is a story of wide-ranging, often class-based values
relating to the countryside, manifest in a disparate number of
pressure groups, philanthropists and radical thinkers, all lobbying
government for legislation. Each was concerned to promote its own
ideas about the countryside, and such was their diversity that they
ranged from the exclusion of the public in the name of scientific
preservation to those of mass public access to private land.
Nevertheless, it was hoped that for many the 1949 Act would be a
people's charter.

This first part of the volume traces these pressures right up to the
Act's Royal Assent, focussing, too, on the deliberations that took
place within both the House of Commons and the House of Lords,
some of the main personalities behind the legislation and the
political processes at work inside Westminster. Thus the Act was
born not only of a wide range of visions of a future country-side, but
also, at a public policy level, of a variety of perspectives about the
extent to which the countryside was truly a national resource.

The second part of the volume calls on the views of four people,
pre-eminent in their field, to reflect upon the successes and
shortcomings different parts of the 1949 legislation. Theo Burrell

provides an analysis of how the implementation of the national parks designation has developed over the forty years of the Act. Roger Smith examines the principal impacts of those parts of the legislation concerned with increasing access to the countryside for the public at large. Gerald Smart then explores the principal achievements and shortcomings of the area of outstanding natural beauty designation and other proposals for the wider countryside. Finally, Richard Steele provides a critique of how the nature conservation components of the Act have been implemented, and what kind of nature conservation planning legacy we have inherited as a result.

In his examination of the birth and development of the Nature Conservancy and subsequently, the Nature Conservancy Council, as the Government's chosen instrument to implement its policy for the conservation of wildlife, we are again reminded of that division inherent in the 1949 Act which separated off to the National Parks Commission and later the Countryside Commission, responsibility for recreation and landscape conservation. Long a contentious division, and one to which we refer in Part III, there are, as this book goes to press, indications from the Government that at least in Wales and Scotland these countryside concerns may be handled by one agency.

However, the final part of this volume, to which we now turn, takes a wider perspective in looking back over all the salient inheritances of the Act, as well as looking prospectively towards its implications for the future of our countryside. This it does in a particular way, for in this section we have returned to the views of pressure groups, some of which were set up in the context of the fight for this piece of legislation. Here, we solicit their views in relation to the impact of the Act on the countryside and why, in most cases, they have remained in existence some 40 years after the passing of the Act.

In compiling this section, we have spoken to Kate Ashbrook of the Open Spaces Society, Amanda Nobbs of the Council for National Parks, Fiona Reynolds of the Council for the Protection of Rural England, Tim Sands of the Royal Society for Nature Conservation, Chris Hall for the Ramblers' Association, Laurence Harwood from the National Trust, Stuart Housden of the Royal Society for the Protection of Birds, and representatives of two relatively new organisations with a different raison d'etre from the others. They were Brian Limbury from UK 2000 and Frances Vernon of Friends of the Earth. From these discussions we have provided a blend of official views and personal reflections about the legacy of the 1949 Act and the future, from essentially, outside of the establishment. Clearly all of these groups feel that there is still a job to be done in caring for, and enhancing the opportunities for our enjoyment of, the countryside. It is this ethos which lies behind much of the rationale for their continued existence today.

Thus the book runs full circle. We start with an evaluation of the actions and values of a range of pressure groups concerned with bringing about this pioneering 1949 legislation for the countryside. We end with their views about what has and has not been achieved, forty years on, as a result of its passing. Has the Act provided a 'charter for the people' in making the countryside a truly public resource, or does our legislative inheritance from 1949 leave the countryside the private province of the privileged few?

PART I

1 *The development of the conservation movement*

Conservation values

If there was one main source of inspiration for national parks, national nature reserves and areas of outstanding natural beauty, all of which found their realisation in the National Parks and Access to the Countryside Act 1949, it could be said to be a desire to conserve the countryside in one way or another. Although such a desire is inextricably linked with the enjoyment of the countryside and suitable access to it, much of the story of the emerging pressures leading to the 1949 Act can be told from these conservation and recreation views separately – a distinction that we make with these first two chapters.

This 'desire to conserve the countryside' came about for many different and quite disparate reasons. It is probably not surprising, therefore, that there was really no such thing as a single 'conservation movement' that provided a clear momentum for pressure to introduce the 1949 legislation. There were actually quite a number of different conservation groups with quite separate interests and values that were often to be at loggerheads in the lead-up to the Act. We shall examine some of the motivations behind these groups and the conflicts that they often engendered later in this chapter, but for now it is important to present a brief review of different motivations for, and values of, conservation. This is because at different times and in different ways these values had distinct roles to play in the conservation arguments leading up to the Act.

Conservation values and motivations are widely discussed in many textbooks on conservation and the natural environment. The first chapter of Bryn Green's book, *Countryside Conservation*, for example, outlines five distinct ones, although they are closely related in many ways. First, ethical values suggest that man has some kind of moral obligation towards the stewardship or custodianship of the countryside environment. These values themselves may range from a belief in man's supremacy over nature to one of man's harmonious coexistence as an integral part of it, but they are all related in that they are much less utilitarian than most other perceived reasons for conserving the countryside. These types of value suggest that there is some kind of obligation to protect nature for its own sake, and they provided at least a secondary inspirational source for many people seeking legislation for conservation in the lead up to the 1949 Act.

Secondly, aesthetic values for conservation essentially concern the enjoyment of the landscape, wildlife and amenity of the countryside. Like ethical values they are illusory, but it is considered that such values increase human well-being and often enhance a desire for countryside recreation or enjoyment. Because aesthetic values are based on sensory utility, they are often considered to be enhanced by rarity and diversity: unusualness and change often stimulate enjoyment. This link between aesthetic values and public enjoyment is considered in this chapter in connection with early conservation pressures for legislation. Aesthetic values were particularly important in England and America as part of the armoury of the 19th century national parks movement. We return to them again in chapter 2, however, since aesthetic values relating to the countryside also had a significant role to play in the influence of the recreation lobby in promoting the 1949 Act.

A third set of values can be classed as cultural and scientific. These motivations for conserving the countryside are linked, it is said, to the intellectual and material development of society. The countryside environment can provide much information both to improve people's understanding of the natural world and to allow actions to steer environmental change. Natural environments are important areas for the scientist to understand human environmental behaviour more fully. Not surprisingly, much of the pressure for the nature conservation elements of the 1949 Act originated in this kind of motivation.

Fourthly, material benefits are considered an important impetus in promoting countryside conservation. Many 'fruits' of the countryside that still occur naturally are exploited for human consumption. Certainly at the start of the 20th century there was much of

this 'natural' environment that was being materially consumed by man. In the case of timber, for example, excessive exploitation led to arguments for greater control over rates of use and the conservation of existing stocks. In material terms too, a diverse reservoir of both plants and animals provides an essential reserve in the development of hybrid species. Again, a desire not to over-exploit natural resources had a role to play in the lobby for national parks.

Finally, a more holistic notion of ecological balance has provided a strong motivation for countryside conservation into the 20th century. This conservation value is essentially concerned with interrelationships within nature and the balance between different living organisms. Ecosystem processes are widely considered to be major determinants of the quality of the environment, and man's involvement with them requires that such processes are not irreversibly corrupted. The nature conservation proponents in the period leading up to the Act were driven by this ecological motivation, but it was often to lead to tensions with those of a more traditional cultural and scientific viewpoint. These notions of conservation value are not necessarily exhaustive, and other such groupings of reasons for conserving the countryside are entirely admissible. They are, though, a useful means of showing that there was not one conservation voice calling for new legislation in the years leading up to 1949. That there were a number of them, and they did not always agree with each other, is something to which we now turn.

Wordsworth, the development of national parks, and social class

If conservation, even as it was manifest in a number of different value systems, was a principal source of inspiration in the designation of special areas of countryside, how was it actually used to bring pressure for change about? In fact, nearly all writings on the development of national parks in England and Wales identify the poet William Wordsworth as the fountainhead of thought about the concept of a designation for natural beauty. But Wordsworth, as we shall see in chapter 2, was simply one person in a wider movement that was to provide a liberalisation of nearly all forms of art during the 19th century, and this in turn was to have a profound impact on the public's attitude towards the countryside. His deliberations were clearly driven by what we have considered above to be aesthetic motivations for conservation.

Wordsworth's *Guide to the Lakes* about parts of what is now the Lake District National Park was published in 1810. In it he claimed the Lake District essentially as a national property for the enjoyment of persons of pure taste. Wordsworth's concept of enjoyment, therefore, was exclusive in character. He felt strongly that artisans, labourers and the humbler class of shopkeepers were in danger of ruining the landscape if they were to arrive in the Lake District in any significant number, particularly after the advent of the steam train and the construction of the branch-line to Windermere.

This brings us straight away to a second set of values that were to cause tensions and differences in both the conservation and the

1.2 Newby Bridge, Windermere railway station
Wordsworth was concerned about mass access to the Lake District.
Source: Francis Frith Collection

recreation lobbies seeking legislative change for the countryside — that of social class. In conservation terms in England, it was essentially a middle class movement that championed the aesthetic worth of the countryside, and it was also an educated middle class caucus that was to promote the cultural, scientific and even ecological values for conservation. All of these pressures were consistent with the exclusion of mass access. In contrast to this, though, one of the most influential conservation pressure groups in the lead up to the 1949 Act, still with scientific and ecological bases to its conservation values, was to be the Royal Society for the Protection of Birds, which had at that time a very strong working class orientation.

In recreation terms too, pressures came from middle class philanthropic liberal quarters, but also from the working class rambling clubs of the northern industrial towns who were often more concerned with direct action than the vagaries of the political process, a point that we examine further in chapter 2. And all of these middle class and working class pressures were aimed essentially at the landowning classes, not only because they were the holders of the 'public goods' of conservation and recreation, but also because they held sway in Parliament. Clearly class differences overlaid differences in conservation and, indeed, recreation values, to create a complex web of pressures for change in the countryside in the lead up to the 1949 Act.

An early example of these class conflicts in conservation comes if we compare Wordsworth's views with the prevailing ethos of developments in the United States of America. The term 'national park' actually originated in North America with the creation of the General Grant National Park in 1901. Again, although there were ethical and cultural overtones to this development, aesthetic values still had a dominant role to play in bringing this national park designation into being. Some 35 years before, Abraham Lincoln had ceded the Yosemite Valley to the State of California to be used as a park, 'inalienable for all time'. The Yellowstone Park had been designated in 1872 as a public park, but soon became the jewel in the crown of the American National parks Service of the US Department of the Interior, set up in 1916.

The purpose of these North American parks was then considered to be to conserve the scenery of natural and historical objects, whilst enjoying them so as to leave them unimpaired for the enjoyment of future generations. There was no hint of class segregation in this ethos. Similar parks were set up in Canada, South Africa and elsewhere before the First World War, but a number of authors have considered the early parks to have been designated, at least as far as governments were concerned, more for national prestige and 'monumentalism' than for any deep desire to conserve nature.

Frederick Law Olmstead is now widely considered to be the American father of the national parks idea, speaking, as he did, in favour of the Yosemite Valley Public Park in 1865 as something that should be accessible to all people. He was critical of the views of Wordsworth and people like him because of their middle class view of conservation. He felt that they were quite condescending about the exposure of the masses to landscape beauty. Olmstead vehemently opposed this kind of exclusivity.

Olmstead, then, unequivocally set the national parks ball rolling as a classless and non-exclusive one. But this was not to be the dominant view. It was very much compromised by the 1949 legislation in England and Wales and, indeed, was never achieved in the Yosemite Park. Even in the middle of the 19th century, the need for transport to reach and enjoy most 'unspoilt' countryside areas entailed a cost that ensured that the majority of such enjoyment would remain the preserve of the relatively better-off.

1.3 The Great Geyser, Yellowstone national park One of the earliest and best known US national parks was established in Wyoming. *Source*: Mansell Collection

Even in the lead up to the 1949 Act, the notion of 'acces
all' was resisted. As we shall see in chapter 3, the Dower Re.
which was to examine the potential of national parks, felt that n.
people by taste and temperament were better suited to the tow
than the country, and the Hobhouse Report, which was to pro-
nounce on the implementation of national parks, sought to
exclude from parks, those whose tastes are for gregarious holiday-
making and urban gaiety.

In America the early development of parks proceeded on otherwise worthless land. Although the customs of land ownership
were never entrenched in the way that they were, and still are, in
Britain, the notion of a national heritage to be the responsibility of
government, and 'access for all' as a public responsibility was still a
residual priority relative to commercial interests, particularly of
timber and mining. Material values for conservation were clearly a
dominant influence in this priority, and aesthetic values took very
much a back seat.

It really was not until the establishment of the US National
Parks Service that the purposes and position of such parks in aesthetic and access terms were accorded a much higher priority.
Even then, though, as with national parks in their international
context, they were essentially wilderness areas — very much different from those national parks that became the concern of the 1949
Act in England and Wales.

Aesthetic and scientific conservation: a divergence

The early drive for national parks, then, was essentially aesthetic
and there was a divergence of view across the Atlantic about the
degree of access that should be accorded to such parks. But
national parks were only one part of the drive for the 1949 Act.
Their proponents were concerned principally with the appearance
and experience of the landscape and not so much with its cultural,
scientific, material and ecological worth. In fact, the beginning of
the development of organisations to champion conservation causes
probably originated in North America from material motivations.
Concern for 18th and 19th century resource depletion, the whole-

felling of trees and the near extinction of the bison, for exam-
provided a powerful stimulus to this development. The
ource conservation movement proceeded in parallel, and some-
mes in conflict with, the national parks movement.

These material motivations were not quite so dominant in
Britain since a crude kind of balance between resource conservation and exploitation had been in operation since Norman times.
It is important to note, however, that such a balance was born out
of a need to conserve hunting lands for the upper classes and the
aristocracy. It owed little to any notion of the common good.

A more powerful drive for conservation grew out of the industrial revolution. As we shall consider in more detail in chapter 2,
the 'drift to the town' as a result of rapid industrialisation and
urbanisation quite naturally turned the minds of a large number of
ordinary people to the great outdoors and the welfare of much of
its wildlife and habitat. To this end, a number of conservation
groups with consistent, but distinct, purposes came into being in
the late 19th century, such as the Royal Society for the Protection
of Birds and the National Trust for Places of Historic Interest and
Natural Beauty.

The formation of the Royal Society for the Protection of Birds
was inspired very much by ethical notions of the unnecessary
slaughter of birds of prey on sporting estates. It became successful
in lobbying for a number of Acts during the early 1900s, aimed at
controlling the worst ravages of gamekeeping and the over-collect-
ing of birds eggs and plumage. The National Trust was inspired
more by aesthetic and cultural values, but was also successful in
gaining statutory protection for its lands following concern over
the growth of the holiday trade in the Lake District. This was done
through the 1907 National Trust Act which gave statutory recognition to the Trust. The Trust was also able to secure sites of special interest to naturalists. Indeed, the 1907 Act specified that the
Trust should promote the conservation of animals and plant life on
its many holdings. By 1910 it had some 13 nature reserve sites.

One of its earliest land holdings, Wicken Fenn in Cambridgeshire
which had come to the Trust in 1899, was one of the last undrained
remnants of what had once been the Great Level. Even today it

supports the largest population of fen violet and is host to ⌐
different kinds of butterfly and moth. Despite these early accessi⌐
many people felt that the Trust was rather slow at developin₋
acquisition of sites of interest to natural scientists and they ＼⎽⎽
being secured in a rather random fashion and with little regard to
national importance.

If the Royal Society for the Protection of Birds had a strong
working class following, with its origins in the industrial revolution,
the National Trust succeeded more by virtue of a core of middle-class

**1.4 'The
Extinction of
Species'**
Turn of the century
concern about the
unnecessary
exploitation of
birds by the
millinery trade
became the subject
of satire.
Source: Punch

intellectuals. Much of the Trust's early parliamentary success was due in no small measure to the adoption of conservation causes, in a variety of forms, by such people. A number of eminent Victorians was closely involved in the Trust's development. These included the English art and social critic and the first Slade Professor of the Fine Arts at Oxford, John Ruskin; the Pre-Raphaelite painter Holman Hunt; the artist and designer William Morris; and Thomas Huxley, a biologist and educational reformer. It had actually been founded in 1895 by Octavia Hill, a social and housing reformer and a pupil of Ruskin who had been involved in the Commons, Open Spaces and Footpaths Preservation Society; a lawyer and amateur botanist by the name of Robert Hunter; and a Church of England canon, Hardwicke Rawnsley, who was also much influenced by Ruskin while at Oxford.

The dominant interest of these influential people still lay with aesthetic and cultural values associated with the landscape, historical

1.5 'Our Plea For Open Spaces' Octavia Hill is heroically portrayed here in her campaign for open spaces, especially for the urban poor. *Source: Punch*

monuments and buildings. This very dominance of interest, however, heralded a divergence between the aesthetic landscape conservationists and those concerned with the value of the countryside for its scientific worth. Although the aesthetes held sway at this time, competition was growing through the development of natural history — through Charles Darwin, the originator of the theory of evolution by natural selection, and Thomas Huxley — into the discrete academic discipline of ecology. Ecological values for conservation joined cultural and scientific motivations to vie with the aesthetic and ethical.

As an interest in ecology grew, naturalists began to extend their concern for wildlife to systems rather than just species. Arthur Tansley, a distinguished plant ecologist, formed the British Vegetation Committee in 1904 to map the country's vegetation. This led to the formation of the British Ecological Society in 1913, of which he was the first president. This began to identify threatened habitats and natural systems, particularly as a result of agricultural and urban developments. In turn, this allowed the development of persuasive arguments in support of some kind of 'nature reserve' habitat protection.

Such arguments were taken up by the Society for the Promotion of Nature Reserves which was set up in 1913 to assist the National Trust develop a more rational policy for the acquisition of reserves. The Society presented a list of 273 important sites in the British Isles to the Board of Agriculture in 1915 in anticipation of a possible war-time ploughing campaign. Unfortunately, the Society was not to champion the nature reserves cause through to the 1949 Act. Its relationship with the National Trust deteriorated after the first war and its influence declined, particularly after the death of Lord Rothschild, an important patron of the Society, in 1923. Although it submitted a conference memorandum on nature preservation in the context of post-war reconstruction to the war-time coalition government later in 1941, the Society for the Promotion of Nature Reserves, like a number of other scientific conservation organisations had suffered in its political influence by having views which would deny some people access to the country-side. Because there was no desire for scientific conservation to be popularist, it was always difficult for such organisations to enlist popular support.

		1.6 Conservation organisations and their dates of formation *Source*: Nigel Curry
The Royal Society for the Protection of Birds —	1889	
The National Trust —	1895	
The British Vegetation Committee —	1904	
The Society for the Promotion of Nature Reserves —	1912	
The British Ecological Society —	1913	
The British Correlating Committee —	1924	
The Council for the Preservation of Rural England —	1926	
The Council for the Preservation of Rural Wales —	1928	
The Standing Committee on National Parks —	1936	

Further threats to the countryside

After the First World War, new threats to the countryside environment emerged. The aggressive developments in timber production by the newly formed Forestry Commission, particularly in upland areas such as the Lake District, caused open opposition on amenity and habitat grounds. Post-war reconstruction also took place in a period of agricultural depression. With few effective planning laws and farmers only too keen to sell their land for development, urban sprawl began to be manifest in the countryside on a significant scale. Clough Williams-Ellis, who was a landscape architect and builder of Portmeirion in Wales, was one of many who spoke out vehemently against this rural despoilation. In his 1928 book *England and the Octopus* he berated builders and planners for their destruction of the countryside, which he termed the common background of beauty.

Effective opposition was still considered best achieved through land acquisition, but this was haphazard and always vulnerable to the competition of commercial interests. The need to coordinate environmental opposition to all of these pressures led to the formation in January 1924 of the Central (later British) Correlating Committee, representing some ten scientific and naturalist groups, and the Councils for the Preservation (later Protection) of Rural England and Wales which, from their founding in 1926 and 1928 respectively, acted as mouth pieces for a number of amenity organisations.

These Councils strongly favoured some form of designation a means of protecting vulnerable landscapes and habitats. They were aware, as we noted earlier in this chapter, that extensive tracts of land in America and Africa had been designated national parks for the preservation of wildlife and for recreation. This concept was appealing to them for the more attractive and remote parts of England and Wales, despite the fact that there was little true wilderness in these countries and the land was not in public ownership. Certainly it was a concept that they were to keep alive by participating in the formation of the Standing Committee National Parks in 1936 after proposals of the Addison Committee were not acted upon because of economic recession, a point we return to in chapter 3.

In many ways, this Standing Committee on National Parks broke the mould of separatism in both conservation and recreation pressure groups. This is because it did not have its roots in any conservation ethos at all. It had only one purpose — the creation of national parks. With this goal, different allegiances could fight their own corner later. As well as being non-separatist, it rapidly became a formidable organisation by virtue of its social and political breadth. It could draw on conservation organisations with their roots in the countryside, and ramblers' groups with their core support mainly in urban areas.

The membership of the committee was impressive. For the recreationists, T.A. Leonard, a cleric with a strong concern for the provision of holidays in the country for the working classes, represented the Ramblers' Association; Sir Lawrence Chubb, the first secretary of the National Trust and recently knighted for his services to the English countryside, represented the Commons, Open Spaces and Footpaths Preservation Society; Professor (later Lord) Chorley, although Honorary Secretary of the Council for the Preservation of Rural England, represented the Fell and Rock Climbing Club; and the Reverend H.H. Symonds, who often described his hobby as 'rescuing scraps of natural beauty', nevertheless represented the Youth Hostels Association. For the amenity conservationists, Patrick Abercrombie, professor of architecture in the University of London and destined to become one of the great post-war city planners, represented the Council for

1.7 Members of the Standing Committee on National Parks They were drawn from a wide range of interest groups. Clockwise (from the top left) they are: Julian Huxley, Sir Lawrence Chubb, Norman Birkett, and T. A. Leonard. *Source*: Council for National Parks

Preservation of Rural England. For the scientific conservationists, Julian Huxley, then a professor of zoology from King's College in London, represented the Zoological Society. The Chairman of the Standing Committee on National Parks was Norman (later Lord) Birkett, the eminent QC, and its drafting secretary was an architect, John Dower, who was himself to chair an influential committee set up to examine the feasibility of national parks during the Second World War. We examine the work of this committee further in chapter 3.

19

Whilst the Standing Committee on National Parks was pressing the case for national parks, the Councils for the Preservation of Rural England and Wales were familiarising themselves with the aesthetic conservation potential of the existing statutory land use planning system, particularly for the containment of urban sprawl. The development of this planning system was an approach favoured by governments in the 1920s and was therefore likely to have quite a degree of political mileage. The Councils for the Preservation of Rural England and Wales, however, had been critical of the ineffectual nature of much planning legislation. The Town Planning Act 1925 in particular had made some provision for preserving rural land by local authorities, but this had been largely ineffectual in an economic depression where local authorities had few funds and where farmers were keen to sell their land for development as agricultural incomes plummeted. The story of how this land-use planning system came to be developed is again picked up in chapter 3.

Into the 1930s, then, with the notable exception of the Standing Committee on National Parks, conservation movements that were to push for legislation for the protection of the countryside had quite distinctly fallen into two groups. Although they were never to be totally discrete, landscape and amenity conservation bodies such as the National Trust and the Councils for the Preservation of Rural England and Wales were to champion aesthetic and ethical conservation values. The British Correlating Committee on the other hand, representing a range of scientific groups, was to push much more for cultural, scientific, material and ecological values.

This split was to cause a unique, and some would say false, distinction in the way that conservation came to be organised after the 1949 Act, a point that we return to in chapter 3 and again in chapter 9. In class terms, both of these groups were dominated by educated middle class people. A number of the industrialised 'masses' had an ethical and an aesthetic concern for the welfare of the countryside, but this was more commonly manifest in their membership of recreation organisations, as we shall see in chapter 2.

Public pressures for countryside recreation ✳ 2

Motivations for countryside recreation

We have seen from chapter 1 that an articulate group of essentially middle class people spearheaded the conservation movements that were to lobby government to embrace both amenity and scientific conservation objectives in the 1949 Act. In parallel with these developments, pressures for recreation opportunities in the countryside were also articulated by specific, if somewhat broader, groups. It must be said at the outset that enjoyment of the countryside for recreation purposes has never been universally popular, but the influence of the recreation lobby in bringing about countryside legislation and influencing the 1949 Act in particular is often underplayed. This chapter, in examining the development of the countryside recreation movement in Britain up to the passing of the Act, clearly indicates that the Act was not a success for the conservationists alone.

In terms of the deeper history of the enjoyment of the countryside, romantic notions of rural landscapes and wild areas have been balanced by a more utilitarian apprehension of, or even disinterest in, nature. On the one hand, for example, the prevailing view in Tudor times was that the 'Garden of Eden' was 'a paradise prepared for man', but on the other, mountains, forest and marshes have been regarded in a number of periods of history as places of fear and dread, with the notion of 'the wilderness' being that of a gloomy and uncouth place.

Within these two extremes, access to the countryside had found some kind of balance prior to the parliamentary enclosures of the 18th and early 19th centuries. Common people had been able to roam in a relatively unrestricted way particularly over vast extent of downland and heathland 'wastes'. These areas of common land provided the focus for numerous festivals and feasts and were essentially the geographical centre of village social life. The landowning classes had made, as they continue to make, use of their terrain for 'hunting, shooting and fishing'.

The enclosure movement itself was one of a number of factors of the 18th and 19th centuries that conspired to make an interest in enjoying the countryside dominate over human antipathy. The development of the chequerboard countryside of enclosed fields created a man-made environment that was intrinsically less intimidating than the wild areas that preceded it. It held a new popularity in its security. Access to the countryside became a preoccupation of the many. At the same time it was this enclosed countryside that had created a reduction in the supply of accessible land, particularly through a severe diminution in the country's wild areas. For the more adventurous these wild areas, too, became increasingly precious because of their increasing scarcity. But most significantly of all, the enclosure movement simply caused vast reductions in the amount of countryside available for access,

2.1 The enclosed countryside
Field boundaries complement the old ridge and furrow pattern of the open field system to create a new landscape, now part of our cherished countryside.
Source: Hunting Aerofilms

taming, as it did, much of the country's downland, marshland, woodland and heathland.

Changes in hunting fashions also served to reduce access, coincident and in association with, the enclosures. In essence, 'wasteland', as well as agricultural lands, were enclosed in many parts of the country, specifically for hunting purposes. Working people were increasingly deprived of access to wild areas, both for sport and as a source of food, by successively restrictive and penal Game Laws up to the 1870s. The increasingly dire consequences for poaching and selling game significantly inhibited the use of such lands for leisure purposes. Thus the enclosures served to increase popular demand for countryside recreation at the same time as reducing the supply of readily accessible areas.

A second factor that caused an increase in the popularity of the countryside during this period was the industrial revolution. The mass movement of people from country to town created a sense of longing in many for their rural heritage. The nature of industrial employment too — indoors for long periods and invariably in poor environmental conditions — led to an inclination for the wide open spaces and fresh air in such leisure time as was available. Recognition of these conditions and the concomitant propensity for countryside access and, indeed, access to open spaces in towns, led to positive action on the part of upper class liberals such as the

2.2 Late nineteenth century game laws These made it increasingly dangerous for the working class to supplement their diet by poaching. *Source: Illustrated London News*

barrister and MP George John Shaw-Lefevre (later Lord Eversley), and the philosopher and economist John Stuart Mill. They were instrumental in the formation, in 1865, of the Commons and Open Spaces Preservation Society, which itself spawned the National Trust in 1895, to preserve the commons of Victorian England for public enjoyment. This was to become the Commons, Open Spaces and Footpaths Preservation Society by the turn of the century (now the Open Spaces Society) through amalgamation with a number of individual footpath groups.

A third factor in bringing about a new popularity in countryside recreation in the 19th and indeed the early 20th centuries was the growth in the Romantic and in similar movements of all forms of artistic endeavour. Even at the start of the 19th century, Wordsworth produced his *Guide to the Lakes* extolling the virtus of his beloved Lake District and Lord Byron was waxing lyrical in verse over the virtues of pastoral England.

As composers became less tied to the services of the Church and the Crown and less reliant on their patronage, their attention turned to rural imagery, culminating in many 19th and early 20th century compositions by Elgar, Holst, Delius and particularly, though a little later, by Vaughan Williams. The Victorian novelists

2.3 Turner's Buttermere
Romantic movement artists did much to inspire a wider public interest in the countryside.
Source: Tate Gallery

too — Hardy, the Bröntes — and many artists — Turner, Constable — made the English countryside a backcloth and often even a focus for their representations. And the Romantic movement also extended its interests to the National Trust, with, as we have noted in chapter 1, Ruskin, Hunt and Morris amongst its early members. Importantly, all of these developments were not overtly concerned to conserve the countryside, but rather to enjoy and even celebrate it.

Through the 18th and 19th centuries, then, first the enclosure movement and then the industrial revolution, together with cultural changes strongly inspired by the Romantic movement, nurtured a popular interest in access to the countryside. The corresponding reductions in available areas in which to enjoy such access, chiefly again as the result of enclosures, was bound to lead to friction.

Access and parliamentary conflict

This uneasy relationship between recreation supply and demand led the more vociferous proponents of access into organised resistance. As early as 1826 a number of ancient footpaths societies, footpaths preservation societies and rights of way societies were formed to counteract the often illegal blocking of ancient rights of way by landowners. Many of these groups were eventually to combine to form the Ramblers' Association in 1935. Some legal challenges reached the House of Lords, but for the less affluent groups, wars of attrition with the landowner became more common.

In tandem with this overt opposition to the loss of access, the national parks movement provided another vehicle for organising the public access voice. Initially, the middle class Romantics, with their visions of a rural idyll, began through the 19th century to articulate the need for some kind of formal consideration of our rural heritage. Subsequently the city-bound working population of the late 19th century, many of whom had taken direct action to challenge the gamekeepers of the landowning classes for improved access, began to champion the national parks cause as a less confrontational means of increasing public awareness of the access issue. Many early demands for popular countryside recreation were thus jointly expressed by the middle and working classes, a balance that was to shift eventually towards the more affluent in the 1960s and 1970s when access to the motor car came to have a dominant influence over countryside recreation activity patterns.

Both the more radical access groups and the more conservative national parks movement put pressure on government to pass legislation concerned to increase access to upland and mountainous areas. In 1884, the Aberdeenshire MP and lawyer James Bryce, introduced his first abortive Access to Mountains (Scotland) Bill. Although a keen mountaineer and president of the Alpine Club, he was considerably motivated to bring in his Bill by anti-American sentiment. A great deal of land was being purchased in Scotland by American millionaires at that time. He was proposing, quite simply, free access to mountain and moorland, without hinderance, and that has been the underlying demand sustained by a substantial part of the recreation fraternity ever since. Despite much vociferous argument over his 27 years in parliament, Bryce witnessed 12 such unsuccessful bills, all withdrawn through lack of support, in a parliament dominated by landowning interests.

However, in 1908, Charles Trevelyan, a lawyer and Liberal MP, introduced an Access to Mountains Bill which successfully completed a second reading, but failed in Committee. He tried again without success in 1926, 1927 and 1928. Further bills were introduced in 1931 (promoted by Ellen Wilkinson, later to become the Labour MP for Jarrow), 1937 (promoted by Geoffrey Mander, the Liberal MP for Wolverhampton) and 1938. The 1931 Bill in particular had more or less been guaranteed the support of the first Labour Prime Minister, Ramsey MacDonald, who then refused enough parliamentary time for it to be discussed. Eventually, an Access to Mountains Act did reach statute in 1939, but in fact this simply strengthened the resolve of the recreation lobby to fight harder for more effective legislation.

The Act came from a Private Member's Bill introduced in 1938 by Arthur Creech-Jones, the Labour MP for Shipley in Yorkshire, who was to become a Labour minister after the Second World War. This Bill was the first access bill to receive a second reading since

2.4 Epping Forest's royal accolade
Queen Victoria celebrates the acquisition of the forest by the City of London for public enjoyment in May 1882.
Source: The Graphic

Trevelyan's Bill of 1908. It originally sought simply to give access to uncultivated land, but this was something that the landowning lobby would not tolerate. They found a willing ally in Lawrence Chubb, then, as we noted in chapter 1, secretary of the Commons, Open Spaces and Footpaths Preservation Society and a founding member of the Standing Committee on National Parks. With Chubb's help and guidance, the Bill was distorted in Committee through the introduction of the 'trespass clause', which would have made it a criminal offence simply to be on open moorland that was classed as private land — the very areas to which ramblers most wanted free access.

After bitter negotiations, the trespass clause was removed, but in its place came a tortuous arrangement which might, in certain circumstances, give controlled access to specific areas. The ramblers agreed, very reluctantly, to this measure being incorporated into the Bill, and in due course it passed into law as the Access to Mountains Act 1939. It contained no fewer than 14 separate offences carrying fines ranging from £2 to £5, not inconsiderable sums in those days, especially for working class people, which many ramblers were.

Thus the Bill was so watered down during its passage through parliament that it became much more an Act for the landowner than the rambler. Fortunately, in some ways, the Act was never brought into effect, because of the Second World War, and was repealed by the 1949 Act anyway. Clearly the landowning, and, indeed, hunting interests in parliament, particularly of the uplands, held sway over the access lobby. But outside of this uplands legislation, other public authorities were responding to the move for increased access. This was particularly so in the City of London where the council bought Epping Forest in 1882 for the purposes of public enjoyment.

Early risings

During this long period of parliamentary frustration, the increasing popularity of the countryside for leisure purposes led quite naturally to the formation of a wide range of recreation organisations, first locally and then nationally. The times of formation of the more important of these national organisations are indicated in figure 2.5. Some of these, like the Ramblers' Federation and its successor the Ramblers' Association, were concerned, not only with rural enjoyment, but also explicitly with organised pressure for legal reform. These groups clearly had identifiable working class origins.

Other organisations such as the Commons, Open Spaces and Footpaths Preservation Society and the National Trust which it spawned, the Cyclists' Touring Club, the Caravan and Camping Club and the Youth Hostels' Association, all formed before the Second World War, were more conservative organisations and lent more covert pressure for access reform. It was these more conservative organisations, particularly the Commons, Open Spaces and Footpaths Preservation Society, that scored some early 19th century successes where they were more at home in the south of England. Many urban commons and places of public recreation, particularly in London, were preserved through these groups. They were active in persuading the City of London to procure the public ownership of Epping Forest, for example. Membership of these organisations was largely middle class and they effectively used litigation, personal influence and connections with the Establishment to further their ends.

The more radical groups were not only to fight for access through the parliamentary process, but they were also to find themselves at loggerheads with the counterbalancing recreation organisations of the landowners, such as the British Association for Shooting and Conservation and the British Field Sports Society. This was to be a conflict that remained at the core of all access pressures and legislation both up to the 1949 Act and well beyond, and remains with us today as we shall see in chapter 10. It is a conflict between public access and private property rights.

This more radical cause, in contrast to the commons preservation movement, was a northern working class rather than southern middle class one. It began with the Hayfield and Kinder Scout Ancient Footpaths Association founded in 1876, which sought to establish a freedom to roam across wild upland and open parts of Britain. It made little progress in the parliamentary system and this frustration combined with a climate of idealism after the First World War, concerned with increased rights for the population at large, spurred on more direct action.

'Popular'	
The Commons, Open Spaces and Footpaths Preservation Society —1865	
The Hayfield and Kinder Scout Ancient Footpaths Association —1876	
The Cyclist's Touring Club —	1878
The National Trust —	1895
The Youth Hostels' Association —	1930
The Ramblers' Federation —	1930
The Ramblers' Association —	1935
'Landowning'	
The British Assocation for Conservation and Shooting —	1908
The British Field Sports Society —	1930

2.5 **Recreation organisations** and their dates of formation
Source: **Nigel Curry**

In the 1930s there was a clear post-war ethos of a 'land fit for heroes' and an expectation of social change that would embrace wider access to the countryside. Men who had fought in the 'war to end wars' felt that it was their right to walk on their own land in search of simple refreshment at the weekends and on holidays. In 1922, the Manchester and Staffordshire Ramblers' Federations circulated candidates in the general election asking if they would support a bill 'to give free access to moors and mountains'. The same Federation had set up a special committee to 'mould public opinion to our way of thinking', which they recognised was no easy task. In 1930, with legislative success as far away as ever, the movement united in the Ramblers' Federation, the forerunner of the Ramblers' Association. As it became clear that the ideals fought for in the First World War were not to come to pass effortlessly, these more radical recreation groups in the federation took on an aggressive mood.

By 1931 rambling had become a mass sport. There were estimated to be over half a million regular walkers at this time with some 10,000 on the Derbyshire Peak on a summer weekend. Such levels of activity undoubtedly were due to the introduction of paid holidays and increases in mass transport. The close geographical proximity of the more wild upland parts of Britain with centres of heavy industrial development, led many of the local walking and rambling clubs that were formed during the late 19th and early 20th centuries to be based in the industrial towns of the north. These usually had some association with the Young Men's Christian Association or with groups more directly associated with left-wing politics such as the Co-operative, Trades Union, Clarion and Labour movements. The formation of the Holiday Fellowship and the Co-operative Holidays Association also gave working people the opportunity to spend short periods in countryside areas.

2.6 Limited access to the Peaks
A lack of roads and footpaths on the high moors is well portrayed in this 1934 map.
Source: Willow Publishing

But in addition to these working class clubs and societies, middle class groups, again often with their national counterparts that we have already mentioned, were being formed more generally across the country. Both were beginning to experience increased problems of access, and there were numerous clashes with gamekeepers. Gentlemen's clubs often coped with this well, as exemplified in a quote from an article by Peter Donelly writing in *Leisure Studies* in 1986:

> 'Some of the gentlemen's clubs devised novel ways of dealing with gamekeepers. Leslie Stephen's group, who called themselves the Sunday Tramps, would

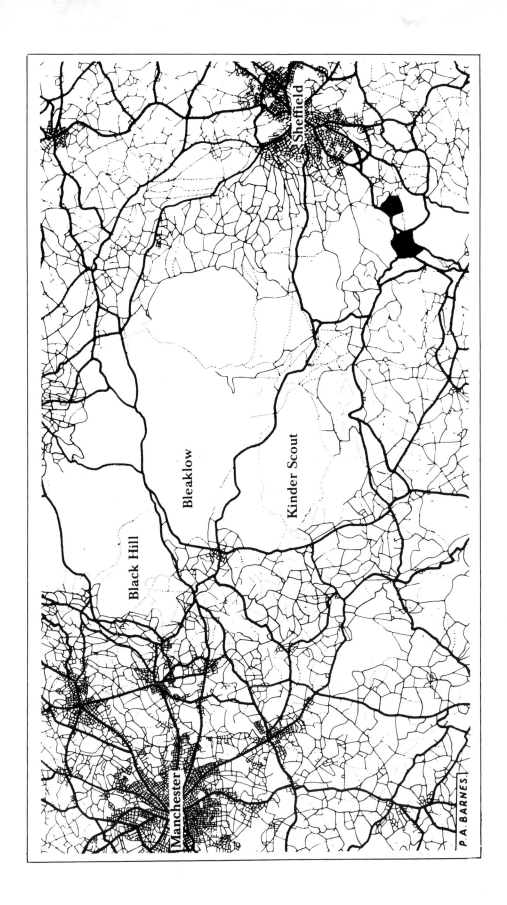

P. A. BARNES.

face the gamekeeper and chant in unison: "We hereby give you notice that we do not, nor doth any of us, claim any right of way or other easement over these lands and we tender you this shilling by way of amends" (*The Times*, 1930). Middle class groups could afford such arrogance, intimidating the gamekeeper with both their obvious social status and their pseudo-legal formula, and confusing him further by offering him a tip'.

Such bravado, however, was overtaken by more serious developments. As mass unemployment began to bite in the 1920s and into the 1930s, many working class people were looking for inexpensive ways to spend their enforced leisure time. The rural heritage of many of them reinforced a feeling that they should have a right to access in the countryside. As a consequence, the attention of the access movement began to focus on the Peak District where, in the early 1930s, there were about 62,000 hectares of open moorland, less than 1 per cent of which had access to it. At the time it was estimated that over half the population of England lived within a 50 mile radius of the area.

The idea of a mass trespass came at a camp organised by the Lancashire District of the British Workers' Sports Federation. On that occasion a small-scale trespass had been undertaken, a not uncommon occurrence by the 1930s. But after the trespass had been turned back by gamekeepers, it was suggested that if it had been of a large enough scale, the gamekeepers simply would not have been able to stop it. As a result, plans were made and publicised for a peaceful mass trespass to be held on 24 April 1932 over land held by the Duke of Devonshire, known as Kinder Scout.

Even before the event, some newspapers had branded it an 'assault', and the Manchester Ramblers' Federation urged its members not to take part. Nearly 800 of them did, however. The trespass took place with opposition from both gamekeepers and the police, but on the whole it was peaceful, as had been intended. Six arrests were made for unlawful assembly and committing a breach of the peace, five of whom were members of the Young Communist League. They were tried by a jury comprising eleven

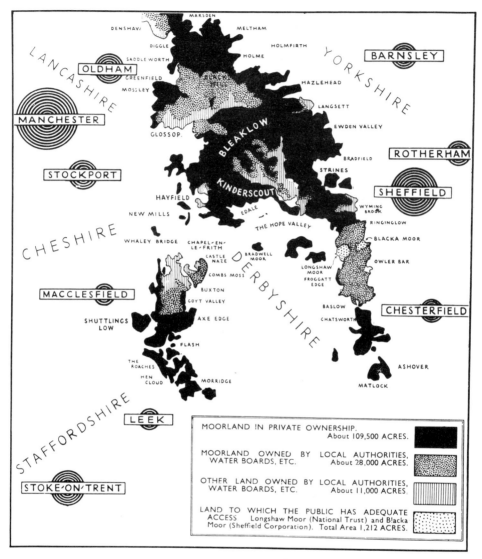

MOORLAND IN PRIVATE OWNERSHIP.
About 109,500 ACRES.

MOORLAND OWNED BY LOCAL AUTHORITIES,
WATER BOARDS, ETC.   About 28,000 ACRES.

OTHER LAND OWNED BY LOCAL AUTHORITIES,
WATER BOARDS, ETC.   About 11,000 ACRES.

LAND TO WHICH THE PUBLIC HAS ADEQUATE
ACCESS   Longshaw Moor (National Trust) and Blacka
Moor (Sheffield Corporation). Total Area 1,212 ACRES.

country landowners and sentences were passed ranging from two to six months.

From the other side of the Pennines, a second mass trespass was organised later in 1932 by the Sheffield Ramblers' Federation, but it is now felt that this did little more than assist in the early abandonment of yet another Access to Mountains Bill proposed for that year. Indeed, it had been described as being a 'vicious and Bolshevik attack on the rights of private property'.

2.7 Ownership and access in the Peaks

Landed interests largely precluded access in an area adjacent to the homes of half the population of England, as this 1934 map shows.
Source: Willow Publishing

2.8 The Kinder Scout trespass, 1932
A mass demonstration against a lack of access to the open country of the Peaks crystallised popular support for th ramblers' ovement. *ource*: Willow Publishing

After the mass trespass movement

From these trespasses, there was some confusion over loyalties amongst different groups of ramblers. The Ramblers' Federation, which had been formed in 1930 with between 30 and 40 affiliated clubs, sided with the activists and continued to press vociferously for open access. The middle classes were slightly more torn between the position of the militant worker and the revered landowner, but it was through these more acquiescent groups and particularly the conservative Commons, Open Spaces and Footpaths Preservation Society, which had done much through their secretary, Lawrence Chubb, to frustrate the 1939 Act, that a negotiated progress with landowners came about. Landowners began to realise that public opinion favoured more access, and they opted for some limited access to specific areas on a permit system.

As landowners were softening their somewhat entrenched attitudes a little, those years after the mass trespass provided times of consolidation for the more militant approaches of the Ramblers' Federation. Personalities in the ramblers' movement began to develop their public profile. Tom Stephenson, for example, was editing a magazine called *Hiker and Camper* in 1933 after a brief career with the Labour Party at Transport House. Through this work he became acquainted with Arthur Leonard, founder of the Co-operative Holidays Association and the Holiday Fellowship.

34

Other activists such as Edwin Royce, G.R. Mitchell, the first honorary secretary of the Ramblers' Association, Benny Rothman and Alfred Embleton, honorary treasurer to the Ramblers' Association until 1961, were numbered among his associates, as was Stephen Moreton and G.B.H. Ward who had convened the first meeting of the National Council of Ramblers' Federations.

These people were to spearhead the campaign for access during the 1930s and were instrumental in organising demonstrations such as the one at Winnats Pass at Castleton in the Peak District in 1934, which attracted more than 3,000 people. Tom Stephenson in particular was to take this militant view of the right to access back into 'the corridors of power', when he joined the new Ministry of Town and Country Planning as Press Officer in 1943, at the same time as he was elected to the executive committee of the Ramblers' Association.

Two years later, in 1945, a former Independent Labour Party colleague of Stephenson, Lewis Silkin, became the Minister of Town and Country Planning, and early contacts between the two of them did much to promote the cause of the access radicals. When Silkin received a deputation from the Ramblers' Association in December 1945, he was very susceptible to Stephenson's ideas of facilities for access to wild parts of Britain, drastic revisions of footpath law and the creation of national parks and long distance footpaths such as the Pennine Way. Stephenson had forcefully made out the case for this particular long distance route in his 1935 article, *The Long Green Trail.*

Even when he began his 21 years as secretary to the Ramblers' Association in 1948, Stephenson was able to press his access case to government by taking part with prominent Labour Government members — Hugh Dalton (who was president of the Ramblers' Association that year), Barbara Castle and Arthur Blenkinsop amongst others — on a three-day walking holiday on the Pennine Way. Although the walk was devised as a political stunt following the redrawing of the boundaries of Dalton's Bishop Auckland constituency, it nevertheless provided an unrivalled opportunity for lobbying in the lead up to the 1949 Act.

Thus the mass trespasses and the events that followed on from them did play a vital part in developing public awareness of the access issue and really provided the starting point for both the landowners, who began formally to negotiate with access groups, and for the consolidation of individual rambling clubs into the Federation and ultimately Ramblers' Association. Such developments were not sufficient to spur significant legislation, and, as we have seen, further bills for access failed during the 1930s. Even the 1939 Act had a sting in its tail, because, as we noted, the landowners' lobby had managed to insert a penalty clause into the Act, allowing landowners to charge for damage to property for actions that had never previously been chargeable offences.

If in fact, the 1949 Act did little to improve upon the Act of a decade earlier regarding access — a situation that persists to the present day — this is because it retained the idea of negotiations for access with individual landowners in the creation of national parks. This was to be realised either through the negotiation of outright purchase or the payment of compensation for access. As a result, only 2 per cent of Britain's open country has had public access secured for it by these means.

The history of access to the countryside, then, is clearly not simply a chronology of reconciling supply with demand. It is essentially a political issue in a social and cultural (and often class) context. In retrospect, in this milieu, the access lobby has never really succeeded in its primary goal. There is still no legal right of public access to open or uncultivated land in England and Wales, not even to common land and, as we shall see in chapter 3, access still sustains a residual priority to conservation in countryside policy and legislation. We explore this issue further in evaluating the implementation of the 1949 Act in parts two and three of this book.

The response of the establishment: reports in profusion

3

A groundswell of public pressure

So far the story of the drive for countryside legislation has centred on the development of a wide range of pressure groups, all with slightly different motivations for change in the countryside. On the conservation front there were those concerned with scientific conservation often at the expense of public access, but in contrast there were also groups concerned with the amenity value of the rural landscape. For these conservationists, public access was part of their ethos. But largely distinct groups provided the spearhead of recreation pressure. The issue of public access over private land was an important ideological one for many, particularly northern working class rambling associations. Recreation pressures, too, came from slightly more acquiescent middle class groups, well away from the concentrations of industrial populations in the north, and where access to the countryside was often not so restricted.

Clearly, there was no one point at which governments began to take this groundswell of pressure on board. It was a gradual process, gaining momentum after the First World War. The amenity conservation groups probably scored the first significant victory in bringing the Addison Committee into being. But Addison had something to say for recreationists, too, and his was the first of quite a staggering number of committees and reports that were produced in the 20 years leading up to the 1949 Act. It is to these that we turn in this chapter.

The Addison Committee was appointed by Ramsay Macdonald's second Labour Government in 1929, chiefly as a result of lobbying on the part of the Councils for the Preservation of Rural England and Wales for special powers for landscape protection. It was chaired by Christopher Addison, MP, Parliamentary Secretary to the Ministry of Agriculture, but perhaps more distinguished as the very first Minister of Health between 1919 and 1921. Its terms of reference were:

> 'To consider and report if it is desirable and feasible to establish one or more national parks in Great Britain with a view to the preservation of the natural characteristics, including flora and fauna, and to the improvement of recreational facilities for the people: and to advise generally, and in particular as to the areas, if any, that are most suitable for the purpose'.

At this stage in the development of the national park concept the principal divergence of view amongst interest groups was about the relative priorities of conservation and preservation on the one hand and recreation and access on the other. These two priorities were considered to be largely irreconcilable and organisations such as the British Correlating Committee, representing scientific conservation interests and the National Trust, representing amenity conservation interests, strongly favoured areas of high value in national parks to be closed to the public. Ramblers' groups, on the other hand, in making representations to the Addison Committee, stated that extending access should be the prime purpose of national parks.

The Addison Committee's compromise was a suggestion of two types of national park. Firstly, 'national reserves' were to be selected by virtue of their outstanding scenic and wildlife interest to the nation as a whole and were to have a primary purpose of preservation, requiring a degree of exclusion. 'Regional reserves', on the other hand, were to be areas of pleasant countryside conveniently situated near to towns, with a primary purpose of public access. A central national parks authority would be needed to designate both of these types of area. Thus Addison was to make for the first time this distinctive hierarchy of designated areas, which many now consider to be the forerunners of national parks and areas of outstanding natural beauty respectively.

Although these proposals met with favour in government, action was stalled until the passing of the Town and Country

3.1 The South Downs in the 1930s
Now an AONB, this area was considered by Addison, along with Dower and Hobhouse, as worthy of special protection. *Source*: Royal Photographic Society

Planning Act 1932, after which time the recession in the economy and a more specific budgetary crisis, allowed no resources to be disposed to the development of new initiatives in this area. Addison's proposals were not implemented.

In response to this government inactivity, the Standing Committee on National Parks was formed in 1936, as we have noted in chapter 1, to sustain an interest in national parks and promote increased access to the countryside. By the time the national economy was emerging from recession, the government was more hesitant about implementing the proposals of the Addison Committee, despite lobbying from the Standing Committee on National Parks. It was argued that the new town and country planning system introduced in the 1932 Act, when fully operational, would effectively embrace the preservation of high value landscapes and any new separate designations at the time actually would be counter-productive.

The Ministry of Health, which, at that time, was responsible for town and country planning matters, defended the ability of the planning system set up in 1932 to protect the countryside. In a 1938 report, *The Preservation of the Countryside*, it claimed that developments in rural areas had taken place only in response to people's housing needs after the First World War, and anyway it was really too soon to condemn the planning system as being inadequate to control sporadic development since it had not really had time to prove itself.

The national park protagonists were not happy with this complacency. Agricultural land loss to development had been unprecedentedly high during the 1930s. Although local authorities had wide-ranging powers to control development under the 1932 Act, they were also liable to pay compensation to those who chose to dispute planning refusals. The Standing Committee on National Parks, in particular, objected to this local authority control in rural areas since they felt that the rural heritage was a national rather than a local responsibility and that local authorities were often too poor in remote rural areas to withstand compensation claims anyway. They were, also, impotent to control the activities of statutory undertakers and the government itself who collectively were often responsible for the most radical landscape changes in remote rural areas — an accusation that was to resurface when the 1949 Bill had its second reading in parliament.

In partial recognition of these problems the 1938 report, *The Preservation of the Countryside*, suggested strengthening the planning system through the designation of 'rural zones' outside of village boundaries. These would tolerate agriculture and forestry developments and some small-scale industrial activity, but design qualifications would be needed outside of agricultural proposals. This attempt to shore up the planning system did not persuade the Standing Committee on National Parks. It responded by mounting a publicity campaign for specially designated areas, no small part of which was a booklet by John Dower entitled *The Case for National Parks*. It was argued here that it was precisely our precious remote areas where local authorities were too poor to pay compensation to stem development that were most vulnerable to despoilation. At the same time these were areas where public access was most restricted. Special powers were therefore required, through the formation of national park authorities.

The Committee's publicity campaign was accompanied by films, a roadshow and a number of articles, and it even began to work on a parliamentary bill to submit to the Ministry of Health. Although these arguments did hold some sway with central government, the outbreak of the Second World War again forestalled action.

The run up to reconstruction: Barlow, Scott and Uthwatt ·

As Britain emerged from its economic recession in the 1930s the conservation of the natural heritage was not the only countryside issue that was preoccupying public interest. There had been significant agricultural land losses to development which the Town and Country Planning Acts of the 1920s and 1930s had done little to ameliorate. This was not surprising since the agricultural depression had left farmers only too keen to pursue the financial gains of releasing their land for building. The onset of war brought this issue sharply into focus in the context of the need to plan comprehensively for post-war reconstruction. When Lord Reith was appointed Minister of Works in 1940 in a coalition government under Winston Churchill, he set about preparing a national plan for the optimum use of all land and a comprehensive planning system that would implement it.

In doing this he drew heavily on the report of the Royal Commission on the Geographical Distribution of the Industrial Population which was produced in the year of his appointment and was known as the Barlow Report. This really provided the basis for the post-war planning system in the areas of industrial location, new towns and land use planning. Its influence embraced an attitude to rural areas that has permeated the planning system that we have today. This is essentially that town and country should be seen as opposites — the former a place for development and the latter a place to be conserved and where any land-based activity should be largely autonomous.

This attitude was due very much to the influence of Patrick Abercrombie, who was a prominent member of the Barlow Commission, but whose views on the countryside had involved him as a founder member of the (then) Council for the Preservation of Rural England, which was openly opposed to urban encroachment in the countryside. His championing of the green belts cause further served to reinforce the preservationist ethic towards the countryside generally that was the prevailing ethos in post-war reconstruction.

3.2 Box Hill, Surrey
A prime example of London's green belt landscape for which preservation was a high priority even before the Second World War. *Source*: Francis Frith Collection

A second report that contributed to the reconstruction drive appeared in August 1942, and was that of the Committee on Land Utilisation in Rural Areas chaired by Lord Justice Scott. This Committee was originally intended by Lord Reith to look only at development and planning controls in the countryside, but it stretched its terms of reference to embrace both conservation and enjoyment. In spite of this it produced its findings in ten months. The Scott Report has been called essentially an appendix to Barlow and very much reinforced the ethos of non-intervention in the countryside. Any developments in rural areas should be allowed only in the case of a proven national need. Agricultural land should be preserved in productive use and agricultural developments should generally not be subject to planning controls.

It was the clear assumption here that the proposed town and country planning system would be strong enough to reconcile private and public interests in the countryside and ensure an appropriately conserved landscape. It was also assumed that a prosperous agriculture was bound to enhance the landscape (and the welfare of its rural communities) rather than lead to its deterioration. This was based on the Scott Committee's recognition that the landscape characteristics of the countryside were man-made and that 'it must be farmed if it is to retain those features that give

3.3 Derelict farm buildings in the 1930s
The Scott Committee felt that agricultural growth was the best means of remedying rural neglect.
Source: MERL

it distinctive charm and character'. These kinds of extreme recommendations for the countryside were perhaps understandable in the context of the wartime economy, and particularly a wartime that followed an agricultural depression that caused much landscape and economic deterioration in the countryside. But they also provided the preservationist and non-interventionist inheritance for the countryside in the planning system that we still have today.

Although more briefly, the Scott Committee also championed the cause of public access to the countryside, not least because of pressure from the Ramblers' Association. The Associations' memorandum to the Scott Committee urged that there should be free public access to all open land, including coastal areas. It also recommended the creation of a number of long distance footpaths, taking up the challenge set down by Tom Stephenson in his *Long Green Trail* article of 1935.

Accepting that the countryside was the heritage of all, it followed that there must be a facility for access for all, but this must not interfere with 'the proper use of land in the national interest'. Also included in the Report's recommendations was the idea that local authorities should keep maps recording all public footpaths — a proposal that was to become one of the most important provisions of the 1949 Act. The Scott Committee also acceded to the need for national parks which it considered to be long overdue. These would be principally for recreation purposes and would have a national body to control them. Although the Committee also proposed the establishment of nature reserves, these were to be separate from national parks. It was the Scott Committee's notion of agricultural autonomy, however, that was to have the most pervasive impact on post-war planning legislation, if not the 1949 Act itself.

In tandem with these two reports came, also in 1942, the Uthwatt report on compensation and betterment. This was concerned to address the problem of how to deal with the huge gains in the value of land, or betterment, that accrued as a result of the granting of planning permission. In the countryside, this was a particularly significant problem since, as Barlow and Scott had both argued, planning permission was to be exceptional outside of the towns so the scarcity value of such permission in rural areas created huge gains for those lucky enough to possess it. The Committee proposed the nationalisation of development rights on the urban fringe, but this and other subsequent proposals to solve the betterment phenomenon have always proved notoriously difficult to implement.

Planning for parks and reserves: Dower, Hobhouse and Huxley

The commitment of the wartime coalition government to a firm policy for land use planning through Scott, Barlow and Uthwatt spurred a number of voluntary groups into petitioning further for national parks. After preparing a paper on the provisions of a bill establishing these, the Standing Committee on National Parks sent it to Lord Reith, the Minister for Town and Country Planning. At a meeting held a few weeks later, in January 1942, the Standing Committee was not only able to persuade him of the need for national parks, but also to look favourably upon the setting up of a national parks commission with wide executive responsibilities for these and financed by government. At that meeting too, the Society for the Promotion of Nature Reserves successfully lobbied for the nature reserves concept.

They had convened a meeting in 1941 entitled 'Conference on Nature Preservation in Post-war Reconstruction' and had decided to divorce themselves from broader issues of conservation that very much embraced the range of values that we considered in chapter 1, to concentrate specifically on scientific aspects of nature conservation. This conference was actually invited to set up a Nature Reserves Investigation Committee at the meeting with Lord Reith in 1942. This developed its work in tandem with a committee called together by the British Ecological Society in March 1943 to examine ecological research and the role of nature conservation in it. These two committees were successfully to shunt nature conservation out of the realms of planning and into the sphere of the natural sciences, which had a separate representation in government as chapter 4 makes clear.

During this wartime government the civil service was composed of an unusual mix of temporary civil servants. Generally, they were less used to the ways of the civil service and were largely drawn from a different kind of background. They were certainly much less negative in their approach than their peace-time counterparts, as chapter 4 again shows. One of these happened to be John Dower who was, as we have seen earlier, an architect and a member of the Ramblers' Association. He had written the Standing Committee on National Parks' influential report *The Case for National Parks* in 1938 and was himself related by marriage to Charles Trevelyan who had sponsored a number of Access to Mountains Bills in parliament through the first 30 years of the century.

He managed to convince Lord Reith of the need to pursue the idea of national parks further in government. As a result in August 1942, John Dower was commissioned to produce the *Report on National Parks in England and Wales,* which was to examine the practical problems, needs and potentials of the parks. His initial definition of a national park was:

> 'An extensive area of beautiful and relatively wild country in which, for the nation's benefit and by appropriate national decisions and action,
> (a) the characteristic landscape beauty is strictly preserved,

3.4 John Dower
Architect and wartime civil servant, his role was crucial in shaping the provisions of the 1949 Act.
Source: Council for National Parks

(b) access and facilities for public open-air enjoyment are amply provided,

(c) wildlife and buildings and places of architectural and historic interest are suitably protected, while

(d) established farming use is effectively maintained'.

Using this definition he surveyed possible national park areas for Reith's Ministry, describing in his field records their characteristics, boundaries, problems and requirements. This resulted in the identification of a primary list of ten delineated national parks amounting to more than 2 million hectares, 'those areas which I consider most suitable and desirable for establishment as national parks during the first period of operations (say five years)'. There was a second list of twelve covering more than 930,000 hectares

'which it will be desirable to establish as such at a later stage', plus a third list of other amenity areas.

Over the next two years, although frequently interrupted by illness, he laid down most of the fundamental principles on which a subsequent national parks programme might be based. Dower importantly concluded that if national parks were to be provided *for* the nation, they should be provided *by* the nation with their costs met from national funds. Unlike Addison, he did not accept the need for two separate parks for recreation on the one hand and conservation on the other. He felt that public access was the justification for wildlife and landscape conservation. He proposed, too, the setting up of a single preparatory national parks commission. According to Dower, this body should consist of a chairman and six to eight members. Besides a headquarters staff, each national park would have its own personnel. The Commission itself would be a body of:

> 'high standing, expert qualification, substantial independence and permanent constitution which will uphold, and be regarded by the public as upholding, the landscape, agricultural and recreational values whose dominance is the essential purpose of national parks'.

This was considered far too controversial when the Dower Report was published in 1945 for a government which was just about to begin instituting a comprehensive town and county planning system. Indeed, it was regarded with extreme suspicion by both the Ministry of Agriculture and the Forestry Commission since it threatened to diminish their responsibilities. By July of that year, though, a general election brought a Labour Government into power that was particularly committed to the national parks idea, mindful of its earlier embarrassment over the Access to Mountains Act 1939. Many of Dower's proposals were to take on a new importance as a result. Some of the Government's new ministers even had explicit associations with the ramblers' movement — Lewis Silkin, the Minister of Town and Country Planning and Hugh Dalton, the Chancellor of the Exchequer, for example.

Caution over the Dower Report was thus overridden and Lewis Silkin, within days of taking office, decided that Dower's proposals

**3.5 Sir Arthur
Hobhouse**
An influential
figure in the
Association of
County Councils,
he chaired the
committee
responsible for
refining Dower's
ideas.
Source: Education

should be developed further. A National Parks Committee was appointed by government in July under the chairmanship of Sir Arthur Hobhouse, a landowner from the south-west of England and Chairman of the County Council's Association, to make specific recommendations arising out of the Dower Reports for England and Wales. (Scotland was to be considered separately by a committee chaired by Douglas Ramsay.) By the time the Hobhouse Committee began its work in August 1945 it had mustered a familiar set of names, many of whom had been members of the Standing Committee on National Parks. Julian Huxley, from the Zoological Society, was a member, as was Lord Chorley, who had represented the Fell and Rock Climbing Club on the Standing Committee on National Parks in 1936. Clough Williams-Ellis, the architect, who had been so critical of sporadic built development in the inter-war years, was also a member, as was Ethel Haythornthwaite, an important figure, with her husband Gerald, in the later development of the Peak National Park as we shall see in chapter 5. John Dower, too, had an official position on the Committee, but sadly this was to be his last contribution to the national parks movement. He died of tuberculosis in 1947.

On the nature reserves front, the wartime coalition government had invited the Society for the Promotion of Nature Reserves to set

up a Nature Reserves Investigation Committee in 1942. This set about identifying potential nature reserves both inside and outside national parks. The British Ecological Society and the Royal Society were both involved in this initiative and were instrumental in persuading Hobhouse (because these reserves were to be considered outside of national parks) that a separate nature conservation committee was required. As a result, a committee parallel to that of Hobhouse — the Wildlife Conservation Special Committee chaired by Julian Huxley — was set up by Hobhouse himself to consider the national requirements of nature reserves. (A similar committee under James Ritchie, a professor of natural history, was set up to consider the special needs of Scotland.) A further sub-committee under Hobhouse also focused on footpaths and access to the countryside.

The Huxley Committee again had associations with personalities involved in earlier pressure group activities, since it was chaired by the grandson of Thomas Huxley, who had been involved in the setting up of the National Trust and was prominent in the academic development of ecology. Its vice-chairman, too, was Arthur Tansley, who had set up the British Vegetation Committee in 1904. Membership of the Committee was made up mainly of professional ecologists and civil servants with an interest in wildlife.

Two types of conservation: two sets of proposals

The Hobhouse, Huxley and Ramsey Committees all reported in 1947, although Ritchie's final deliberations were to take another two years. The fruits of their labours defined a distinction that has remained a key feature in British conservation ever since — between landscape conservation for amenity and habitat conservation for science. The former is about access and the latter is about exclusion, and they exemplify the distinction of conservation values that we discussed in chapter 1. This distinction led to fundamentally different philosophies towards the development of landscape conservation and nature conservation — still represented in the separate existence of the Countryside Commission and the Nature Conservancy Council in 1989.

The Hobhouse Committee, for example felt, like Scott, that the new planning legislation would be quite sufficient to protect the landscape interests of national parks. The Huxley Committee, on the other hand, felt that scientific interests could only be properly served by direct land acquisition. Many people since this time have criticised this, what is often seen as a false distinction in conservation terms, pointing out that such a division is hardly to be found anywhere else in the world.

With regard to landscape conservation, the Hobhouse Committee proposed twelve national park areas, omitting one of Dower's suggestions, North Cornwall, because of its linear nature and adding two from his reserve list, the Broads and the North York Moors, and one from his amenity areas list, the South Downs, because it was near to London. In agreement with Dower, the Committee felt they should be nationally co-ordinated by a National Parks Commission financed by the Exchequer and responsible to the Ministry of Town and Country Planning. Also consistent with Dower, it considered that each park should be administered by a committee separate from the local authority. National parks were for the nation and as a result should not be administered just by local interests. The Hobhouse Committee therefore suggested that parks should be administered by local ad hoc executive bodies which would act on behalf of both the National Parks Commission and the local planning authority. Membership of these bodies should draw equally on both the Commission and the local authority.

It was this organisational structure that was to be the Hobhouse Committee's biggest stumbling block, for the combination of strong central direction and effective local planning was never achieved. The Town and Country Planning Act 1947 gave strong new powers to local authorities, so that two years later, when the 1949 Act came to Parliament, it was not expedient to transfer some of these powers to a new central and non-elected National Parks' Commission, as we shall see in chapter 4. That the Commission was born devoid of any executive status and the reasons for this is a matter we also pursue there.

For nature conservation, the Huxley Committee concluded that 'research and experiment' would be the most appropriate way

3.6 The Hobhouse proposals, 1947
Source: Report of the National Parks Committee

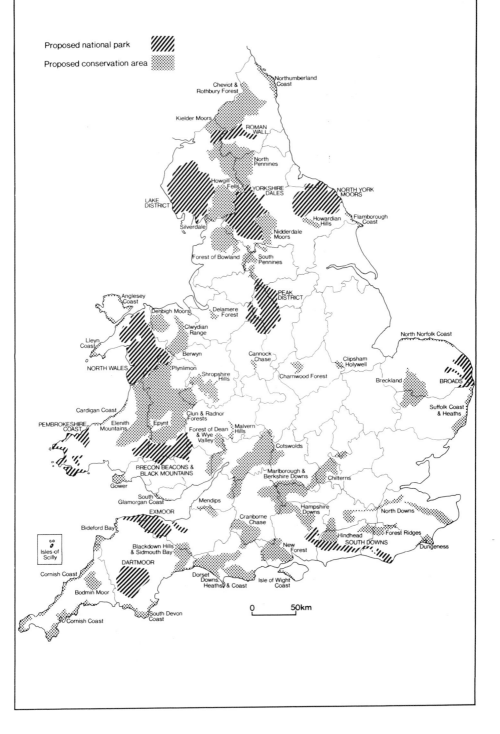

National Parks and Conservation Areas
proposed by the National Parks Committee, 1947

Proposed national park

Proposed conservation area

Northumberland Coast
Cheviot & Rothbury Forest
Kielder Moors
ROMAN WALL
North Pennines
Howgill Fells
YORKSHIRE DALES
NORTH YORK MOORS
LAKE DISTRICT
Howardian Hills
Flamborough Coast
Silverdale
Nidderdale Moors
Forest of Bowland
South Pennines
Anglesey Coast
PEAK DISTRICT
Denbigh Moors
Delamere Forest
Clwydian Range
North Norfolk Coast
Lleyn Coast
Berwyn
Cannock Chase
Clipsham Holywell
NORTH WALES
Plynlimon
Shropshire Hills
Charnwood Forest
Breckland
BROADS
Cardigan Coast
Clun & Radnor Forests
Suffolk Coast & Heaths
PEMBROKESHIRE COAST
Elenith Mountains
Epynt
Forest of Dean & Wye Valley
Malvern Hills
Cotswolds
BRECON BEACONS & BLACK MOUNTAINS
Marlborough & Berkshire Downs
Chilterns
Gower
South Glamorgan Coast
Mendips
Hampshire Downs
North Downs
EXMOOR
Cranborne Chase
Forest Ridges
Bideford Bay
Hindhead
SOUTH DOWNS
Dungeness
Blackdown Hills & Sidmouth Bay
New Forest
Isles of Scilly
DARTMOOR
Dorset Downs Heaths & Coast
Isle of Wight Coast
Cornish Coast
Bodmin Moor
South Devon Coast
Cornish Coast

0   50km

'to control nature so as to maintain or establish a series of varied and most delicately balanced conditions'. The Committee nominated 73 national nature reserves for this purpose. These were to preserve wild species of fauna and flora and were to provide opportunities for research and education. They needed to be actively managed on a scientific basis and because of this they should come under the direct control of a National Biological Service.

This would be a scientific body separate from the planning system (something which Dower did not approve since he had advocated a composite national parks and national nature reserves authority) and responsible to government as a research body. The Huxley Committee, unlike that of Hobhouse, was to be successful in its proposals for an executive management structure. The Nature Conservancy was formed, uncontroversially as it turned out, as a 'biological service' under powers contained in the 1949 Act, but separately by Royal Charter. It was to have both executive and advisory functions, and was to both own and manage land and set up a regional structure and carry out research.

Despite the Huxley and the Hobhouse Committees offering fundamentally different proposals for the setting up and running of national parks and national nature reserves, they exhibited a degree of concordance over other issues. In recognition of a 'second order' of high value landscapes and habitats, which did not require the same intensity of control as national parks and national nature reserves, but nevertheless required special conservation and recreation considerations, both the Huxley and the Hobhouse Committees recommended a further 52 tracts of land, to be known as conservation areas. These were eventually agreed partly to provide a common voice on the conservation front after initial differences between the two committees about the location of a number of different types of land classification. They were to emerge in the 1949 Bill that was placed before parliament as 'areas of outstanding natural beauty'.

These conservation areas were to be administered by local authorities with similar though more flexible principles, as national parks. It was proposed even at this stage that conservation areas should have the protection of natural beauty and interest as a principal consideration above that of open air enjoyment.

The Huxley Committee also proposed the identification both within conservation areas and outside, of 'sites of special scientific interest' simply as a means of allowing scientific interests to be voiced in any significant development proposals. They were to be smaller than conservation areas and national nature reserves and would, it was suggested, provide a good basis for more localised nature conservation in the form of local nature reserves. These might be designated by local authorities as areas of local interest, generally publicly owned, and safeguarded for public education and enjoyment.

Recreation sustains a residual priority

This clear division of the conservation lobby into two distinct parts ensured that it remained at centre stage relative to recreation in official government considerations. Even from the first two chapters of this volume it is evident that the drive for the conservation of the countryside dominated that of the pressure for increased countryside access, at least in terms of political persuasion. The relative importance of these two in government policy remains an issue of contention even today, with the Countryside Commission stating in its policy priorities for the 1980s that 'proportionately more of our resources will go into conservation than to recreation'. Such a prioritisation surfaces throughout this book, as one of the principal legacies of the 1949 Act.

On the surface, the governmental and legislative actions that we have already reviewed in this volume seemed keen to pay due regard to access as a major priority. The earlier unsuccessful access bills that came before parliament championed by Trevelyan and Bryce had a clear recreation thrust. Addressing a countryside recreation conference in 1978, Michael Dower, son of John Dower, cited their principal purpose as being specifically designed so:

> 'that no person should be excluded or molested by the owner or occupier whilst walking or being .... for the purposes of recreations or scientific or artistic study on .... uncultivated mountains or moorland'.

3.7 The Huxley and Ritchie proposals
Respectively, these dealt with England and Wales, and Scotland.
Source: Report of the Wildlife Conservation Special Committee and the Scottish Wild Life Conservation Committee

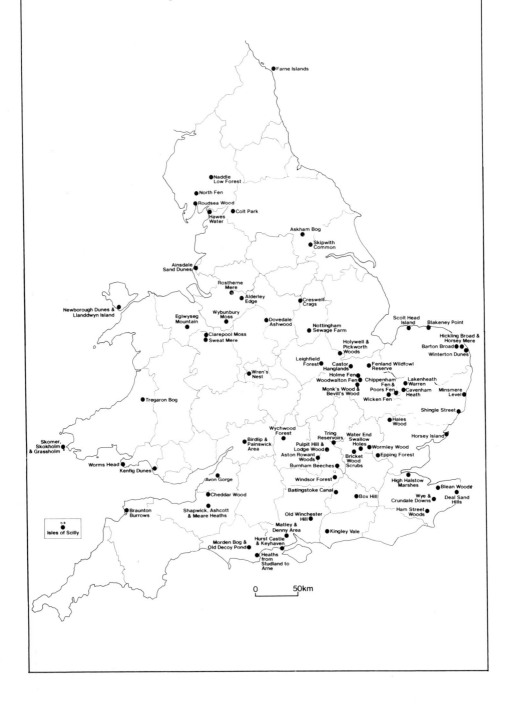

National Nature Reserves

proposed by the Wild Life Conservation
Special Committee, 1947

Farne Islands

Naddle
Low Forest

North Fen

Roudsea Wood

Hawes
Water

Colt Park

Askham Bog

Skipwith
Common

Ainsdale
Sand Dunes

Rostherne
Mere

Alderley
Edge

Creswell
Crags

Newborough Dunes &
Llanddwyn Island

Eglwyseg
Mountain

Wybunbury
Moss

Dovedale
Ashwood

Nottingham
Sewage Farm

Scolt Head
Island

Blakeney Point

Holywell &
Pickworth
Woods

Hickling Broad &
Horsey Mere

Barton Broad

Winterton Dunes

Clarepool Moss
Sweat Mere

Leighfield
Forest

Castor
Hanglands

Fenland Wildfowl
Reserve

Wren's
Nest

Holme Fen

Woodwalton Fen

Chippenham
Fen &
Poors Fen

Lakenheath
Warren

Cavenham
Heath

Minsmere
Level

Monk's Wood &
Bevill's Wood

Tregaron Bog

Wicken Fen

Shingle Street

Hales
Wood

Horsey Island

Skomer,
Skokholm
& Grassholm

Worms Head

Kenfig Dunes

Wychwood
Forest

Birdlip &
Painswick
Area

Tring
Reservoirs

Pulpit Hill &
Lodge Wood

Aston Rowant
Woods

Burnham Beeches

Water End
Swallow
Holes

Wormley Wood

Bricket
Wood
Scrubs

Epping Forest

Avon Gorge

Windsor Forest

Cheddar Wood

Basingstoke Canal

Box Hill

High Halstow
Marshes

Blean Woods

Wye &
Crundale Downs

Deal Sand
Hills

Braunton
Burrows

Shapwick, Ashcott
& Meare Heaths

Old Winchester
Hill

Ham Street
Woods

Isles of Scilly

Matley &
Denny Area

Kingley Vale

Morden Bog &
Old Decoy Pond

Hurst Castle
& Keyhaven

Heaths
from
Studland to
Arne

0   50km

National Nature Reserves
proposed by the
Scottish Nature Reserves Committee, 1949

Hermaness, Unst

Noss

North Rona

St Kilda

Inverpolly Forest & Summer Isles

Bay of Nigg

Newton Estate, Haskeir, Pabbay & Shillay

Loch Druidibeg
Allt Volagir

Estuary of Ythan

Oakwood at Ariundle

St Cyrus

Blackwood of Rannoch

Shingle Islands, Tay & Tummel

Treshnish Isles

Tay Estuary, Mugdrum Island

Tentsmuir

St Serf's Island

Isle of May
Bass Rock
Aberlady–Gullane

Gruinart Loch & Flats

Ailsa Craig

Reach of Solway

0   50km

Although all of these bills were unsuccessful, the Government was still keen to set recreation priorities into the terms of reference of the Addison committee, that would lead to the 'improvement of recreational facilities for the people'. This sentiment in turn was echoed in 1942 by the Scott report which maintained that national parks should be 'for the enjoyment of the whole nation', a sentiment that found its way into the 1944 White Paper *The Control of Land Use* as being a central strand in post-war reconstruction. Access to the countryside was to be for the townsman every bit as much as for the rural dweller.

At this time, too, the Dower report was making statements about the social intentions of recreation policy. Access to the countryside, it maintained, should be for people, and especially the young of every class and kind, from every part of the country and for the public at large, not just some privileged section of the community. It urged that the public should have the right to wander at will, subject only to a minimum of regulations to prevent abuse, and to a minimum of 'excepted areas' where such wandering would clearly be incompatible with some other publicly necessary use of the land. Importantly, the report made it clear that 'excepted areas' were not to include grouse moors, over which there had been such bitter controversy in the inter-war years.

Hobhouse, too, maintained that recreation in national parks should be 'for the whole of the nation'. Generally on the question of access, he maintained that the freedom to wander over mountain, moor and rough grazing, and other uncultivated land, would be of the utmost importance. Instead of the hillwalker being treated as a trespasser, it would be up to the landowner to apply for exemption for the general 'free access' provision if he could show good cause.

Recreation considerations reached a high point in 1946, when the Footpaths and Access Special Committee, also chaired by Hobhouse, followed much the same line as his main Committee. At the same time the Chancellor of the Exchequer, Hugh Dalton, stated that he was prepared to make available the very considerable sum of £50 million, 'which might be used to finance some of the operations necessary in order to give the public permanent access to the national parks'. Yet despite these brave sentiments, it would be nearer the truth to say that the use of the countryside for recreation was to be rather selective. As we noted in chapter 1, access was not quite to be for all, but for certain specific groups. In his report, Dower had indeed suggested that some people would be better off pursuing their interests in an urban setting, while the Hobhouse Committee, in echoing such sentiments, wanted to exclude from national parks, those looking for all kinds of mass entertainment. Clearly, neither Dower nor the Hobhouse Committee was expecting countryside recreation to be to the taste of all.

In fact, if it came to a push, the arguments for conserving the countryside might hold sway over a massive countryside invasion. The Hobhouse Committee proposed that a progressive policy of national park management would be needed to:

> 'ensure the peace and beauty of the countryside and
> the rightful interests of the resident population are
> not menaced by an excessive concentration of visi-
> tors, or disturbed by incongruous pursuits'.

As in so many of the proposals promulgated for the countryside at this time, this sentiment of ambivalence towards the extent of public access was strongly contested by Professor Dennison, a member of the Scott Committee, writing in his minority report of disagreement with the main committee:

> 'In particular it is important not to attempt to pre-
> serve amenities which can only be preserved so long
> as full access to them is denied to those whose her-
> itage they are'.

The more restrictive ethos of the Hobhouse Committee, and of the sentiments common to the Hobhouse Committee and the Dower Report about access for all — as long as it was peaceful and did not disturb anyone — were to find their way into the 1949 Act. In fact, acceptable types of recreation for the countryside were seen by both Dower and the Hobhouse Committee to be for rural refreshment, and, as the Hobhouse Committee put it, 'countryside contentments', rather than the pursuit of activities that owed little to the beauties of the natural environment. Participation was to be dispersed to ensure the peace and beauty of the countryside.

The prevailing ethos even of those of the amenity persuasion,

3.8 Recreation contrasts in national parks
The walker on the Pennine Way is closer to the Dower and Hobhouse vision for the national parks than the mass entertainment of a Derbyshire well-dressing!
Source: Peak National Park

leading up to the 1949 Act, then, was one where public access should take place, but without sacrifice to conservation goals. For the scientific conservationists, and those concerned with the Huxley Committee's nature conservation proposals, recreation was to have an even smaller role to play. Even before the Act reached parliament, then, there were signs that it was not going to be the people's charter for access that many were hoping for.

Even Hugh Dalton's 1946 sentiments, concerned to give the public permanent access to the national parks, eventually came to little, as did those of his Labour Government colleague, Lewis Silkin, the Minister for Town and Country Planning. If, as chapter 4 makes clear, his intentions on access in the 1949 Act were laudible at the start, he was soon to change his approach. 'A person's land is his land', he ultimately concluded. 'I think it is wrong to give the public an automatic right to go over all private land of a certain character.' In the end the 1949 Act's access proposals differed from those in the never-implemented 1939 Act only to the extent that negotiating access now fell to the local authorities, rather than the ramblers themselves.

Acts come to pass: planning, agriculture and forestry

All of these developments concerned with countryside recreation and conservation were taking place alongside a plethora of other initiatives concerned with post-war reconstruction. We have already mentioned that a comprehensive town and country planning system was being constructed, largely by the implementation of the recommendations of the Barlow, Scott and Utthwatt Committees. The 1944 White Paper, *The Control of Land Use*, put operational clothes on the principles of these reports and in deference to the Scott Committee in particular, explicitly included proposals for the establishment of national parks. This White Paper was to culminate in the Distribution of Industry Act 1945, the New Towns Act 1946 and the Town and Country Planning Act 1947.

The first of these Acts was to provide a comprehensive set of controls over the distribution of manufacturing industry through the introduction of Development Areas and building licences. The New Towns Act 1946 designated sites for new towns with their own development plans and development controls that provided the basis of the planning system still in existence today. The town and country planning legislation relinquished much control over the countryside, designating most of it 'white land' where activities could remain in situ, where agricultural and forestry operations could remain largely exempt from planning controls, and where the conservation of the countryside was largely left to chance.

Agriculture and forestry, too, were undergoing comprehensive reforms derived in a wartime climate where strategic needs to grow our own food and timber were paramount and where, as the Scott Committee put it, 'every agricultural acre counts'. The resulting post-war parliamentary Acts, the Hill Farming Act 1946, the Agriculture Act 1947, and the Forestry Acts 1945 and 1947, all reflected this imperative. The Forestry Acts were concerned either to expand production by the public sector directly, in the 1945 Act, or through fiscal concessions and grant-aid to the private sector, in the 1947 Act. The Hill Farming Act 1946 introduced special payments to improve hill and upland farming outputs, whilst the Agriculture Act 1947, in a comparable way to the Town and Country Planning Act of the same year, provided the basis of modern agricultural support through guaranteed payments for products and subsidies for farm modernisation.

Of greatest significance in all of this legislation was the fact that the control of development through the town and country planning system was to have a physical basis, but the development of the primary resource sectors of the countryside was to be governed

3.9 A new deal for farming and forestry
Post-war legislation ensured a stable financial basis for both these sectors.
Source: Countryside Commission

by a much more powerful set of economic incentives. This divergence in the mechanisms for planning in the countryside has created many of the problems that still exist today in our rural areas. Much of the basis for these problems centres on the fact that agriculture in particular, but also forestry, was exempt from most forms of planning control. This severely weakened the planning system's ability to control the development of the rural landscape and countryside habitats.

The Hobhouse and the Huxley Committees both cautioned against some of the possible ravages of agricultural practice — moorland ploughing and hedgerow loss in particular — but neither felt these important enough to require the imposition of controls. They felt that this would interfere with the special planning and management functions in national parks, and inhibit the development of a prosperous agriculture industry. Rather, Hobhouse went for the vaguer notion of 'goodwill' and for land purchase for limited areas of moorland. The former was not to succeed very well with an agricultural lobby much stronger than the conservation one.

In the lead up to 1949, then, the public campaigns for conservation and access in all their disparate forms, that had triggered so much consideration within government circles, were beginning to have an impact on legislation itself. A number of issues remained unresolved for many interests, however. Was the land-use planning process on its own going to be powerful enough in the countryside to serve conservation and recreation ends? Was the autonomy given to agriculture through the 1947 agriculture and planning Acts going to make the implementation of conservation and recreation policies more difficult? What kind of organisational structure was appropriate for the management of our natural heritage? Would the separate interests of amenity and scientific conservation serve to weaken the overall conservation case?

It was with these uncertainties still to be resolved that the campaign for significant new countryside legislation was to find expression in the drawing up of the National Parks and Access to the Countryside Bill and its passage via parliamentary process through the House of Commons and the House of Lords. It is to this that we now turn.

4 *The Bill reaches parliament*

Towards a legislative framework

It was on 17 March 1949 that the final phase of the campaign began. As *The Times* announced, 'The National Parks and Access to the Countryside Bill was formally introduced in the House of Commons yesterday'. With great economy of words — for these were days of post-war paper rationing — it made clear that the Bill would promote 'the creation in England and Wales of national parks in parts of the country famous for their natural beauty and for the designation and special protection of other similar areas. The general purpose of the Bill', it continued, 'is to provide for urban populations fuller access to and enjoyment of the country-side. In addition to the provision of national parks, it will make possible rights of access to the wilder parts of the country any-where. The Bill also provides for a national survey of existing foot-paths and bridle-ways, for the creation of new public rights of way, and for the establishment of nature reserves'.

It concluded that the Bill 'embodies the chief proposals of the Hobhouse Report on national parks and the associated reports on footpaths and access to the countryside and nature conservation'. It was for these reasons that the editorial of that day suggested that the Bill deserved a warm welcome, although *The Times* was circum-spect about the means by which the objectives of the Bill were to be achieved. After all, it had campaigned for a Hobhousian view of what the Bill ought to contain, with strong directive powers in the hands of a National Parks Commission, far removed from any notion of such an organisation acting only in an advisory role. Indeed, in a leading article a year earlier it had specifically sug-gested that 'if out of mistaken tenderness for the supposed suscep-tibilities of the planning authorities to be set up next July, the parks are to be left to be managed piecemeal, little that is effective will remain of the recommendations (of Hobhouse), which less than a year ago, received so friendly a public welcome'. However, *The Times* was sufficiently generous at this later stage to suggest that Mr Silkin's proposals were at least 'good enough to deserve a fair trial'.

For Lewis Silkin, Minister of Town and Country Planning, the day of real satisfaction came, on the occasion of the Bill's Second Reading which began on 31 March 1949. In introducing it and broadly outlining its proposals, he made clear his pride in presenting to the Commons what he called:

> 'a people's charter — a people's charter for the open air, for the hikers and the ramblers, for everyone who loves to get out into the open air and enjoy the countryside. Without it they are fettered, deprived of their powers of access and facilities needed to make

4.1 Lewis Silkin MP
For him, the 1949 Act was to be 'a people's charter'.
Source: Labour Party

holidays enjoyable. With it the countryside is theirs
to preserve, to cherish, to enjoy and to make their own'.

The notion that the protection of the most beautiful parts of the countryside was a key means of 'seeking to promote happiness for ordinary men and women' was undoubtedly part of Silkin's socialist creed which was able to find true expression in his Bill. Equally, at the time of its Second Reading he seemed satisfied to have incorporated '90 per cent of the Hobhouse Report into it'. Some have doubted the validity of such a claim, but even if this is accepted, questions do arise as to why no more was possible, given the acclaim with which the Hobhouse Report had been greeted by a wide range of interest groups. Few were openly hostile to it, other than the entrenched supporters of the sanctity of private property, the landowners. Although *The Times* now felt inclined to gloss over what many considered administrative inadequacies in the Bill which were not present in the Hobhouse Report's proposals, why had Silkin not been more concerned about these and had taken what many saw as the line of least resistance? Indeed, why had it taken the Government so long to come up with relevant legislation?

To provide adequate answers, the appearance of the Bill and in its distinctive form at a particular moment in the legislative programme of the post-war Labour Government has to be seen, not merely as a response to the campaigns of the external pressure groups discussed earlier. It also owes much to the personal proclivities of the Minister himself and his relationships within government and the civil service.

The commitment of the Minister

There can be no doubt about the personal commitment of Silkin as Minister of Town and Country Planning in so far as rural amenities were concerned. Although city born, he acquired a passionate love for the countryside and as a young man he rambled through much of England. Indeed, in 1939 he was so deeply affronted by the emasculation of the Access to Mountains Act that he spoke out against it at a rally at Leith Hill. After his appointment in 1945 he was always actively looking towards the opportunity to translate into legal form the principles for countryside protection that, by then, he had long been brooding over. The setting up of the Hobhouse Committee and its other attendant committees was but one step in this direction. Indeed, as we noted in chapter 2, early meetings with Tom Stephenson, the Ministry's Press Officer, led to wide-ranging discussions about the views of the Ramblers' Association and, in December 1945, to Silkin receiving a deputation from that organisation. It was at this meeting that he made a commitment to introduce fresh legislation to make good the debacle of 1939.

But his wish to go beyond this more limited objective is supported by other evidence. In February 1947 the Treasury indicated its willingness to collaborate over the use of the National Land Fund for the compulsory acquisition of areas suitable as national parks. Then departmental records, also of that month, show that Silkin had decided to 'stake a claim' for a countryside bill 'whatever its content', although he had not 'reached any firm conclusion whether to rely on a national park element, or to go for amenities generally' in terms of legislation.

In June of the same year, his desire to 'legislate in this parliament' to protect the countryside was given public voice in a speech to the Rural District Councils Association. In emphasising the problems of access he said, 'It is not good enough that the only way of enjoying the countryside is from the road'. By now, his ideas had begun to move in the direction of a much more general amenities bill, which would consider not only national parks, footpaths and access, but also the restoration of derelict land and the preservation of historic buildings.

However, the publication of the Hobhouse Report in the summer of 1947 provided no quick resolution of his thinking. Indeed, the processes by which this was to further evolve, finally to find substance in the Bill that was placed before parliament, proved complex and lasted far too long for many enthusiasts of that report. By May 1948, a note of frustration had crept into the tone of Lord Merthyr, a veteran countryside campaigner. In a House of Lords debate on national parks, he castigated the Government for its failure to say what it intended to do following Hobhouse.

4.2 Countryside congestion
Even as early as 1951, enjoying the countryside from the road had its limitations, particularly at 'honeypots' such as Dartmeet in Dartmoor National Park.
Source: National Motor Museum

This was a matter which others outside the House were becoming equally vociferous about; certainly, Sir Patrick Abercrombie, the Chairman of the Council for the Preservation of Rural England, and Sir Norman Birkett, Chairman of the influential Standing Committee on National Parks, together with Lord Crawford, of the National Trust, had all expressed themselves vehemently on the subject. But in the debate in the Upper House, Lord Henderson, replying for the Government, was left to justify the delays. Whilst it was in sympathy with the aims of national parks 'there was a difficulty about the constitutional arrangements contemplated by the national parks report'.

This was undoubtedly at the heart of the problem which Silkin now perceived. He saw legislation on the countryside not in isolation but, as 'constituting the complete trilogy of planning' and taken with the New Towns Act 1946 and the Town and Country Planning Act 1947, 'representing a code fashioned in the one parliament by the same Minister'. Because of this, it is hardly surprising that the planning controls vested in local authorities under the 1947 Act could not be so unceremoniously and speedily divested from national parks and other designated areas of outstanding landscape quality, even though supporters of Hobhouse might wish it otherwise.

Such a move would have smacked of a complete lack of forward planning within the Ministry and have reflected poorly on the Minister. This is not to say that Silkin did not give the Hobhouse proposals on this matter due consideration — indeed, external interests, and not least the Standing Committee on National Parks, were doing all in their power to ensure that he did. But he was also aware of the concern being expressed by county councils. They might have suffered a loss of planning control over what would have constituted some 25 per cent of the land area of England and Wales.

These were not matters to be lightly passed over in spite of Abercrombie's accusation that Silkin was remaining 'ominously silent' about the administrative machinery of the new national parks. This time the Minister responded for himself in an address to the Town Planning Institute in July 1948, making it clear that his reticence was only because he was having 'informal discussions on these matters with interested parties'. In asking newly appointed county planning officers to give up some of their powers, even Abercrombie had to admit that he would 'need to undo what he had just done', an unenviable task.

By the end of August, however, it was evident that he was preparing to give the county councils a major role in the administration of national parks, at least in planning terms. As he said, in an address to the Town and Country Planning Summer School, it would be 'utterly wrong and the negation of democracy' to suggest that they were not capable of carrying out such functions. Such sentiments were to find strong support from the chairmen of influential local planning authorities, notably Lord Gage of East Sussex, Bertram Wilson of the West Riding of Yorkshire, and Henry Slessor of Devon.

Doubts in the departments

However, Silkin's difficulties were not confined to the resolution of the question of who should exercise planning powers. Throughout 1948 other doubts and uncertainties were voiced that helped delay the framing of legislation. These arose inside a number of government departments which were particularly concerned about the nature of a bill based on the Hobhouse Report and the role this might give a National Parks Commission. Indeed, some, especially in his own Ministry, questioned the need to legislate at all.

Responsibility for this negative attitude was partly that of the Permanent Secretary to the Ministry of Town and Country Planning. Sir Thomas Sheepshanks was a career civil servant, cast in the traditional Whitehall mould and nearing the end of a long career which had embraced five other ministries as well as the Treasury. He was much more the norm than the less conventional civil servants, such as John Dower, who peopled the corridors of power during the War years. As Sheepshanks explained to Silkin, 'I more than ever have the feeling that the case for legislation is weak and that so far as administrative merits are concerned, an informed critic could demolish most of our arguments pretty easily'. As to the idea of a Commission he stated that:

> 'I feel bound to repeat the warning I have given you before, that this might quite possibly prejudice the future existence of this Department. As you know we are inevitably regarded by many of the older Departments as a fifth wheel on the coach. It might be said that a sixth wheel in the form of a Commission for the country or amenity planning would be quite intolerable. The concluding argument might be that amenity or country planning is the one function which justified an independent defender of its own and it would be better that that defender might be the proposed new Commission and that the Ministry of Town and Country Planning might therefore cease to exist'.

However, the idea of a National Parks Commission did remain part of Silkin's agenda as Sheepshanks was later to concede. 'In view ... of the general expectations', he wrote:

> 'and because there is a need for some Exchequer assistance which probably can be better disbursed by some independent body than a minister, he (Silkin) thinks that a National Commission should be estab-

lished with responsibility for areas of natural beauty, that is, not only the named national parks, but also some at any rate of the conservation areas'.

Nevertheless, the uncertainties and doubts of this time were to be reflected in a preliminary memorandum produced in April 1948 concerning what might be contained in an amenities bill. This was produced for the government body which vetted all potential legislation, the Lord President of the Council's Committee. Chaired by Herbert Morrison, this Cabinet committee contained most senior Ministers from the domestic departments of government.

By the title of his memorandum *National Parks, Footpaths and Access to Uncultivated Land* Silkin hinted at the ground a bill might cover. However, in reprising its antecedents in the reports of Hobhouse etc, he also appropriately reminded the Committee that the scientific aspects of conservation, outside those that could be secured by the control of land use, had been examined by the Huxley Committee. Its findings were being now considered by the Lord President of the Council 'within whose domain these scientific matters fall'. Whilst he was clear, of course, about supporting the Hobhouse notion of a National Parks Commission, he also made it plain that he did not feel able to accept the ideas in his Committee's report concerning planning in national parks since Silkin was now sure that this should remain a local function. However, he was much less positive about other issues and when

4.3 The Attlee cabinet, 1945
The Lord President of the Council, Herbert Morrison (fifth from the right in the front row) sits next to prime minister, Clement Attlee. *Source*: Labour Party

questioned by the Lord President's Committee admitted that he had not discussed his proposals with the Treasury, other Ministers of State, including agriculture and defence, nor had he consulted the Law Officers.

As the minutes of that meeting at which his memorandum was discussed make clear, so much preliminary work still remained to be done on a bill, that the Lord President 'doubted whether it would be ready in time to be introduced in the 1948/49 session'. Later, in reporting on that same meeting, Evelyn Sharp, the Ministry's Deputy Permanent Secretary, was to write that the Committee, considered the paper 'half-baked'. Not surprisingly the Committee determined on another review of the proposals, after they had been further refined, a process which would certainly entail the inter-departmental consultations.

Silkin's unsatisfactory brush with the Lord President's Committee seemed a turning point for him. From then on he seemed able to formulate a clearer view of the kind of legislation that was needed, tempered only by the demands of practical politics.

A second shot at drafting

By the time the House of Lords debate on national parks had taken place in May 1948, Silkin was, therefore, in a much more decisive frame of mind. Instructions were now given for Evelyn Sharp to prepare a second memorandum. In spite of the continuing scepticism of the civil servants working in the Ministry which she frankly acknowledged at the time in a note to a new colleague, she applied herself to the task of producing a paper that would unequivocally set out the broad lines of what a bill should contain.

On this occasion it began by acknowledging the general expectation that existed concerning the establishment of national parks and their running, but without 'the elaborate machinery proposed' by Hobhouse. As in the earlier memorandum, a series of arguments were rehearsed for a National Commission 'to assist and advise on securing ... a high standard of amenity and improved access and accommodation in the parks and also in the conservation areas', but now it positively proceeded to draft such a commission's terms of reference. These outlined its essentially advisory role, but with powers to disburse monies and exercise reserve powers. The Commission, rather than the Minister, would be the source of financial assistance to individual authorities responsible for the parks to enable their objectives to be achieved under the Act. With respect to footpaths and access, there was a general acceptance of the *Report of the Special Committee on Footpaths and Access* which had been chaired by Hobhouse.

Anticipating Silkin's speech to the Town and Country Planning Summer School in August 1948, the memorandum reaffirmed that the administration of the national parks would remain with the county councils as the planning authorities, but it then dealt particularly with those areas not defined in the submission of April. For example, if a county council did not carry out 'a desirable national park development' the Minister would be able to take any necessary action. These local authorities would also be obliged to consult the Commission on major new developments in a park and to set up special committees responsible for the administration of the park areas. Where special committees involved more than one county, joint arrangements through joint boards or advisory committees, would have to be employed. This was an issue on which Silkin seem to have yielded as a result of sustained pressure from the Standing Committee on National Parks, ably chaired by Sir Norman Birkett who had personally interceded with the Minister. Only months earlier Silkin seemed prepared to rely totally on the new large planning authorities without any kind of compulsory association into joint boards.

In the discussions with the Lord President's Committee that followed, other matters were thrashed out. Contrary to Hobhouse, it was decided that the Commission would primarily act in national parks whilst maintaining only limited functions in conservation areas. The Commission, whilst having powers to finance special schemes in parks, would not hold land of its own, but assist local authorities in its purchase. It would also advise on which parks should be created and their likely boundaries. But government departments, when wanting developments in national parks, would not need to consult the Commission; instead they

4.4 A 'trilogy of planning' for the country
Seen here discussing a new town proposal, Lewis Silkin saw the Acts of 1946, 1947 and 1949 as a coherent code within which responsibility for planning controls was the most difficult problem to resolve.
Source: Topical Press

would directly have the ear of the Minister who might then seek advice from the Commission. On the mapping of rights of way, this should be done by local authorities every four years, although not on an obligatory basis. Local authorities would be allowed to declare a public right of access to a specified area of uncultivated land in a national park and to beaches and foreshores anywhere. On the subject of long distance footpaths, the Commission would now be responsible for their creation and maintenance.

It was with the consideration of this paper that the preparation of the Bill that was to go to parliament in the Spring of 1949 can be said to have begun. Not only did Silkin now feel that he had made considerable progress, but also the recommendations on the scientific aspects of conservation made by the Huxley Committee had already been accepted by the Government. That the Lord President had made such rapid progress in gaining the acceptance of these owed much to their uncontentious nature. For example, the proposed Nature Conservancy, the means by which the scientific aspects of the Bill would be activated, posed no threat to local authorities. Moreover, the land requirement for national nature reserves and sites of special scientific interest was small, affected only a few people and did not involve a heavy financial outlay by the State, with the Treasury proposing to earmark only half a million pounds for the acquisition of such sites. The view taken by the Government then and subsequently by parliament, was that if science needed its small corners of the countryside to get on with its research-oriented tasks, such activities would interfere with few other interests. Thus Silkin now felt justified in asking that the detailed drafting of the Bill by Parliamentary Counsel should begin.

That he was at last in a more buoyant mood was clearly evidenced by his speech to the 1948 Town and Country Planning Summer School. However, his euphoria was short-lived, for if he had had to contend with somewhat qualified support from his own Department during the preparatory stages of the Bill, the Treasury had very little enthusiasm for much of the legislation he was proposing. And it was now to have its say.

Legislative proposals and a hostile Treasury

Satisfied as the Treasury was with the input the Huxley Committee had made to the proposed Bill, the same cannot be said about the Hobhouse Committee which had seemed an anathema from the start. The Treasury had always argued that planning in the national parks could be taken care of under the Town and Country Planning Act 1947, and all executive activity looked after by the park committees acting under the guiding hand of the Minister. But its hostility only became really significant after Silkin's second encounter with the Lord President's Committee. It crystallised particularly around the idea of a National Parks Commission.

The most contentious issue, was the concept of a body, such as a Commission, spending money when the expenditure had been incurred by a local authority. The idea of the Commission contributing to the cost of the extra staff employed by local authorities for national park functions was a particular case in point. Indeed, such was Treasury hostility that the Chancellor of the Exchequer, Sir Stafford Cripps, personally intervened and told Silkin 'that if authorities must employ and control staff, they must also pay for them'. As for some additional subvention to help with this, he pointed out that the poorer local authorities were already being supported by the Exchequer. He would not agree that the:

> 'unimaginative or supine administration of national parks ...justified an Exchequer grant as an induce- ment to the authority to take on the staff necessary for the efficient discharge of its duties. I cannot accept either unwillingness or poverty on the part of local authorities as a reason for agreeing to a grant towards administrative expenses which I regard as wholly undesirable in principle and in no way spe- cially justified by this case'.

The other major Treasury objection was the open-ended nature of much proposed National Park Commission expenditure. One way of controlling escalating costs which the Treasury favoured was for the Bill to lay down a fixed annual sum for the Commission's expenditure with powers to raise this by an Order subject to affirmative resolution. But expenditure limitations of a geographical kind were also demanded by the Treasury. This involved the Commission, in the first instance, limiting the number of national parks and conservation areas.

The negative influence of the Treasury was also evident in many other less significant ways. Certainly, its ethos seemed to be that if it was important not to spread resources too thinly, it was essential at a time of economic stringency to contain expenditure.

Early in 1949 Silkin produced a further outline of the Bill for the Lord President's Committee which for the first time contained a draft section on nature conservation. The Bill appeared under what was to be its final title — the National Parks and Access to the Countryside Bill — much to the distaste of Parliamentary Counsel who thought it too cumbersome. As it had already been scheduled for parliamentary time in that session by the Future Legislation Committee, Silkin was anxious for the widest consultation on its content, but concerned that nothing should hinder its progress.

Of all the responses from the members of the Lord President's Committee, amongst the most positive were those of Hugh Dalton, now no longer Chancellor of the Exchequer, but the

Chancellor of the Duchy of Lancaster, and perhaps no less importantly, President of the Ramblers' Association. Following their previous meeting, Silkin and the Lord President's Committee had finally agreed that the membership of park committees or joint boards should involve the Minister nominating three members, or a greater number, provided it did not exceed 25 per cent of its membership. Under pressure from local authorities, the Minister was now proposing the number of his nominees should be reduced if it proved difficult to find suitable candidates. Dalton, knowing the power of local landowners, argued against anything that might enhance their position at the expense of national interests and called for a 25 per cent nomination by the Minister as a matter of course.

Although he won the day, he knew it was far short of what his Ramblers' Association wanted. As he recorded in his diary, 'the Ramblers won't like the composition of the park committees'. But even less satisfactory from his point of view was his failure to persuade the Lord President's Committee and Silkin to acquire land compulsorily in the national parks in default of action by local authorities. Knowing the record of land owners in the Peak District in resisting access, Dalton was sure 'that we shall have no peace around the Peak until we have paid off the Dukes'.

More Treasury cost cutting

However, before, during and after the discussion by the Lord President's Committee of Silkin's new memorandum, the concern of the Treasury regarding some aspects of the Bill in no way diminished. To begin with, Silkin had felt that the Commission would be more independent if it had freedom to recruit and pay its own staff; it was a matter to which he attached great importance. But the Treasury was anxious that Commission staff remained government employees, a view which ultimately prevailed. As to the Commissioners themselves, there were prolonged negotiations over who should receive remuneration. It was finally agreed in December 1948 that only the Chairman and Vice-Chairman were to be paid, to the evident satisfaction of the Treasury alone.

There was also the difficulty of publicity. The Treasury wanted this handled, not by the National Parks Commission, but by the Central Office of Information and the Stationery Office. For a Minister who had already conceded most of the Commission's executive functions, 'to part with the one direct power which we have left to the Commission' was unacceptable. Even Sheepshanks suggested to the Treasury that 'the great criticism we are undoubtedly going to meet when the Bill is published is that the Commission will not be in a position to achieve anything of its own motion; and although this matter of the information service is a small thing, at least it is something'. The Treasury's only response was to say that the advisory role of the Commission had always been of fundamental importance in the discussion between the Chancellor of the Exchequer and Silkin.

Then there was the matter of the National Trust. Silkin regarded it as essential that the Exchequer should help it acquire and maintain land in national parks. But the Treasury objected on

4.5 Support for the National Trust?
The treasury resisted exchequer grants for properties such as this at Ickworth, Suffolk, as part of the 1949 Act.
Source: National Trust

the ground that the Trust in its then form should not be subsidised by government. Besides, a report from a committee chaired by Sir Ernest Gowers on stately homes was due soon and its findings, some of which would be relevant, should not be prejudged, so the Treasury argued. Whether these were convenient excuses for ducking out of a possible financial commitment is uncertain.

What is clear is that it was equally determined not to give an open-ended commitment to subsidising the acquisition of long distance footpaths. The Minister wanted powers to defray expenditure on these if it was incurred by local authorities. Although the words 'with the consent of the Treasury' were originally to be added to this proposition, the idea that Silkin should subsequently delete these caused a major confrontation between his Ministry and the Treasury. Evelyn Sharp, his Deputy Secretary, bore the brunt of the Treasury attack in which it asserted that Ministry of Town and Country Planning personnel 'are always intolerant of Treasury control in any shape or form', adding that 'a great deal of time and trouble has been wasted on this Bill through constant appeal to higher authority on trivial points'. In a final memorandum on the subject, the Treasury peevishly insisted that the wording must stand.

Legislation and the bargaining process

Thus the hand of the Treasury can be seen to lay heavily upon the proposed legislation from the time of its consideration by the Lord President's Committee (on which its interests were represented by the Chancellor of the Exchequer) through to its drafting stages, to its consideration by the Legislation Committee, and its subsequent publication as a Bill. Whilst there will always be differences of opinion about the nature of legislation between outside pressure groups, all of whom will be anxious to persuade the Minister in one direction or another, to many it may seem curious that there are inter-departmental differences within a government where it might be assumed that there is communality of purpose. But there are many paths to achieving common political objectives.

Moreover, it has to be remembered that the Treasury has to

fund a wide range of government policies. Its Ministers must make choices. No government has unlimited access to revenues, let alone one of a country that had recently emerged from an economically debilitating war. Unfortunately, the overwhelming mandate for major social and economic change that followed the 1945 election did not provide the wherewithal for its achievement. When choices have to be made and priorities established, the Treasury can seem vindictive and small-minded in the eyes of a Minister who does not want to see his cherished scheme emasculated. Certainly, in the case of the legislation in question, the Treasury never saw it as having a very high priority. But each interest group inside government, whether it is the Treasury or another department, has to fight its corner for what it will justify as the common good.

However, the role of civil servants in the process of evolving legislation cannot be reduced to one of neutrality, merely carrying out the will of their political masters. Even if this would seem the

4.6 The run-up to the 1949 Act! As well as pursuing the cause of the 1949 Act in parliament, some members of the Labour Party were active ramblers. *Source*: Ramblers' Association

constitutional ideal, it cannot necessarily be assumed that civil servants share the enthusiasms of their Ministers or are likely to be as ready as they ought to embrace the policies of a new administration. These may be radically different from the one that preceded it and on which they may have worked hard and invested much intellectual capital.

Hugh Dalton found the corps of senior civil servants with whom he came into contact as a Minister rather negative in their approach. He described them as a set of 'congenital snag-hunters', whilst Shirley Williams, a Labour Minister of later years, spoke of the civil service as 'a beautifully designed and effective braking mechanism'. Both of these judgements might justly have been applied to Sheepshanks and others in the Ministry of Town and Country Planning.

Finally, the bargaining processes which precede legislation must also be dependent for their effectiveness on the ability of the Minister in charge and his position in the government. That Silkin was not a full member of the Cabinet inevitably added to his difficulties, especially in dealing with the Treasury. In summary, it is then possible to see that any Bill brought before parliament for the first time must inevitably be the outcome of various inter-acting forces, some external to the government and some intra-governmental. Even then, as it is subjected to due parliamentary process, it is unlikely to emerge totally unscathed, whatever the Government's majority in the two Houses. On both counts Silkin's Bill was no exception.

Second Reading in the Commons

It must be now clear that the National Parks and Access to the Countryside Bill as presented to parliament, was not quite that which had been lobbied for outside, nor that which enthusiasts for the Hobhouse Report would have wanted. Indeed, throughout the period in which the Minister had been in discussion about it with the Government, conservationists and the recreation lobby had not let up in their attempts to push their case. It is not surprising, therefore, that although there was some genuine cause for satisfaction when the Bill came to the House of Commons for its Second Reading, it did not receive universal praise. Thus, in spite of Silkin's attempt in his opening speech to put a good face on it through his claim that it represented 90 per cent of Hobhouse, he was soon attacked.

The Conservative member for Twickenham, E.H. Keeling, remarked that since the Hobhouse Report had been published 'the Government mountain has been in labour for a period of eighteen months, quite a long period of gestation, but has produced only a very small mouse' and he was astonished at the Minister's claim that the Bill 'was 90 per cent of the Hobhouse recommendations'. Although he objected to what had happened to the National Parks Commission, it was W.S. Morrison, Silkin's Conservative predecessor as Minister, who best caught the mood of the House. In welcoming the Bill on behalf of the Opposition, he said that they 'rejoiced in anything which made an understanding of the countryside a more general possession of the people'.

About those parts of the Bill which dealt with nature conservation, Morrison was generally pleased, as, in the event, were most of his parliamentary colleagues. Aspects of it covering public footpaths and rights of way, and access to the open countryside, also found favour. However, he felt that the downgrading of the National Parks Commission to the point at which its functions were largely advisory had:

> 'caused the express displeasure of some of the voluntary societies ..... If the Minister feels a little nettled at the criticisms of the voluntary societies, he must ... appreciate that these enthusiasts, who had worked so long and zealously for national as distinct from local parks, feel a certain disappointment ... No doubt they feel that to the Commission recommended by the Dower and Hobhouse reports, this Commission bears about the same relation as what is called a baby's comforter to a real feeding bottle'.

As Morrison added, 'It may have a superficial resemblance to attract and soothe the innocent, but it stops short and there is nothing behind it'.

This was a sentiment echoed again and again in the two-day

debate. Even if many MPs were not aware of the background to the internal government debate that had led to the decision to give the National Parks Commission an advisory role, D.L. Lipson, the Conservative member for Cheltenham, quite remarkably summed up the thinking of many when he said, 'I really cannot understand how a progressive government could hand over to reactionary local authorities the administration of the measures passed by this House'.

The Labour member for Blackburn, Barbara Castle, also took up a matter first aired by Morrison at the beginning of the debate and of popular concern, as it turned out, to a whole cross-section of members of the House. This was that the Commission had no way of effectively dealing with proposed developments in national parks put forward by the Government or its agencies. Indeed Sir Arthur Salter, the Independent member for Oxford University, had already stated that in construing the threat to these areas as being 'the ill-regulated and insufficiently controlled activities of industries or companies rather than public authorities', the Bill was misconceived.

Although Hugh Dalton was later to propose that the solution to this problem might lie in all such developments being subject to consideration by a cabinet committee, Barbara Castle's contribution on this point was at the time ably supported by Emrys Roberts, the Labour member for Merioneth. Speaking in particular of his own part of North Wales, he forcefully maintained that

4.7 Military use of national parks
Fears about the use of such areas by the War Office at the time of the 1949 Act anticipated an enduring problem. Wilsworthy Camp, Dartmoor.
Source: John Weir

'the gravest threat to a national park ... comes from the activities of government, with the worst trespasser, the War Office'. However, apart from W.M.F. Vane, the Conservative member for Westmorland, Roberts was one of the few MPs to offer support for the notion of allowing power to rest, not so much with the Commission, but with the local authorities in the parks. This was a subject to which E.M. King, the Parliamentary Secretary to the Ministry of Town and Country Planning, returned in his closing speech further to justify the abandonment of the precepts of the Hobhouse Report over questions of planning control.

Of the other contributions to the debate, Sir Arthur Salter, like Hugh Dalton, wanted a permanent Cabinet committee, if only to be the final line of defence for the interests of the national parks in general. E.H. Keeling also drew attention to what he called one of the Bill's 'most serious defects' — its failure to insist that where a park is partly in one area and partly in another 'it need not be planned as a whole'. Like Emrys Roberts and D.L. Lipson, he, too, had wanted the parks, if they were truly national, to be paid for totally by the nation.

At a more prosaic level, Hugh Molson, the Conservative member for the High Peak, regretted the absence of a warden service in national parks which might act as a police force to deter vandals. Over the more important question of the line to be drawn between industry and amenity, like Vane, he was not anxious to see quarrying unduly forced into decline — economic diversity was important. But the Peak District was also Dalton's stamping ground and his Ramblers' Association affiliations made him warmly welcome the access provisions of the Bill, as well as repeat again the views he had already expressed in the formative stages of the Bill regarding the need for the public acquisition of land in the national parks and the role the National Land Fund might play in this.

Reviewing the debate as a whole, it is often difficult to recognise divisions of opinions along partly lines. For example, Colonel Clarke, the Tory member for East Grinstead, was a strong supporter of the Minister's views on the make-up of the parks committees. If there was a tendency for Conservatives like the Leeds North member, Osbert Peake, and Sir Ian Fraser of Lonsdale, to proffer some doubts about the possible adverse effects of visitors to the countryside on traditional rural activities such as farming, supporting, as it were, the land-owning interests, there was Tom Fraser, Under Secretary of State for Scotland, speaking of the need not to prejudice food production. Moreover, M. Philips Price, the Labour member for the Forest of Dean, called for the development of agriculture and forestry in balance with conservation and recreation. Even the Chancellor of the Duchy of Lancaster suggested that if food and timber production were adversely affected by numbers, access might need to be limited.

However, where Labour members found common cause was in the general spirit of the Bill. As H.D. Hughes, the member for Wolverhampton West, put it, the Bill represents 'a very important step in the long struggle of the common people to establish their right to the freedom of their own land'. But was such a sentiment really very different from that expressed at the beginning of the debate by W.S. Morrison on behalf of the Opposition?

In Committee and on Report

With the Second Reading the debate about the principles of the Bill was over. The Committee and Report stages, which involved looking at the Bill clause by clause and making any necessary amendments, took place between late April and July.

Proceedings in Standing Committee began with a bipartisan approach to the discussion apparent from the start. The Conservative, Hugh Molson, who had publicly campaigned for a strong National Parks Commission with centralised planning powers, at once complained that the National Parks Commission would not have the powers, authority or standing that was contemplated by the Hobhouse Report. He therefore put forward an amendment seeking to allow the Commission to hold land. In this he was supported by Barbara Castle, who said that it seemed as if the Minister had gone out of his way in the Bill to try to bypass the Commission in a number of important matters. 'We have cause for great concern as to the type of central authority that is going to emerge from this Bill if the powers we ask for are not given us', she added. Silkin, in response, did not feel he could agree that the Commission should hold land generally for the purpose of access. But whilst the amendment was rejected, he did concede that he was prepared to look again at some matters pertaining to the National Parks Commission.

Evidence that this might be proving to be the case can be found in a letter written to *The Times* after a morning session of the Committee on 19 May. It was signed by a number of its members keen to show publicly their desire to have the Bill strengthened. They maintained that over the discussion of Parts I and II of the Bill, which dealt with the setting up of national parks and the Commission and had just been completed:

> 'the Minister, while standing firm by the main struc-
> ture of the Bill, has gone a long way to meet propos-
> als put forward by the amenity societies. The
> proportion of national members on authorities
> respectively for each park has been raised to a mini-
> mum of thirty-three and one-third per cent; an
> amendment has been promised to clarify and consol-
> idate the powers of the Commission; and many assur-
> ances have been given as to its status and
> responsibilities'.

More positive proof of Silkin's intentions, though, had to await the recommittal of the Bill to the Committee of the Whole House and its Report stage (both taken on the Floor of the House of Commons), when tabled amendments could be considered. Here it was evident that out of the Bill's now 115 clauses, 67 were up for revision. If only a very small number of these was put forward by the Opposition, it was clear that the Minister had tried to do more than merely put right errors and omissions and to tidy up inade-quacies of drafting apparent at the Second Reading. There were, indeed, many genuine attempts to keep the promises made at the time of the Bill's clause by clause discussion, not only by amend-ments, but also in the 17 entirely new clauses he tabled.

Notable amongst these was that which encompassed his promised undertaking to bring all of the functions and duties of the Commission into one clause instead of leaving them dis-tributed through the Bill. If this was acceptable to many, to some this new clause seemed opportunistic and once again Barbara Castle was to be found casting doubts on the Minister's integrity. She reminded the House that although one of the chief purposes of the new clause, when promised in Standing Committee, was to increase the authority of the National Parks Commission, the Minister had used it to slip in a new power by which he could direct the timing and the designation of national parks. Barbara Castle suggested that such an action on the part of the Minister would be like saying to the Commission 'Your final power, your last remnant of authority, shall be stripped from you and you shall emerge finally as merely an advisory body and nothing else'. But without the sup-

4.8 Barbara Castle – thirty years on Although a parliamentary activist during the passage of the 1949 Act, she was still championing the ramblers' cause at a Pennine Way celebration in 1985. *Source*: Ramblers' Association

port she needed on this, her effort to overturn the offending section of the new clause through a suitably worded amendment was negatived.

Much greater support came for another amendment to this new clause permitting the setting up of a Welsh national parks subcommittee, which according to its proposer, Emrys Roberts, would further the interests of national parks in Wales and ensure an effective voice for the people of Wales concerning their national parks. Although wide cross-party support was forthcoming from Welsh members, Silkin was against what he saw an an amendment which said more about Welsh nationalism than national parks. As with most of the amendments which were not his own, his effective arguments caused their withdrawal.

Other new clauses tabled and ultimately accepted by the House included those making provision for accommodation, meals and refreshment on long distance routes, and for penalties to be imposed on those who would display notices deterring the public from using footpaths. As one member of the House had said in Standing Committee: 'Should farmers be allowed to say "Beware of the Bull", when there was, in fact, no bull?' But most important of all were the new clauses which had resulted largely from the lobbying of interested parties outside parliament. These dealt with the need to exempt Epping Forest and Burnham Beeches from the provisions of the Bill and the need to withdraw from the threat of compulsory purchase all inalienable land owned by the National Trust. By 21 July the Bill had uneventfully been given its entirely formal Third Reading.

Their Lordships' Second Reading

But the debate in the House of Lords was yet to come and although Silkin, as he intimated to the Cabinet, would have liked to have had the Bill passed into law before the long summer recess, this was not to prove possible. On the advice of the Lord Privy Seal, Lord Addison, the crucial Second Reading was delayed until autumn.

When the Second Reading debate eventually did begin on 18

October, it was at once apparent that the tone of the proceedings was to be very different from those of the Commons with a clearer reflection of the uncertainties and hesitations of the landowning classes so well represented in this House. Although Lord Macdonald, Post-Master General, introduced the debate with the expected rhetoric about the Bill and its capacity to enable thousands to enjoy the peace and quiet of the countryside, their noble lordships were soon voicing their feelings about it.

The Earl of Radnor and the Duke of Rutland both doubted the wisdom of spending money on national parks, with the Bill itself leading, in their eyes, to a conflict with agriculture and increasing unnecessary bureaucracy. Lord Winster was adamant that the Bill should not publicise national parks, some of the probable sites which had already been damaged by visitor pressure, whilst Lord Cranworth envisaged that 'an orgy of destruction' could result from legislation that encouraged visitors to the countryside. In a rare moment of controversy in either House concerning the scientific aspects of the Bill, Lord Llewellin said that nature reserves could prove a breeding ground for vermin with all that this meant for agriculture and other traditional rural pursuits.

The Earl de la Warr, in opening the debate for the Opposition, was also worried about the impact of visitors on farming, but he followed a more positive line in calling for the Government to respond to this problem by publishing a countryside code to be enforced by a warden service. He also pursued the more reasoned attacks on the Bill of 'the other place'. The lack of power to be enjoyed by the National Parks Commission particularly bothered him as it did the Socialist peer, Lord Chorley, who as a member of the Hobhouse Committee was now at least prepared to see if Silkin's alternatives could work. But de la Warr also expressed his concern about the damage government and public agencies could do in national parks unless effective ways were found to prevent them, a point explored by other lords including Llewellin, Hylton, Harlech and Rochdale.

In his closing speech for the Government, Lord Macdonald was moved to grasp this nettle and gave an assurance that the Minister would 'do all he could to safeguard the beauty of the countryside' where it was likely to be thus affected. He also made promises regarding the need to protect forestry and agricultural interests, since in doing so he was hardly striking at the heart of the Bill. He would see that planning officers were made aware of the importance of both of these traditional occupations.

However, Macdonald's words were not enough and at the Committee stage Earl de la Warr moved an amendment to have two members appointed to the National Parks Commission with practical knowledge of agriculture and forestry. Further consultation followed and at the Report stage a new clause to the Bill was introduced to the effect that the National Parks Commission and the Nature Conservancy, in exercising their duties should pay 'due regard to the needs of agriculture and forestry'.

The Committee stage saw evidence of the Government's own sensitivity to pressure, for Lord Macdonald moved a new clause on access to woodlands. He said the Minister had been sympathetic to the contention that the public should not be automatically admitted to woodland where access would threaten or endanger timber production. At the same time the public should not be automatically barred from entry where no danger was feared. What he did not say was that this clause went some way to meet the intense lobbying on this issue from the Forestry Commission.

Other substantial amendments were successfully made, but usually as a result of the efforts of the Opposition. In Committee Lord Llewellin insisted that the National Parks Commission should be charged with the preparation of a uniform model of by-laws for local parks authorities which would ensure the preservation of order and the prevention of damage. Lord Carrington was able to amend the Bill so that a local planning authority could offer water recreation facilities only where no one else was prepared to provide them.

4.9 The Country Code
This code, familiar to the countryside visitor of the late 1980s, owes its existence to pressure exerted in the House of Lords during the debate on the 1949 Act.
Source:
Countryside Commission

In a similar vein, Earl de la Warr also returned to the fray with a fresh clause which recognised that local planning authorities should not introduce new catering and accommodation facilities unless they were assured that there was inadequate private provision. But perhaps of greater importance was that he again raised the question of the publication of a country code, this time ably supported by Viscount Maugham, Lord Hawke, Lord Merthyr and the Archbishop of York. Such was the pressure now exerted

FOLLOW THE COUNTRY CODE

Countryside COMMISSION

Enjoy the countryside and
respect its life and work.
Guard against all risk of fire.
Fasten all gates.
Keep your dogs under close control.
Keep to public paths across farmland.
Use gates and stiles to cross fences,
hedges and walls.
Leave livestock, crops and machinery alone.
Take your litter home.
Help to keep all water clean.
Protect wildlife, plants and trees.
Take special care on country roads.
Make no unnecessary noise.

TAKE CARE OF THE COUNTRY

on the Government that it was forced to carry discussion on after the Committee stage, finally conceding this matter on Report in late November when this proposal was written into the Bill.

In addition to the rather more substantial changes already discussed, there were many others mostly of a drafting character, or were consequential on drafting amendments, or represented minor improvements in the machinery of the Bill, making up a total of 140 Lords amendments in all. As Silkin told the House of Commons on 9 December 1948 'we do not disagree with any of them'. The passage of the Bill into law a week later was, therefore, a mere formality.

Establishing the Commission

Quite early on in the progress of the Bill through parliament, Silkin had begun to look to its future as an Act. He would need to have in place, as a top priority, his appointments to the National Parks Commission. First attempts to address the question came as early as April 1949 with the Permanent Secretary, Sir Thomas Sheepshanks, offering suggestions of his own. These included the name of Lord Portal, on the grounds that whilst at school 'he had created a bit of a sensation by keeping hawks'. Later deliberations on the subject were more considered, so that by the time the Royal Assent was given to the Bill on 16 December 1949, the Minister was able to announce its first members.

The choice seemed to avoid the obvious charges of extremism that might have been raised by critics. On the one hand, there were no preservationists who were likely to want to see the total cessation of most forms of economic activity in national parks. On the other, those whose interests would be purely local and unlikely to address the national need for recreation and enjoyment were also not in evidence. On the whole the Commissioners seemed to be those with a known interest and concern for countryside both in the practical and academic sense.

Some argued that the composition of the Commission erred on the side of the political, but with Sir Patrick Duff, an experienced diplomat, civil servant, member of the Council for the Preservation

4.10 The Pennine Way
A popular recreation path, it was designated a long distance route under the 1949 Act.
Source: Countryside Commission

of Rural England and the British Trust for Ornithology as its chairman, and Lord Merthyr, president of the Royal Forestry Society and an active critic of the Bill on its way through the Lords, as a member, it seemed unlikely that they had been appointed to do the bidding of the Minister.

Others appointed included J.J. Lawson, a Labour MP, as vice-chairman; Sir Ifan ab Owen Edwards, a member of the Welsh Committee of the National Trust; Professor R.C. McLean, a botanist and member of the Nature Conservancy; Francis Ritchie, chairman of the Rights of Way Committee of the Ramblers' Association; John Wilmot MP, a founder member of the Workers' Travel Association; Mr E.W. Wimble, of the British Tourist and

Holidays Board; and Pauline Dower, widow of the author of the report that had helped prepare the way for the National Parks and Access to the Countryside Act 1949.

There was certainly important work for the Commission to expedite without delay. A small but expert permanent staff was required to service the Commission; the precise areas, locations and numbers of the future national parks had to be settled and then other areas of outstanding natural beauty which were to come under special control had to be determined. The Commissioners had to scrutinise schemes for the protection and improvement of the national parks prepared by local authorities; they also had to compile lists of people from which the Minister could select national nominees to occupy one-third of the seats on the special local committees controlling each park. There were the plans to be prepared for the establishment of long distance routes, such as the then projected Pennine Way, by which the public were to make 'extensive journeys on foot or horseback'.

Fears for the future

In a sense there was all to play for, with the degree of success accruing to the Commission inside the powers given it under the Act, depending a great deal on its treatment by government and the local authorities. In comparison with the powers of compulsion given the Nature Conservancy covering nature reserves, it was obvious that it was much less well off. In the light of what went into the Act it was apparent to many protagonists of the national parks movement that the activities of other government departments and agencies were likely to be a major threat to the work of the Commission.

Not least among these was Sir Norman Birkett. For many years the highly effective chairman of the Standing Committee on National Parks and a brilliant advocate, he was to make the fight against such intrusions the major preoccupation of his retirement. Indeed, the successful battle to preserve Ullswater in the Lake District from the depredations of Manchester Corporation,

proved, in the eyes of many, to be the last and greatest of his many courtroom triumphs.

Fears were also voiced at the time about the possible short-sightedness of some local authorities that might disregard national needs, whilst others might refuse to cooperate in managing a park that spread beyond its own boundaries. Given the Act that was eventually passed, the last word over such matters would have to rest with the Minister or indeed the Cabinet. Certainly, if there were grave doubts about the distribution of powers and duties between the Minister, the Commission and the local authorities during the discussion of the Bill in parliament, these remained

4.11 Ullswater after Birkett
Sir Norman played a critical role in the preservation of this national park lake in its natural state.
Source:
Countryside Commission

much in evidence as the new decade began. A strong feeling outside government that the Commission might have been given much more authority persisted.

As *The Times* leader of 19 December 1949 stated, the Commission by

> 'their own abilities and prestige may gain for themselves the needed authority, but it will be an uphill struggle unless they can rely on the firm support of the Minister and on an enlightened attitude from the local authorities who have seldom been willing to combine efficiency for the joint control of a service beyond their separate capacities. The danger is that the Minister will be tempted to discover special circumstances to explain why he should not set up joint boards for the control of national parks which cannot well be managed in any other way'.

The fears so expressed were to prove, in the years that followed, all too real.

PART II

5 The national parks

Designating national parks

The problems of the early years of the national parks were to prove three-fold — weak administrations, lack of money and over-compromise by central government. If *The Times* in December 1949 had speculated with some perspicacity about the difficulties that would emerge and had foreseen the likely broad compromises, the *Manchester Guardian* was already reporting from its own backyard the particulars that would ultimately feed such compromises. As its columns made clear, Derbyshire was at the time advocating county opposition to boards as it had done when the Hobhouse Report was published, and it had the support of all the Peak District planning authorities except Sheffield. There was opposition to national parks appointing their own staff separate from those of the county councils. In the Lakes, whilst Cumberland and Westmorland supported boards, Lancashire had suggested a compromise administrative structure, but, as the newspaper recorded, all three counties were against the boards appointing their own staff.

The Peak District and the Lake District were the first national parks to be designated and in 1951 were formed, as joint boards, just as the Act intended. Independent of the counties, parks could precept on them; that is, they could send the counties a bill for their costs; although with two-thirds of their members from those counties — three in the Lakes and five in the Peak — they were not likely to be all that extravagant. The Lakes set a limit on its precept, but in practice it provided enough money when needed.

The Peak employed its own staff, the only park to do so for over 20 years, but all the other parks made use of county staff, each giving advice for their own 'patch'. The Lakes accepted the need for a clerk and gave the job to the Clerk of Westmorland County

Council. That turned out well, for the Clerk was Kenneth Himsworth, an enthusiast for the national park, and a fell walker who knew the area and understood its problems. He was a very positive administrator who took a keen interest in the effective use of the Act and, over the years, the need for its modification.

Early preparatory work by the Sheffield branch of the Council for the Preservation of Rural England was the most likely reason why the Peak was the first to be designated. With other voluntary organisations, it had already defined boundaries for a national park. Because of this, the Peak got ahead of the compromise that was to be accepted elsewhere. Indeed, had they not acted so quickly, there might not have been a Peak Board.

Thus the effectiveness of legislation can depend on a few key personalities in its history. In the foundation of the Peak National Park, the key personalities were the leaders of the Council for the Preservation of Rural England's initiative, Lt Col Gerald Haythornthwaite and his wife, Ethel. Ethel, as we noted in chapter 3, had been a member of the Hobhouse Committee and, with her husband, who was an architect and planner, had fought valiantly in the inter-war years for better town and country planning and for the establishment of national parks. They did much to defend the unique character of the Peak District, a point we return to in chapter 9, particularly demanding that modern buildings should follow

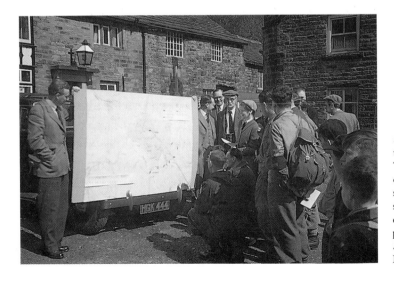

5.1 Early days of the Peak Park
The inauguration of the warden service at Edale shortly after the designation of the park in 1951.
Source: Gerald Haythornthwaite

97

architectural tradition by building in stone and should not be part of the dreary surburbia so common elsewhere. Before the war they had even employed, at their own expense, their own staff to produce better house designs and they had helped the National Trust buy land to protect it from development.

In the Lake District a strong leader was the Rev. H.H. Symonds. A founder member of the influential Standing Committee on National Parks, which we discussed in chapter 2, he proved to be a leading force in developing public support from the Friends of the Lake District. Not only was he very knowledgeable, but also he became an important and effective influence on the Lakes Board.

For a time, because of the differences of background, there was suspicion between county members and nominated members serving national park administrations, but as time went on relations improved. Nominated members discovered politics, and elected members had a new perspective on a part of their county. The consequent debate often developed new ideas. There was, too, in the boards a healthy interaction between nominated members who came from a variety of backgrounds. In the Peak District, as well as Gerald Haythornthwaite, two other members were to prove an important influence. One was Paddy Monkhouse whose paper the *Manchester Guardian* took a great deal of interest in national parks and who followed Gerald Haythornthwaite as Vice-Chairman of the Board. The other was Ivor Morten, whose contribution was different and unique. He was a hill farmer, a member of the Country Landowners' Association (CLA) and the National Farmers' Union (NFU) and while other farmers opposed the establishment of the national park, he welcomed it, recognising the reasons for it, including the extent of urban demand for access. From the beginning he saw farming as being the means of protecting scenery by traditional management. His role has been much misunderstood because of his way of working. With ramblers he argued the farmer's case, and with farmers that of the ramblers. This is not the way to be universally popular, but once one had the eye to see the two sides, reconciliation was in sight, with a wider perspective for all concerned. This was later to become an essential element in the development of a new style of administration. He was a man many years ahead of his time.

Seventeen months after its first meeting, the Peak Board was able to report that: '...There has emerged among members of the Board a singleness of purpose and an enthusiasm which augurs well for its future... '.

The Lake District Board also, had been busy. It had its first meeting less than seven days after its designation, and by the time of its first annual report, in March 1953, it had assessed problems reasonably thoroughly. Important among these were the loss of hedgerows, the need to extend the area of Forestry Commission consultation, the need to help the farmers with the maintenance of footpaths, and the need to create new paths and to cover the costs itself. It had reviewed the access position generally and the common land situation; it had asked for consultation on road widening and realignment; it had decided to make its own provision of caravan sites and to try to assist financially in providing hostel accommodation; and, in the light of its experience, it was concerned that government departments should be under the same amenity obligations as other developers.

5.2 A national park board on tour
The elected members of the Peak National Park joint board undertook regular journeys around their domain. This 1961 picture shows Col. Haythornthwaite at the front on the left.
Source: Gerald Haythornthwaite

Administrative compromises

But there were to be no more boards. While eight more national parks were designated in the 1950s, none was given a board with executive powers, and even now, in 1989, the situation remains the same. Thus the counties who had opposed the establishment of national parks were given the job of administering them. In a report for the Countryside Commission in 1971, Sir Jack Longland explained how the compromise started in the case of Snowdonia. The Minister, now no longer of Town and Country Planning, but of Housing and Local Government, had apparently told the three county councils in June 1951 that there were no exceptional circumstances for dispensing with a joint board in Snowdonia. But the counties brought further pressure to bear and even refused to accept the Minister's nominated members. In 1952 the Minister, by now the Conservative, Harold MacMillan, although admitting a board would be better, accepted a Joint Advisory Committee for an experimental period of three years. The executive powers, including those for planning, were to be left with each of the three counties.

These actions brought protests from the Standing Committee on National Parks. It had already protested on staffing and other matters, but these had been dismissed by Hugh Dalton who had followed Silkin as Minister. He suggested it should '...concentrate on what needs to be done ...rather than worrying about whether the machinery will be adequate...'. A similar view was expressed by his successor, Harold MacMillan, but subsequent events showed the Standing Committee's concern was well founded. Snowdonia's Joint Advisory Committee was to have no executive powers, but would have a part-time planning consultant. The National Parks Commission said rather weakly that it '...will, of course, refer to the Advisory Committee any matter that would not otherwise come to it, but upon which the Commission think the opinion of the Advisory Committee should be obtained...'. After three years the life of that Committee was extended, and so it remained until 1974 when a new Act required a proper National Park Committee.

In 1951 the Dartmoor National Park had its designation confirmed, the Pembrokeshire Coast and North York Moors following in 1952, and the Yorkshire Dales and Exmoor in 1954. For other national parks a planning consultant was not even demanded to give an overall view. The three original objectives of an independent joint board, a full-time planning officer and the planning of each national park as a single geographical unit, were thus abandoned. The administrative structure that remained was, as a consequence, inadequate for the task it had to perform.

There were sometimes good local reasons why little was done. Northumberland, for example, had actually welcomed its national park when it had been established in 1956, but its resources were minute. With major industrial problems and ambitious plans for the south-east of the county, there was little time available for a county planning department to consider the national park.

The last national park to be established was the Brecon Beacons, which had its status confirmed in 1957, and although two other areas had been suggested by Hobhouse, they were not designated. Because one of these, the South Downs, had been ploughed during the war, the National Parks Commission considered it no longer warranted consideration. The other area that had been suggested was the Broads. In his first briefing of the National Parks Commission, Hugh Dalton had stressed this as a priority for designation in order to prevent any further deterioration in its physical condition. Members of the Commission, however, were rather divided over the issue of whether it should be designated. While accepting that the area nearest the water had scenic and natural importance, they were doubtful whether the rest of the area was up to national park standard. Proposals for proper management, when later prepared, proved costly and this proved to be the final deterrent.

Thus, by the end of the 1950s the pattern of national parks was set. But positive action was not very great, a problem that the National Parks Commission had realised by the middle of the decade. Clearly, the Act was not proving very effective. Sensing the counties' reluctance to face the cost of greater activity, in 1956 it suggested to Duncan Sandys, the Minister at the time, that all expenditure, including administration, should be grant earning and that grant should not be limited to 75 per cent. The

National Parks in England and Wales

as at Autumn 1989

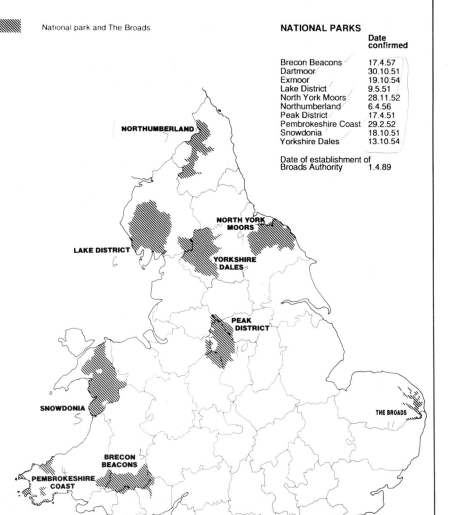

National park and The Broads

NATIONAL PARKS

	Date confirmed
Brecon Beacons	17.4.57
Dartmoor	30.10.51
Exmoor	19.10.54
Lake District	9.5.51
North York Moors	28.11.52
Northumberland	6.4.56
Peak District	17.4.51
Pembrokeshire Coast	29.2.52
Snowdonia	18.10.51
Yorkshire Dales	13.10.54

Date of establishment of
Broads Authority 1.4.89

NORTHUMBERLAND

NORTH YORK MOORS

LAKE DISTRICT

YORKSHIRE DALES

PEAK DISTRICT

SNOWDONIA

THE BROADS

BRECON BEACONS

PEMBROKESHIRE COAST

EXMOOR

DARTMOOR

0   50km

Commission even suggested (rashly, it later considered) that developers should be compensated for complying with extra conditions in national parks. It foresaw in its 1955 report that a 'great work of education' will be needed before the importance of national parks is widely understood.

5.3 National parks in 1989
Source: Countryside Commission

The need for education, the Commission must have thought, certainly applied to government for it was in 1958 that three proposals alien to national parks were projected. They were the Esso Oil Refinery in Milford Haven; a large ore-stocking ground at Angle, also in the Pembrokeshire Coast Park; and in Snowdonia the Trawsfynydd Nuclear Power Station. The Commission accepted the refinery because it felt it was set as low as possible in the landscape, but it was much opposed to the other proposals, though it would have accepted the ore store on a better site. In Snowdonia there was local support for the nuclear power station. The Minister approved all three projects.

Limited resources and new pressures

In 1959 the first national park conference was held and, rather surprisingly considering all the discouragements, it proved to be most successful, giving the National Parks Commission fresh heart. In

5.4 Alien developments in a national park Although designed not to break the sky-line, Trawsfynydd power station in Snowdonia still over-powers the landscape. *Source*: John Blunden

103

its Annual Report it suggested more money for national parks. The new spirit seemed eventually to reach the Minister, for speaking at the third national park conference in 1961, ten years after the first designations, Mr Henry Brooke pleaded to have submitted to him for grant something other than car parks. 'It is not I, but you, who must initiate', he said, adding '...I would be happier if authorities were putting forward more schemes and more imaginative schemes than they are actually doing'. Lord Strang, Chairman of the Commission pointed out that 'In no case that I know of has grant so far been refused, and the Commission has every reason to believe that grant would be liberally afforded if more ambitious proposals than those put forward in the past could now be submitted'.

The challenge was not taken up and soon it was too late, for the Government later restricted its financial support. Each year's budget was judged on what had been spent in the previous year, and, as budgets were small, increases were even smaller. Besides, there was another financial snag, since each project had to be approved for grant by the National Parks Commission. Each item was part of a national park's budget that had only been agreed a few months before the year started. If the money was not spent within the year, it was lost. Yet, for each project, authority had to be obtained, meetings arranged, land bought, estimates sought, contracts signed and works completed. As a result, underspending became inevitable. Ironically, this was sometimes used as an excuse for not providing the greater resources that national parks needed.

As the Commission had previously noted, the administrative work involved in the process of grant approvals was not even covered by the resulting grant. In practice, the unenthusiastic counties found themselves paying more than half the cost. Yet, in the 1950s, an internal briefing note for the Minister warned that national payment of administrative costs was 'not a proposition the Treasury are ever likely to yield to without great pressure'. Thus, it was not surprising that by 1971, 20 years after the first designations, the total expenditure for all ten parks was little more than £1.2 million, and half of that was spent by the two boards.

There had been another radical change from the original intention for national parks. It was notable that in the Minister's comment in 1961 there was no talk of government initiatives for he did not say what needed to be done. He merely suggested to the counties, who had not wanted national parks, that they should submit more imaginative proposals. When the Hobhouse Committee proposed boards it had said: 'Clearly national parks must be national in fact as well as in name'. Yet now they were not regarded as a national responsibility. This attitude continued to be reflected in government decisions on planning appeals; parks became just one of the parties to which the Minister might have regard. As Gerald Haythornthwaite was to point out, national parks had to fight for their corner and to do so with very small resources. The approach could hardly have been further from the 'national decision and action...' that Hobhouse had envisaged. Indeed, the attitude nationally was so lax that some of the early planning consents for mineral extraction given by the Minister have few effective conditions on them.

There were national park successes too, although usually after a battle. For example, in the 1960s when the Central Electricity Generating Board proposed a 400kv power line across the moors

5.5 A blot on the landscape
Despite some successes in routing power lines underground, they can still have a pervasive impact in some national parks, as in this Snowdonia example.
Source: John Blunden

of the northern Peak District, a government Minister insisted, in spite of the considerable extra cost entailed, that for three miles it should go underground using an old railway tunnel.

In the late 1960s there was a new pressure. The growth in recreation had been greater than expected and, with increasing car ownership, took new forms. Access to the countryside was part of this trend. In 1968 came the Countryside Act, and the National Parks Commission became the Countryside Commission with a much wider remit. The new Act also provided powers of value to national parks. Apart from the establishment of country parks elsewhere to relieve the pressure, there were to be powers to provide study centres, the ability to control boating on national park lakes (widely used in the Lake District by the mid 1970s), a rather flimsy power to control the ploughing of moorland, and new powers for traffic regulation. But, in spite of these improvements, many of the national park pioneers resented the change of emphasis in the work of the Commission, interpreting it as a downgrading of the relative role of the parks.

This reaction was understandable. As we saw in chapter 4, the pioneers had seen a massive dilution of the recommendations of the Hobhouse Committee: they had also experienced since the 1949 Act inaction from the counties and weakness from government, with budgets that bore little relation to the original intentions or the much increased pressures. For example, the £50,000,000 that had been promised by Hugh Dalton in 1946 to help with land acquisitions for access, as we mentioned in chapter 3, seemed to have disappeared altogether. Moreover, national parks had been under pressure for mineral extraction, afforestation, reservoirs, roads, housing development and tourist development. These pioneers had to fight all the way, but the pioneers fought willingly, for they had seen before the Second World War what could happen without adequate planning control. They were also old enough to know that in all planning there is an element of fashion, and that for recreation was particularly strong at the time. So it was not surprising that their reaction was both defensive and distrusting. In return it was not surprising that others saw them as backward-looking, neither part of the swinging sixties, nor even realistic about change and current concerns.

The early seventies and Sandford

The year 1970 was European Conservation Year. As a result there began to be an increased public awareness that resources were limited, that we needed to husband them well, to manage what we already had. It offered a new set of ground rules for national parks. Three things were also new at that year's national parks conference. The Countryside Commission invited other Europeans; a nature conservation theme was introduced; and for the first time the press was invited.

An interest in the dynamics of conservation was particularly significant. As we noted in Part I of this book, prior to the 1949 Act there had been a division between the scientific business of nature conservation and the concept of 'national parks'. The roots of the latter were in development control and architectural conservation and in access for open air recreation. The ploughing of moorland and afforestation had caused concern in the national parks, but to a large extent the motive was scenic rather than a concern for the dynamics of conservation. The fact that the two might combine had rarely been considered, for the divisions of the National Parks and Access to the Countryside Act 1949 were too strong. Also a

5.6 Exmoor under the plough The ploughing of Exmoor was to become a much greater preoccupation for the national park authorities from the 1970s. *Source*: Countryside Commission

107

sort of professional apartheid frequently existed, the product of educational separate development. And there were, as we also recognised earlier, differences of interest within the voluntary sector.

Within the membership of the national parks, Ivor Morten, by now (and for 14 years) the Peak Park's Vice-Chairman, did much to try to bring nature conservation increasingly into national park thinking. He operated in a lot of subtle ways. It was he who advocated a small Nature Conservancy sub-office within the national park office, so that greater integration came at an informal level. It was he who introduced the nature conservation element into the 1970 conference. And it was he who, as a farmer, did not demand better concessions for farmers as the National Farmers' Union tended to do, but rather better integration of effort.

John Dunning, a hill farmer appointed member in the Lake District, also did much to further this integrated view, including taking a very sound interest in the relationship of national park hill farming to action going on in the European Economic Community. In the national parks themselves, two other groups of people were beginning to take the stage. First there were the voluntary rangers or wardens. Originally intended as a link between the townsman seeking access and the landowner, their knowledge of country life increased. With new full-time ranger services, training began to develop and many of those recruited came with interests (and possibly degrees) in geography, the natural sciences and various new courses of study involving environmental and recreational management. In effect they became a much needed new generation of national park supporters.

The second group that grew in the 1970s was the conservation volunteers, following in the wake of the national park voluntary warden services. Often the initial emphasis for these new volunteers was on jobs such as footpath clearance, which hikers wanted, but could lead to concern about problems of erosion caused by bad land drainage, to stile building, and to the whole process of land management. Perhaps these groups seem of insufficient significance to influence national parks. To begin with perhaps they were, but later they were to become a new congregation for a reformed church and one that might no longer be on the retreat.

There would develop a new way of working which would show that national parks were even more relevant than the pioneers of the 1930s and 1940s had expected.

Administrations had not changed much by the early 1970s, but the shortcomings of the system were being voiced. Sir Jack Longland's report of 1971 for the Countryside Commission has already been mentioned. It made clear the need for boards with full planning powers in all parks; the need for proper national park staff and a right of precept; and the need for central government to pay for national park administrative costs. The Countryside Commission supported the Longland recommendations, but a little later effected a compromise with the County Council's Association, agreeing not to press for more boards although demanding national park staff and national park plans. Sir Jack Longland, a Countryside Commissioner, strongly dissented from this view and most supporters of national parks were very displeased with this compromise. The Commission however, pointed to some gains.

At that time the whole future of local government was under review. In 1969 a Royal Commission under Lord Redcliffe-Maud had recommended radical changes, and these included boards for national parks, but in 1971 the Government's proposals were in most respects different from the Royal Commission's recommendations and the idea of further boards was dropped. It did, however, set up a committee under a government Minister, the Right Rev. Lord Sandford, and asked it to see if national parks had fulfilled their purpose, and to consider what now needed doing.

The Sandford Committee made a tour of the parks and reported widespread public concern about park protection. It had noted increasing conflict between recreation and conservation, and between national parks and other government agencies. The problem was that scenery depended on land management which was largely outside national park control, although it was much influenced by government grants for other purposes. Afforestation and the ploughing of moorland caused particular concern. It also reported that 'many large-scale intrusions of an incongruous nature had been allowed, usually by decisions taken at a national level'. For the future, whilst it thought mineral and water demands meant parks could not be inviolate 'the presumption against development which would be out of accord with parks must be strong...; in the most beautiful parts... it should amount to a prohibition to be breached only in the case of a most compelling necessity'.

Traffic planning was piecemeal and traffic often too heavy. Recreational traffic was not catered for in a way that was sympathetic with the environment. Investment in trunk roads, the Committee believed, should aim at developing routes for long distance traffic that avoided national parks. Widening and realigning roads should be brought under planning control. There was also concern for local people and the local economy. With a limited supply of houses in beautiful areas, prices were more than local people could afford. The Committee concluded that more help was needed from local councils.

Much more sympathetic planning of national parks was needed if authorities were to succeed in the way that Sandford envisaged. It had been originally intended that this would come in two ways — from the development plans of the park authorities prepared under the Planning Act 1947; and by means of the parks' annual reports to the National Parks Commission under Section 10 of the National Parks and Access to the Countryside Act 1949 about the action needed to realise park objectives. But, in practice, the devel-

5.7 New roads in national parks
The construction and improvement of major trunk roads, such as the A66 through the Lake District, has always been controversial.
Source: Countryside Commission

opment plans and the structure plans that followed, lacked the clear management programme that was needed. The statutory process took a long time to complete, the documents were verbose, and the plans lacked the vision, courage and clarity the pioneers had envisaged. Too often, both in national parks and outside them, planning was thought of as the vetting of other people's plans rather than the implementation of a bold strategy. What was needed was a new sort of plan — an assessment and systematic statement of the management measures needed and what was to be done about them and when. Such a plan needed to be non-statutory and, if combined with a national park block grant, would leave the national parks much freer to get on with the job and would make it clearer if they did not do so. It would also provide central government with a reasoned case as to the money needed to achieve national park objectives.

The Sandford Report was published just before local government changes in the spring of 1974. Amongst the innovations wrought, central government now agreed to pay 75 per cent of 'accepted' national park expenditure. The Local Government Act 1972, which was implemented two years later, reconstituted the Peak and Lakes Boards, but, for the rest, it contented itself with requiring that each national park should have a single committee which was to appoint its own official, a national park officer. Each park had to prepare a national park plan indicating the practical measures that were to be undertaken. The national park expenditure for 1974/75, rose to £2.3 million, although this was not quite as impressive as it sounds compared with £25 million for sport and recreation in 1973/74 and £15 million expenditure by the Arts Council.

Thus there was in 1974 a new attitude to national parks. The new committees, the appointment of a national park officer in each park and an increased acceptance of public support for national parks, all contributed to this change in attitude and a willingness on the part of national park committees to view problems freshly and positively. But it is useful at this stage to take a wider look at the sort of initiatives that have been developed in the full 40 years of the National Parks and Access to the Countryside Act 1949 and particularly the period since 1974.

Evolving national park working styles

The 1949 Act, and the Dower and Hobhouse reports before it, put a lot of faith in the planning system. Indeed, it was the context in which much of the work of the national parks had been set. In all of the circumstances it was asking too much of that system for when the test came on major planning issues, planning control was not strong enough. In any case, success also depended not just on control, but on positive action. It depended not on formal Acts of parliament, but on tackling problems where they were seen to exist. That there was a reluctance to tackle such problems also owes much to the presence of major organisational snags in the years up to 1974, which included the lack of enthusiasm on the part of most of the counties for national parks; the extent to which the cost of the provision for visitors fell on the recipient counties; and the administrative complexities relating to claims for grants. Fortunately, the national park idea survived these vicissitudes, leaving the reorganisation of 1974 to bring opportunities for those who had kept the vision alive. But these were opportunities that had to be seen in the context of the inherent advantages that the national parks had always had — that is, a clear definition of aims, boundaries defined to suit their objectives and the park itself, the prime resource. The challenge of the post 1974 period was, therefore, to find a means of combining conservation, recreation and local livelihoods— do that and the parks could be to the benefit of all.

The response to the challenge has undoubtedly lain in the concept of integration. Whilst the 1949 Act aims could not be separated from farming and forestry policy or from economic and social policy, and these were treated as rival interests, the consequence was frustration and high cost. What was needed was a view of the world as people see it in its totality, not as a series of disparate elements. That national park work thus became adapted to this need is evident enough if we look at examples.

Firstly, let us consider some aspects of the built environment. In theory buildings of interest can be protected with a building preservation order, but to protect them effectively there needs to be a benefit to the owner. He needs to share that protection goal, even if he is motivated by other factors. Frequently, too, the building cannot be considered in isolation; it is part of the village. A village, in turn, is not merely a collection of buildings, it is a community. To protect Dower's 'buildings and places of historic interest' therefore, a start must be made not from the buildings, but from the community, involving people in the heritage of which they are part. The problem is not so much a legal one, but more of a social one. Thus, imagination and an awful lot of dialogue become more important than writ. That there has been a gradual understanding of this wider perspective can be appreciated by reading recent national park annual reports. There you will find stories of town grant schemes in Staithes and Robin Hood's Bay; tougher grass to cut erosion on the green at Widecombe-in-the-Moor, and new seats; a new pedestrian square in front of Bakewell market hall. There are dozens of examples — 25 in a year on Dartmoor alone. Whole village schemes have been carried out, with the local council contributing to the cost and sometimes to the work as well. And to make future jobs easier, national parks collect and store traditional materials so that they are there when needed.

The protection of trees offers another example. To do this a tree preservation order can be used, but good management of woodlands has proved better. Fencing to keep the sheep out enables new trees to grow, and so on. Deciduous trees are tradi-

5.8 Conservation of the village Settlements as well as scenery are protected in national parks. Robin Hood's Bay in the North York Moors has been given financial assistance by the park authority. *Source*: Countryside Commission

tional, but do not make money, so parks have taken on woodland management themselves. Sometimes this management has been combined with recreation provision as at Aysgarth in the Yorkshire Dales. When the woodland management job proved too large, they developed grant schemes, which enable others to protect those woodlands that the Forestry Commission grants would not reach. Management agreements, too, have been used to ensure that woods and copses remain as an element of scenery, a provision of shelter, a source of timber. The Brecon Beacons, for example, negotiated 38 woodland management agreements from 1980, until the Wildlife and Countryside Act, 1981, increased the cost beyond what it could afford. Only 12 agreements having been made since then.

Consider, too, information services. There are now 65 centres, plus three larger day centres, in all visited by more than 3.5 million people a year. The largest is Brockhole in the Lake District with 150,000 visitors a year. The smallest are information points in village shops, a supplement to local income. There are talks, publications and guided walks — not just for the immediate pleasure they give, but also for the better understanding they create. At the peak of an experiment in 1979, a total of 872 guided walks were led on Dartmoor, with 10,000 people taking part.

People are involved in many ways. Rangers help the visitors, and provide on-the-spot contact, deal with emergencies and supervise voluntary help to farmers and others. In 1986/87, Dartmoor, for example, provided 22,000 hours of voluntary assistance from 1,750 individuals. Thus rangers form a bridge between the demands of the townsman and the needs of the countryman.

As for transport, the 40 years since 1949 have seen the number of private cars in the UK increase from just over 2 million to about 17.5 million. In that time most branch railway lines have closed and most bus services have been curtailed. As a result of these changes, recreational car traffic has often destroyed the very solitude its owners had set off to find.

Laybys and car parks were first put in places where cars already caused problems. Later, parking was moved back from beauty spots, as at the Tarr Steps on Exmoor. But a more radical approach was traffic management, providing parking space at the point of arrival to a valley and an alternative — mini-bus, cycle hire, new trails etc — beyond. Such were the schemes, initiated with the active encouragement of the Countryside Commission, in the Goyt and Upper Derwent Valleys in the Peak District. Not only did this ensure that the attractions of the area were protected, but also it proved extremely popular once the scheme was under way.

Support for public transport alternatives to the car provided another solution. More than half of the national parks were involved in the 1970s in running special bus services at peak visitor times with such exotic titles as Snowdon Sherpa and Pony Express. The national parks were pioneers in attempts to coordinate services and provide comprehensive timetables; and, with Countryside Commission support, all-day tickets became available on many routes throughout a park.

The most notable example of national park public transport was the chartered 'Dalesrail' train service from Leeds and Bradford which not only linked with guided trails through the Yorkshire Dales, but also helped to keep the line open and, in the opposite direction, provided cheap rail shoppers' returns to West Yorkshire cities for those who lived in remoter parts of the national park. It was a 'package' with which no car could compete! But there have been more recent and less desirable changes. Shire counties were given a transport coordinating role from 1974, but when licensing

5.9 Public transport in the national park 'Dalesrail' in the Yorkshire Dales provides both recreational access and a service to the locals who want to visit the shops in Leeds and Bradford. *Source*: Countryside Commission

restrictions were reduced in 1987, opportunities for coordination diminished.

Turning now to conservation and recreation, one of the greatest clichés by way of comment on the National Parks and Access to the Countryside Act 1949 used to be that the two purposes of preserving and enhancing natural beauty, and of encouraging its enjoyment, are in conflict. The statement was frequently made at early national park conferences, but solutions were rarely offered. They were, however, very sensible objectives and therefore the task which has remained is to find ways to reconcile them. Much progress has more recently been made towards this end.

The Sandford Report noted this conflict and said that, as we noted in chapter 3, where reconciliation was impossible conservation must take precedence, for the very good reason that if a park is not conserved it no longer remains to be enjoyed as a national park. But, having said that, reconciliation is possible more often than is commonly supposed. To a large extent it has been a matter of how provision is made. The Goyt and Upper Derwent traffic schemes quoted above are good examples of providing for more recreation, both by increasing considerably the parking space for motorists and by creating traffic-free areas, while at the same time, ensuring the qualities people come to enjoy are conserved and indeed improved. In other ways, too, conservation and recreation can be combined. Thus Countryside Commission funded 'camping barn' experiments in the Yorkshire Dales and the Peak District conserve historical barns by adapting them to provide simple overnight accommodation. Elsewhere, derelict old railway lines have had a new lease of life as walking and cycling trails, new scenic and natural values thus being created by this recreational provision.

Some areas can take pressure better than others, and national park plans can identify which can and which cannot. Often this is a matter of land management, a subject to which we now turn.

Towards shared objectives in land management

We live in a world of specialisation and consequently both government departments and landowners will have their own sets of goals. All react badly if others tell them what to do, but a single area needs a single plan and it makes sense to agree objectives. Achieving this has become a national park priority.

As we noted above, it became clear quite early on in the life of the 1949 Act that there was a limit to what could be achieved by control, even if powers existed, and often they did not, being available only to deal with urban or industrial incursions. Thus, if housing or industrial development or the extension of a quarry could be controlled, land management for farming, forestry or water catchment could not. Yet the national park itself needed management, for the scenery and recreation depended on the form of husbandry. To realise the national park plan, owners and authorities needed to work together.

A good example of such a joint plan is that which has been implemented in the Upper Derwent Valley. The valley was the fourth most popular place in the Peak District, with its forest, three reservoir lakes, and moorland. The range of recreational demands was wide and there was conflict between them. Access by road was down an eight mile cul-de-sac and congestion had been considerable at weekends in summer. Most of the reservoir banks and the forest had been fenced off by the very protectionist water authority which had existed before water authorities were amalgamated in 1974. However, the Peak National Park Board produced a management plan in collaboration with the others, and the three landowners — the new Severn-Trent Water Authority, the Forestry Commission and the National Trust — agreed a timetable for its achievement with the Park and the highway authority, Derbyshire County Council. Each did their part of the plan and in this way the job was completed quickly, cheaply and easily.

The water authority built a large car and coach park with a picnic area at Fairholmes at the top of the first reservoir with a Countryside Commission grant. Beyond this a traffic-free area was established by the County Council to operate at peak periods. The Peak National Park Board provided an information centre, a ranger base, cycle hire facilities and a frequent mini-bus service to the upper reservoirs on a 'park and ride' basis. New bus services were arranged to nearby cities by the urban transport authorities. The water authority also provided new toilets, while the English Tourist

5.10 Peak Park and ride!
The upper Derwent valley recreation experiment was an innovative way of coping with competing demands on a recreational resource.
Source: Peak National Park

Board and Sports Council provided cash for the cycle hire scheme. More than three miles of conspicuous concrete posts and wire fencing were removed by the water authority and it opened up new views, created new footpaths and fenced off a nature reserve. With the Forestry Commission it improved the appearance of its woodlands by softening geometric boundaries and planting many deciduous trees. Finally, a single ranger served the water, forestry and national park authorities.

Although schemes like that for the Upper Derwent Valley were achieved by negotiation at a local level, this is not always possible, for sometimes a government decision taken at the national level has to be dealt with. The Department of the Environment, advised by the Countryside Commission, may represent the national park interest, but the development proposed can be the product of a different government department acting under different Acts of parliament; or it may be a private development strongly backed by another department because of that department's duties. It is certainly not inconceivable, for example, that the Department of Trade and Industry's view may be different from that of the Department of the Environment. Thus while conservation duties exist in a national park, they may be regarded as of secondary importance by those concerned with that development.

118

This is a problem which has occurred several times in relation to routes for highways. When a motorway was suggested through the Peak District, the national park authority was not even allowed a copy of the feasibility study. When the new A66 was constructed through the Lake District in the 1970s and the Okehampton by-pass through the Dartmoor National Park in the 1980s, in each case good alternatives existed that avoided the national park. In the Okehampton case the highway authority had for 12 years actually protected a route in the Development Plan avoiding the National Park. And in 1976, government had said no new road for long distance traffic would be constructed through a national park if a reasonable alternative existed. Similarly, there have been differences over matters of afforestation (which is not subject to planning control) because the Forestry Commission's duties and traditional ways of working have differed from those of the National Park authorities.

Agriculture and the national parks: a conflict of objectives

Although the scenery of the national parks depends largely on farming, the Ministry of Agriculture, Fisheries and Food (MAFF) and the national park authorities have had different policies from the start. Unfortunately, the Hobhouse Committee showed no special concern at the consequences for the national parks of changes in agricultural practice and laid no great stress on providing the means by which nature conservation interests might be protected from it. Yet until recently MAFF had supported a continued expansion of food production, even after there were commodity surpluses. Thus if national park land was fortunate enough to continue to be managed in a traditional way, it was partly because many farms were small and not eligible for grants, and because, being an independent breed, farmers preferred this style of farming. However, the adverse impact of farming is to be seen in national parks and nowhere is this more clearly in evidence than on Exmoor.

In 1947, moorland covered one-third of the national park, but by 1976 it had been reduced to one-quarter of the park, through enclosure and 'improvement', a loss of some 4,800 hectares. This was a matter much publicised by Malcolm and Ann MacEwen whose book *National Parks: Conservation or Cosmetics?* in 1982 provided the most comprehensive and critical examination of national park administration. The Exmoor battle became such a bitter one that in 1976 Lord Porchester was asked to investigate the situation. As a major recommendation he suggested a power to make Moorland Conservation Orders, though in practice he expected there mainly to be voluntary agreements. Although government then gave 90 per cent grants for agreements on Exmoor, which would involve the maintenance of the traditional landscape, nonetheless, 600 hectares have been lost since 1976.

But there are other examples of moorland loss. In its first 25 years, the North York Moors National Park lost to afforestation and agricultural reclamation more than 15,500 hectares of the open country that had been the reason for its designation in the first place. In 1976 the Park bought Lewisham Moor, so that something was at last done about the one-third of the 690 hectare moorland that was infested with bracken. Also in the North York Moors, the Trustees of the 6,000 hectare estate around Bransdale were exempted from capital transfer tax on condition that the moorland character was maintained to a management plan prepared by the Park. Such measures as these were developed generally in national parks; for example, the 1988 Dartmoor Annual Report lists more than 40 management agreements in operation, and parks have generally benefitted from capital transfer tax legislation.

In the 1970s the Countryside Commission had backed upland management experiments in the Lake District and in Snowdonia, where farmers were assisted in small tasks of benefit to both farmer and visitor — jobs such as improved drainage across muddy footpaths and the repair of stiles and walls. A local project man was able to get on with practical jobs without fuss or bureaucracy. The scheme became permanent and other parks developed similar forms of assistance. But if up to 1980 national parks never knew when MAFF was giving grants for agricultural improvement, thereafter, the parks had to be consulted. Any modification was usually quickly agreed on site, though very occasionally a management agreement might be entered into as an alternative. The system proved simple and effective and offered greater rapport between park and farmer.

More controversial, however, was the Wildlife and Countryside Act 1981, for if a farmer's agricultural grant was refused, a management agreement *had* to be made, the park being liable to pay compensation to the farmer for the grant he had not received. It could be a payment to do nothing. Since then many parks have found it cheaper to buy land than to pay compensation which increases as the years go by.

In the Agriculture Act 1986, and the Wildlife and Countryside Amendment Act of the same year, conservation and recreation objectives were at last placed on the Ministry of Agriculture. Grants have been changed and the Ministry has begun to define Environmentally Sensitive Areas (ESAs) where grants can provide for the support of traditional farming practices. Only parts of two national parks have been defined as ESAs, but parks have been promised 'top up' grants which they can pass to farmers keen to undertake environmental improvement.

Meanwhile, other initiatives have been going on. For example, the Prince of Wales (as Duke of Cornwall) took a personal interest in work with Dartmoor National Park on a long-term plan for his

5.11 Experiments in upland management
The restoration of stone walls has been one of the many successes of management schemes in Snowdonia and here in the Lake District.
Source: Countryside Commission

estate (which covers about one-third of the park) with conservation as a key element in the plan. Also the Dartmoor Commons Act 1985 brought the possibility of better planning and management of common land in that Park. The Brecon Beacons National Park has acquired about 1,820 hectares of common land, some of it for a nominal sum. This has provided management advantages and given the opportunity to develop excellent liaison with the farmers who use the land.

The North York Moors is now working with owners and graziers on a five-year moorland management scheme to improve the landscape and the wildlife and economic quality of the moors. Programmes are drawn up with the owners, and grants are available for burning, cutting, bracken eradication and, where necessary, heather reinstatement. Whole farm conservation plans have added extra environmental improvements to farmers' own plans, and in 1988 a pilot scheme was launched aimed at combining the incentives from the National Park, MAFF, the Forestry Commission and other agencies to produce an integrated scheme with conservation as one of the prime objectives.

Integrated rural development

Integration, but this time of a comprehensive kind, remains the one other issue which has begun to be tackled in the 40 years since the Act. This involves providing for the needs of all who live in the national parks, for it makes no sense to treat the different aspects of social and economic actively as separate matters. The Yorkshire Dales now has a member of the Yorkshire Rural Community Council staff working in its office, half of the cost being paid by the Park, and the Brecon Beacons has a full-time member of staff with a brief on community matters. A major social problem in the parks is housing, local people being priced out of the market by those seeking second homes. The Lake District has tried to link new housing approvals to legal agreements to ensure that they would remain in local hands; elsewhere the use of housing associations has proved to be a partial solution.

Of course, success economically and socially depends on more than support in difficult circumstances. There has to be the climate for local action, and on this an experiment involving two villages in the Peak District is of interest. The scheme came from a group set up to help implement the Board's structure plan. Realising the limits to its own powers on land management, in the 1970s the Peak Park Board assembled a small group of officials who represented implementors and grant payers. The purpose of this Rural Land Management Executive Group was to try to encourage work towards common objectives within the targets of the structure plan. In discussion, it became clear that there was a need for alternative grant systems which worked to common objectives. Up until then grant aid had often been at cross purposes: for example, MAFF offered grants for drainage whilst the Nature Conservancy Council offered them for wetland retention!

5.12 A tale of two villages? Monyash (seen here) together with Longnor, both in the Peak District, were involved in an early and successful attempt at integrated rural development. *Source*: Peak National Park

In 1981 the Peak Park Board obtained European Community finance to try an alternative grant system, under which each grant had secondary advantages. Thus, for example, an agricultural grant could have conservation advantages; tourism, by making good use of existing buildings could have architectural advantages; and so on. This was to be tried in two or three villages. The government departments and agencies involved agreed to back the experiment, the Peak National Park providing the project officer. But as the law already laid down grant entitlements on a non-coordinated basis, the problem was how such a grant system could be implemented. It was decided to involve the villages in devising a suitable system to meet their needs, and village meetings and 'surgeries' were held at which ideas were asked for and queries answered.

Based on ideas from the villages and on policies sought in the structure and national park plans, a grant system was set up tailored to the needs of each village. The system included, for example, grants, not for new fences, but for miles of maintained drystone wall; it included grants for herb-rich meadows based on the number of species retained; it included social provision and it included new jobs in industry housed in unused and under-used buildings. It was above all payment by results.

Having devised the scheme the initiative was passed to the villagers. It was up to individuals to apply; they had to put in effort and money themselves and if they opted for the alternative they had to forgo the normal grant. The response was tremendous. Most opted for the alternative system, though grants were generally modest. At low cost the revitalisation of the villages was soon clear for all to see, and the gain in confidence was very noticeable. There had been a coordination of effort between agencies and between National Park and local community. In two villages at least, the joint board which the National Parks and Access to the Countryside Act 1949 had made possible was an integral part of the life of the area, as well as a conservation body in its own right. It may have taken a long time to be realised, but without the provisions of the 1949 Act that had set up such a board, this kind of integration would have been unlikely.

After a year's gap, the scheme was extended for a further three years with the financial support of six government departments and agencies. Towards the end of that time, the Peak National Park Board reported 50 jobs created, nearly 175 km of stone-walled field boundaries maintained, the management of 80 hectares of flower-rich fields secured, and a wide variety of community projects carried out, all in keeping with the environment. All this in two villages whose total population was under 800.

National parks: success or failure?

> 'Planning legislation does not solve problems; it only
> produces a framework within which solutions can be
> found; and the Ministry's chief aim since it was set up
> in 1943 has been to contrive such a legislative frame-
> work.'

Thus reads a report by Hugh Dalton from 1951 on the eight years of the Ministry of Town and Country Planning. But was the framework of the 1949 Act adequate to the task? The establishment of our national parks is an achievement which the Act made possible and, although it did not ensure action in the early days, when there was a desire to solve problems, the framework of the Act did prove useful. Administrative shortcomings of the Act, such as the lack of a plan and a block grant system, however, took 25 years to rectify.

The purpose of national parks set out in the Act remains valid in spite of the difficulties of implementation. Where conservation and recreation have been combined with a concern for local livelihood, imaginative solutions have recently emerged, and this would not have happened without a National Parks and Access to the Countryside Act 1949. Where it has occurred, the formation of joint boards proved most successful, but where they have not been established, difficulties have ensued, committees taking less action in the first 25 years and running into some conflicts over autonomy since, a point we pursue further in chapter 9. This was a consequence of Section 8 of the Act, which provided a weaker alternative to boards and made no requirements as to staff. It was, however, as much a weakness of interpretation as of legislation.

There has also been a weakness in not requiring greater commitment from other government departments. The 1949 Act said that the National Parks Commission should give advice '...where any Minister consults the Commission...'. It does not say the Minister *has* to consult, let alone take some notice! Two important omissions from the 1949 Act's consideration of national parks were concern for the local community and coordination with agriculture. In part, the Act merely followed the emphasis of the Dower and Hobhouse reports which left such concerns to other quarters. Local involvement and land management were to prove to be major issues and, with imagination, major opportunities.

The 1949 Act thus has been like a thin thread that has carried the planning hopes of the 1940s through to the more conservation-minded 1980s. The fortieth birthday celebration of the 1949 Act is probably only possible because of the enthusiasm of the few — the pioneers who had fought for national parks and kept their vision, generally with the support of public opinion. Threats of alien development concentrated the mind earlier than thoughts of a strategy; they usually do. But this has led to a public defensiveness, when really more positive thinking has been needed. It is surely best to get ahead of problems by a clear strategy, a good technique and imaginative ideas. Fortunately, the national parks are increasingly producing these.

The conclusion that stands out most strongly from the first 40 years of the Act is that where there has been merely lobbying, jockeying for position and little commitment, progress has been slow, for arguments are endless and consequences negative. However, where there is the will, national parks have a unique skill in environmental management to make the most of our finest landscapes. But until the achievement of that objective is universally recognised and while conflict of departmental objectives remains, the potential will not be realised and our best assets could be lost one by one.

The Broads — a tailpiece

The fortieth anniversary of the 1949 Act has seen the designation of a new protected area with a special authority given powers for its

management, for the Norfolk and Suffolk Act 1988 became effective on 1 April 1989. The Hobhouse Committee, as we saw in chapter 3, intended the Broads as a national park and Hugh Dalton thought it might be the first one. The idea was revived in the 1970s and in 1978 there was established a joint planning committee of local authorities, national representatives, and water and navigation interests. The new Broads Authority will take over from this.

The draining of wetland for arable use has been a particular problem in the Broads area and drew considerable public attention to the effect of previous agricultural policies in an area worthy of

5.13 Wetlands in danger? Halvergate marshes in the Broads provided the focus for what were to become environmentally sensitive areas (ESAs). *Source*: Countryside Commission

protection. It was the Broads controversy over the Halvergate area, in particular, that gave rise, in the first instance, to the pioneer grazing marshland scheme run jointly by the Countryside Commission and MAFF. With the aid of cash payments, this encouraged traditional farming practices in the area rather than the draining and ploughing of land for arable use. This, in turn, led to the formal recognition by MAFF of ESAs, areas in which farmers could receive positive incentives for farming in environmentally sensitive ways. The ESA designation for the Broads covers it completely, an area larger than that in any individual national park.

Although not declared a national park under the 1949 Act, the Broads Authority has a similar role, inside a legislative framework that has been designed for an area of rivers, lakes and wetland. Thus we now have eleven areas with a national park type of status and eleven administrations dedicated to practical measures to realise the national park objectives of the 1940s. With the Broads defined by MAFF as an ESA, with excellent cooperation there between MAFF and Broads authority, and with other recent trends, the signs are that park policy is beginning to be recognised and followed by bodies other than those with a specific national park responsibility. That, 40 years on, is the big 'break through'.

Access

6

Disappointments for the access movement

Of the various provisions of the 1949 Act, those concerning access were amongst the most controversial. On them were based great hopes and they aroused fierce passion. Their appearance in the legislation was greeted with relief in some quarters and with a keen sense of frustration in others, as chapter 4 has already suggested. But if they were not deemed adequate, in the opinion of some, as regards demands for public access to the wider countryside, where did they fail?

It must be said that the 1949 Act was a great improvement over the ill-starred Creech Jones Access to Mountains Act of ten years earlier, which, as a result of the new legislation, was repealed. There was certainly little mourning over its corpse. The setting up of the national parks was a major step forward and on the access front, the withdrawal of the penalties for various forms of transgression through trespass was a positive and helpful move. Perhaps Lewis Silkin, the then Minister of Town and Country Planning in the post-war Labour Government, felt that getting the Act through was ultimately sufficient achievement in itself without forcing the issue by trying to include within it provision for unfettered access to moor and mountain. Undoubtedly, the landowning interests did their best to exert their not inconsiderable influence on the Bill. But whatever his final reasons, all we can be sure of, as chapters 3 and 4 show, is that over a period of months leading up to the introduction of the Bill to the House of Commons, his attitudes shifted from a firm commitment to provide automatic 'access for all' to one where landowner's rights were much more to the fore. Certainly, once the Act was committed to the statute book in its final form, the die was cast: and it has remained unbroken since. Access, unless provided by enlightened ownership, such as that of the National Trust, was to be won through negotiation (undertaken by local authorities, or the planning boards of the Peak and Lake District National Parks) and agreement and the transfer of money to those providing it, that is, the landowners. Here was no ramblers' charter to roam at will.

The exception was, of course, the rights of way network, to which were to be added in time, the long-distance footpaths. Our rights of way are a precious and invaluable resource, and the Act ensured that they would (in principle at least) be committed to record in a definitive form, and that regular revisions to the network were to be made. If only this had been as straightforward as it sounds. Over the years, many hundreds of miles of path have been lost through development — or more often default — and precious few miles of new path have been created, a process that continues to this day.

What would have been the result if free access to open country had been given by the 1949 Act? One can only hazard a guess: per-

6.1 Our rights of way network
The recording and sign posting of footpaths such as this one along the coast of east Devon was one of the most important responsibilities imposed on county councils by the 1949 Act.
Source: Countryside Commission

haps the situation would have settled down quite rapidly, and landowners would have been disadvantaged little if at all. Certainly, negotiating the costs of individual access agreements could have been avoided. It could be argued that a mistake was made, and it is one we are now very unlikely to ever put right. Another mistake was made in assuming that the local authorities would find sufficient resources, in either manpower or money, to carry out satisfactorily or promptly their new task of preparing the definitive maps of rights of way, of signposting the network throughout, and of maintaining it in good order. But how effective were the early years of the implementation of the Act in access terms?

Fighting for rights of way

It is important to understand that a footpath or bridleway is as much a part of the Queen's Highway as any trunk road. Its position in law is perfectly clear, and the responsibility for maintaining it rests, as it does for roads, with the local authority acting in its capacity as highway authority. Yet in practice, rights of way open to those on foot, cycle or horseback have consistently been short-changed in terms of the resources devoted to them. The pattern was set at the beginning, when local authorities began the task imposed on them by the 1949 Act of preparing the 'definitive maps' which would show rights of way. Once a path was on the published definitive map, its status was legally secure. It was surely, therefore, most important that the definitive maps were just that — truly definitive, and as accurate as possible.

But how was this to be achieved? In many parts of the country, footpath societies and ramblers' groups were less vigorous and less numerous than they are today. To most of the local authorities, the obvious place to go for advice and local knowledge was the parish council, and blank maps were therefore sent to parishes asking them to mark known paths and bridleways believed to be rights of way. These maps were collated by the larger authority (usually at that time the county council) onto a draft definitive map, which could be challenged by anybody either to say a path had been left off or that a path put on the map was not a right of way.

The response from the parishes was, as might be expected, uneven. Some were diligent and marked all known paths. Others did a much more superficial job. A considerable number of parishes — one estimate puts the figure as high as 20 per cent — had no parish council at all, but simply an annual 'parish meeting' at which only the chairman was elected, making the task much more difficult to perform. And in many cases that chairman, whether of council or meeting, was the largest local landowner — the traditional 'squire' — and likely to have mixed feelings about including every footpath on the parish map.

In *This Land Is Our Land*, Marion Shoard quotes the example of Macclesfield in Cheshire, where the published definitive map showed a total of 986 rights of way, amounting to 620 km of footpaths and bridleways. Since this map was first published, no fewer than 260 other paths have been claimed as being omitted. So the supposedly 'definitive' map for that one area could have been in error by as much as 25 per cent! If this picture was repeated nationally then we could have lost by default in the order of more than 48,000 km of rights of way since 1949.

The basic task of preparing parish maps was carried out by unpaid local people. The highway authorities simply did not have the resources to check thoroughly what was laid before them within the timespan set down in the Act for the first set of definitive maps to be agreed and published. They had their work cut out marrying up all the parish maps and getting a draft definitive map drawn up and agreed. Little wonder then that mistakes were made, both of omissions and of paths inserted in error. Unfortunately, once a path was omitted, the process of getting it back had to wait until the map was reviewed and in many places this was to be many years later. Nor did the authorities show any great enthusiasm for the possibility made available to them through the Act for new paths to be created. They had their hands full sorting out the existing network, without trying to add anything to it.

Further, the parish view of what constituted a right of way was understandably still underlain by the path's utilitarian purpose, rather than its function as a recreational resource. The latter view was in its infancy in the early 1950s, so paths which simply went to 'beauty spots', to fine viewpoints or to the tops of hills were left off

6.2 Battling for access
Disputes over access have been a significant legacy of the 1949 Act of which Land's End is amongst the most notable examples.
Source: Camera Craft Photography

by the parishes. One such path, over which a battle has been fought virtually ever since, is the path from the A30 road to Land's End in Cornwall. It was never claimed as a right of way, despite being used by very large numbers of people, and at the time of writing its status is still unclear. Yet it must be a path that virtually everybody in the country, and many abroad, know about even if they have not actually used it.

Recreation was certainly in the minds of those who drafted the 1949 Act, and it was for that purpose that they foresaw local authorities creating new stretches of path and bridleway. In practice, few new stretches of path have been created: the official long-distance paths rely in the main on existing rights of way, as do the vast majority of local recreational paths which have been devised in recent years. Perhaps this is not surprising given the existence on the definitive maps of 225,000 km of rights of way.

Nevertheless, there are still numerous places where more paths would have been of immense benefit, but even when local authorities have been minded to create them, they have faced difficulties. Wychwood Forest in Oxfordshire is one example. Wychwood, and the adjoining Cornbury Park, fine countryside with some very beautiful woodland, together amount to 870 hectares. Yet in all of that area the only public right of way is one footpath that crosses a corner of Cornbury. Public access to Wychwood Forest is allowed on one day a year, and not surprisingly, it is very well used on that day. In 1983, West Oxfordshire District Council, faced with mounting pressure from the Council for the Protection of Rural England and the Ramblers' Association, formally approached Lord Rotherwick to allow public access — but not through the creation of rights of way, merely with a 'permissive path'. In 1986, Oxfordshire County Council took things further by making a creation order for a public path through Wychwood Forest. This was confirmed after a local inquiry. On the banks of the Test river in Hampshire, too, there are paths, but only for anglers on these exclusive stretches of water, not for the public. Such paths as do reach the best stretches of the Test, between Stockbridge and Romsey, do so in order to cross the river rather than run with it.

In fact the number of kilometres of path appears to increase little from one year to the next, and in some years, actually declines. According to figures collected by the Ramblers' Association for the Countryside Commission, about 1,500 formal proposals to create, divert or extinguish paths in England and Wales are made every year affecting 500 km of the network, and of that total about three-quarters go through unopposed. In the four years 1983-1986, the Countryside Commission estimates that the overall length of the rights of way network declined by 5 and 35 km in the first two years and increased by 5 and 28 km in the second two.

When we turn to maintenance, we find a very similar story — lack of resources or of interest on the part of the authorities in general, leading to paths becoming blocked or impassable, sometimes with little effort made to restore or clear them. The legal position is perfectly clear. Landowners who wilfully obstruct paths or block them with crops or through ploughing are committing an offence. Highway authorities have a legal duty to secure the removal of obstacles and also to maintain paths in a passable condition. Yet evidence collected by the Ramblers' Association for the Countryside Commission has indicated that well over half our public rights of way, as shown on the definitive maps, are unavailable to all but the most determined and agile person.

Part of the problem is undoubtedly the change in the use of paths that has occurred this century. From being vital highways used by local people in their work, and for recreation when they had the time to take any, paths have become almost exclusively the preserve of the recreational user. As a result, many of them are used less frequently even than in 1949, so they deteriorate more quickly. If they are blocked, most people will turn back rather than try to force a way through — there is little pleasure in tackling an assault course when you are looking for a pleasant country ramble. And this is part of a downward spiral, since blocked paths deteriorate further.

6.3 Restricting access
This gate bars one of the entrances to Wychwood Forest, Oxfordshire.
Source: John Blunden

Overall then, problems with the distribution and maintenance of, and changes to, public rights of way remain significant 40 years after the 1949 Act.

The 'official' long distance paths have secured some fine stretches, but even here there have been problems, and the first of these paths to open, the Pennine Way, did not do so until 1965 — a full 16 years after the Act came into law. Since then a dozen further long distance paths have been opened, with a total length of about 2,800 km. In all they represent just over 1 per cent of the total path network, and in a number of cases, as we shall see later in this chapter, they have not been able to follow the best routes.

Negotiating access agreements

A substantial section of the Act was devoted to the provision of access agreements to enable people to walk over open country. This was the chosen method by which the true defenders of the faith of 'freedom to roam' were to be mollified. It was envisaged that local authorities, and the national parks themselves, would negotiate such agreements over the best walking countryside they possessed. Again, this fine aim has not been realised. Indeed, access agreements under the Act presently cover only about 34,000 hectares of open country in England and Wales — a very small figure. Almost without exception, they have been shunned by the authorities which were meant to negotiate and use them. It seems they were either too much bother, since the authorities felt they had enough to do defining and trying to maintain the rights of way network, or there was felt to be no need.

In responding to the requirements of the 1949 Act, local authorities had to indicate where in their areas they felt access agreements could be negotiated. No fewer than 38 authorities in England and every one in Wales responded by saying that no action was necessary, or that they considered they had no 'open country'. This was even true of a county such as Devon, despite the fact that anyone with eyes could see that large areas of moorland were closed off to the public. It has to be realised that the negotiation of access agreements was something entirely new to these authorities. It is perhaps little wonder that they were hesitant to tackle major landowners, who were often very influential figures in local government. And with the change to a Conservative Government in 1951 the mood became even more compliant.

There were some successes, however. One of the best-known is in what was the West Riding of Yorkshire, where in 1960 the Duke of Devonshire's estate concluded an access agreement for public use of Barden Moor and Barden Fell, part of the Bolton Abbey estate. The land was previously kept as a private sporting estate, with no public access. It is possible now to wander these grassy heights and enjoy the fine views across the dales untroubled by gamekeepers. But the Barden agreements were not entirely due to the efforts of the local authority. The reaction of the then West Riding County Council to the 1949 Act was that no access agreements were needed anywhere in the county, despite obvious cases like Barden from which the public were excluded. This was quite a typical response from an authority at that time, and it was only after considerable pressure had been exerted by amenity groups, notably the Ramblers' Association, that authorities such as that in West Riding of Yorkshire were moved into action at all. And Barden is an exception. There are still very substantial areas of moorland in West Yorkshire with no legal public right of access.

6.4 Getting access agreed
It was only after pressure from the Ramblers' Association that Barden Fell, part of the Duke of Devonshire's estate, was opened to the public.
Source: Derek Widdicombe

Of course, the definition of open country excludes cultivated and most pasture land. So the access agreement provisions have always had limited relevance in the lowlands. Only the one access agreement for example has been concluded in Oxfordshire. Out of a total land area of 260,000 hectares, the area of negotiation for public access — apart from that on public footpaths and bridle-ways, and the relatively small amount of common land — was just 53 hectares, in an area called the Sinodun Hills, owned by the Northmoor Trust, a private charity.

Efforts were made by some of the national parks. Access agreements have been concluded in the Brecon Beacons, on parts of Dartmoor, and in the Lake District. But overall the picture is one of sparse usage and a great lack of enthusiasm for the access agreement principle. Such agreements as were concluded were mostly negotiated before 1960. Since then what little enthusiasm there was has all but evaporated. Local authorities and national parks alike seem to believe that the access agreement has had its day and that there is little point in pursuing this line any further.

The official view has been to promote the 1949 provisions where appropriate. In its 1987 policy statement *Enjoying the Countryside*, the Countryside Commission called for local author-ities to recognise the significance of customary access that already occurred, to support such access and be ready to negotiate access agreements if required. Its objective was stated as 'to provide and manage appropriate access to wider areas of countryside'. This view is supported by major voluntary conservation bodies such as the Council for the Protection of Rural England. In its response to *Enjoying the Countryside*, the Council urged the Commission to 'lean towards encouraging more general unstructured, informal public use of the countryside. This implies a general emphasis on enhancing public rights of way and extending access by agreement and legislation'. But however many reports and recommendations are produced, it is still down to individual authorities and landown-ers to come together to make access agreements and thereby to provide a proper framework for the access that so many people want and feel they should have. There seems to be little enthusi-asm on the part of most authorities for negotiating such agree-ments.

6.5 What they have and what they want
The situation with regard access as the Ramblers' Association saw it for the Peak District in 1980.
Source: Howard Hill

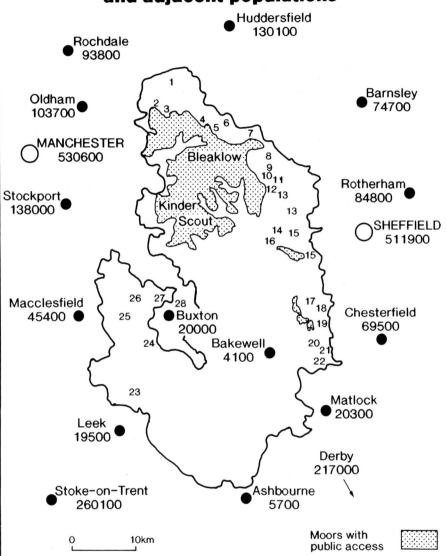

Access agreements in the Peak District National Park and adjacent populations

Huddersfield 130100

Rochdale 93800

Oldham 103700

Barnsley 74700

MANCHESTER 530600

Bleaklow

Rotherham 84800

Stockport 138000

Kinder Scout

SHEFFIELD 511900

Macclesfield 45400

Buxton 20000

Chesterfield 69500

Bakewell 4100

Matlock 20300

Leek 19500

Derby 217000

Stoke-on-Trent 260100

Ashbourne 5700

0   10km

Moors with public access

Moors to which access is sought by the Ramblers Association

1 Wessenden Moor
2 Saddleworth Moor(N)
3 Middle Edge Moss
4 Twizzlehead Moss
5 Grains Moss
6 Snailsden
7 Thurlestone Moor
8 Midhope Moor
9 Pike Low

10 Upper Commons
11 Broomhead Moor
12 Middle Moss
13 Bradfield Moors
14 Moscar Moor
15 Hallam Moor
16 Bamford Moor
17 Big Moor
18 Ramsley Moor

19 Leash Fenn
20 Gibbet Moor
21 Brompton East Moor
22 Beeley Moor
23 The Roaches
24 Axe Edge
25 Shining Tor
26 Hoo Moor
27 Coombs Moss
28 Black Edge

There is, however, one notable exception — the Peak District National Park, and it is worth looking in some detail at what the Park Board has achieved by sensible use of the access agreement mechanism. At present, 19 access agreements in the Peak cover some 20,000 hectares of open country — nearly 60 per cent of the total for the whole of England and Wales! In 1988, these agreements were costing the Peak Park Joint Planning Board about £13,000 per year in compensation and maintenance payments, and a further £11,000 incurred in providing a ranger service for the land. This works out at £1.22 per hectare per year — hardly an excessive amount when weighed against the pleasure given to untold thousands of people.

The Peak Park was quickly into action following the passing of the Act. By 1952, a map had been prepared showing the extent of 'open country' (as defined in the Act) within the Park. Negotiations then began to secure access to 'areas of moorland which were not open to the public and where there was a plain need'. Many of these were, of course, the very areas over which, as we saw in chapter 2, such bitter battles had been fought in the 1920s and 1930s, so it is perhaps not surprising that they were given high priority.

In the years up to 1970, all of the agreements currently in force were concluded. Since then there have been no new agreements, the feeling being that 'having met the main needs for access to open country, the board's efforts should focus upon other opportunities to improve public enjoyment of the park'. The Peak Park Board will shortly need to focus its attention back onto access agreements. Those presently in force are all up for re-negotiation in 1993. Let us hope there is no difficulty in renewing them.

An ominous note is sounded here in a 1989 statement from the Board through Roland Smith, Head of Information Services. He says:

> 'The evidence of our existing agreements is that for the board, the 1949 Act worked quite well and provided a basis for the successful negotiation of access agreements in the 1950s and 1960s. In recent years any attempts at negotiation have been received far less favourably by most owners who have been

approached. As the numbers using access areas have grown, so have some of the attendant problems they create, particularly erosion and the thoughtlessness of some dog owners in relation to the behaviour of their pets. Some landowners have been reluctant to discuss traditional access agreements at all, others have only been prepared to discuss very limited additional provision, affected in their judgement by a wide range of issues directly and indirectly related to the effects of public access as they perceive them'.

What does this mean for the future? Roland Smith goes on: '...it will be an exceptional set of circumstances which allows an agreement providing traditional "wander at will" public access to the whole of an area which is the subject of any new proposal... Far more likely is the achievement of a compromise package taking careful account of the owner's genuine aspirations as owner and manager, balanced against the need for more access provision and conservation issues. Creative negotiation can achieve such compromises, but the Act does not *per se* make provision for them and in that respect it can be considered outdated'.

Having been used little in the past 40 years, it would seem that the access agreement, such a fundamental part of the 1949 Act, will be used less and less in the future. If the Peak Park is finding it so difficult to negotiate satisfactory new agreements, with all its experience in this field, what chance do other authorities have? Here the Act can certainly be seen to be lacking in its relevance to the present situation. Hardly surprising, perhaps, after 40 years.

Access problems in profusion

Campaigning not only for greater access to open country, but also for the maintenance of existing access provisions, and enhancement of the rights of way system, has gone on unceasingly since the 1949 Act was passed. Few, if any, of the demands made by the more outspoken members of the campaigning bodies have been withdrawn or diluted, and it is still official Ramblers' Association policy to press for a 'right to roam' on all areas of uncultivated moorland and mountain. Some commentators go even further, calling for an end to restrictions laid down for the purposes of sports such as shooting, and for free access to all of the country-side, be it agricultural land, forest, or whatever. Legislation to this end is no nearer now than it was in 1949, and although the Labour Party manifesto for the 1987 general election contained a promise that access for all would be given by a Labour government, it remains to be seen if the promise would be backed by parliamentary action. The obstacles would still be formidable.

Making better use of the existing path network has become a prominent issue in recent years following the Countryside Commission's 1987 policy statement *Policies for Enjoying the Countryside*. This singled out the rights of way network as the 'most important means by which the public can enjoy the country-side' and set as its target 'the entire rights of way network to be legally defined, properly maintained and well publicised by the turn of the century'. The Commission has followed this up in 1989 with *Paths, Routes and Trails : Policies and Priorities,* which suggests that the network should be planned and promoted for recreational use around four categories of path. Not surprisingly, access organisations are worried that this might lead to the contin-ued neglect of those paths not selected for promotion.

The Ramblers' Association has continued to express itself forthrightly: 'The main point which we wish to impress upon the Commission is that its over-riding priority should be to improve the basic network of public paths in England and Wales'. The Cyclists' Touring Club, which has fought long and hard to get greater access to the countryside away from roads for cyclists, also expressed concern that any attempt to 'rationalise' the rights of way network would result in overall losses rather than gains. But the farming and land-owning organisations, notably the National Farmers' Union and the Country Landowners' Association, have consistently opposed any move towards more freedom of access, and have indeed tried more than once to have the laws relating to trespass tightened up. As we move into an era when agriculture faces a less certain future and farmers are being urged to diversify

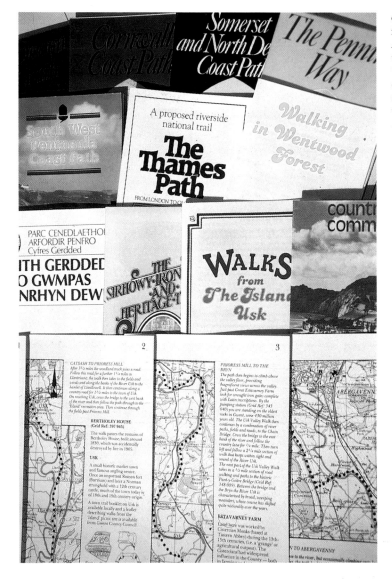

6.6 Guide books for named walks
A large number of these, both for 'official' and 'un-official' paths are now available for all who wish to use them.
Source: Nigel Curry

into leisure activities, it may be that attitudes will change, but it is most unlikely that relaxation to the point of welcoming free access will be achieved. Rather, the land-based organisations will want to permit more access only under conditions which they could control.

Many of the problems that have arisen over access since 1949 have been fundamentally concerned with finance. The opening of the Pennine Way in 1965, for example, was hailed as the beginning of a new chapter in the rights of way story — Tom Stephenson's *Long Green Trail*, first promoted in 1935, had at last become a reality. Since then a dozen further long distance paths have been created by the Countryside Commission, plus dozens of 'unofficial' named walks put together by enthusiasts. The Commission now plans a further programme of four new paths to be called 'national trails', a name also now being given, somewhat controversially, to existing paths too. Articles by the hundred have appeared in publications of all kinds, the production of guidebooks has become a cottage industry, and publicity material has been produced by the Countryside Commission, by bodies such as the Ramblers' Association and the Cyclists' Touring Club, and by local authorities and tourist bodies. The result has been in most cases an increase in the numbers of people walking these routes. While this has been welcome in terms of the enjoyment of the countryside provided and also in revenue brought in to country areas, it has brought serious problems in certain places as paths, unsuited to this kind of continual pressure of use, have become physically impaired.

The Pennine Way has been the principal sufferer, particularly at its southern end on the peaty ground of the Kinder and Bleaklow heights and in the Three Peaks area of the Yorkshire Dales. On Kinder and Bleaklow, experiments of several kinds have been carried out, from extensive stretches of boardwalk over the worst-eroded peat hags to a large-scale revegetation programme. None can be said to have been more than partially successful so far, and still walkers come, so at best what is being carried out is a damage limitation exercise. The same is true in the Yorkshire Dales National Park.

Sums amounting in total to more than a million pounds are being talked about here to combat the present erosion and check further damage. On Pen-y-Ghent, the prominent hill above Horton-in-Ribblesdale, which is on both the Pennine Way and the Three Peaks circuit, the path to the summit had become eroded in places to a depth of nearly a metre and was twenty metres wide. The problem in all such places is to direct walkers onto one line that can be maintained relatively easily, without creating a pathway that looks artificial. In the Snowdonia National Park, for example,

Snowdon is climbed by upwards of a quarter of a million people every year, and the National Park Committee decided that a substantial stone pathway was the best solution to the growing erosion problem. The result is certainly substantial, but to many people it looks anything but natural.

More such problems will arise. They are not insurmountable, but they need forethought and a realisation by funding agencies that very considerable sums of money need to be set aside at the outset in order to keep paths in good order. The provision of public access has never been accompanied by anything remotely like adequate funding, although there are signs at present of that situation changing. In the Yorkshire Dales in 1986, for example, the budget for paths within the national park for that year — excluding the Three Peaks Project, which was funded separately — was approximately £1 for every mile of public right of way within the park. This is hardly adequate.

There are, too, one or two examples of long-distance routes having to divert around places they should logically pass through because of the difficulties faced by authorities in creating new rights of way. When the Wolds Way, an 80-mile path through East Yorkshire, was opened in 1982, it missed one of the most interesting places on the route, the deserted village of Wharram Percy, because of the opposition of the landowner, Lord Middleton. The same gentleman was invited to perform the official opening of the path, which so incensed the Ramblers' Association that they held their own 'alternative opening' on the same day. There is now a right of way linking the Wolds Way to Wharram Percy, but the route still does not pass through it. The South West Coast Path around the coasts of Somerset, Devon, Cornwall and Dorset has met with similar problems, with the path diverted away from the coast in a number of places to accommodate objections from farmers, house owners and the Ministry of Defence.

The access lobby does not always speak with one voice, however. A proposal to create a Cambrian Way route through the best mountain areas in Wales was dropped in 1982 after sustained objections not only from farming and landowning bodies, but also from the British Mountaineering Council, who felt that the provision of a path through the high mountains was unwise and could

6.7 Access wear and tear
Tom Stephenson, father of the long distance path, tries an artificial surface on the Pennine Way. *Source*: Peak National Park

lead to problems with safety as well as with erosion.

The most frustrating case is that of the Arans, a range of hills which provide (or should) exhilarating walking and splendid views, placed as they are at the south-east corner of the Snowdonia National Park. No public paths were recorded on the definitive maps here — another case of recreational use missing out, as the workaday paths in the area not unnaturally avoided the high ground. Despite the ever-increasing numbers of visitors to the park as a whole, it was not until 1982 that the Snowdonia National Park Authority secured any public access to the Arans, and then it was only a 'courtesy footpath' with no legal backing, and with the Park Authority agreeing to make an annual payment to the landowners and to provide a ranger service. Walkers have to keep to the path, dogs are not permitted, and the agreement for the path to remain available has to be renewed every year. It should be remembered that national park authorities have a legal duty to promote and provide means for public recreation.

Common land

Common land is not specifically covered in the 1949 Act. However, much open country is common land and it is right that it should be considered here along with the rest of our open land.

146

The history of common land is a long and complicated one, stretching back a thousand years, but there is no need to go into it in detail. Suffice to say that commons are areas of open land over which people (the commoners) other than the owners have certain rights, such as grazing stock or cutting wood for fuel. Upland commons often remain in agricultural use, but most low land commons are no longer grazed, and those not managed for public use are often neglected. Others, however, are well managed for the good of the community. Some of our best-known and most-used commons, such as Wimbledon in south-west London, fall into the last category. In addition, important recreational areas such as large parts of Dartmoor (some 40 per cent of which is common), Epping Forest and Hampstead Heath in Greater London, and the Malvern Hills are all common. But free access for the public is only legally granted on about 25 per cent of the 540,000 hectares of common land. Legal access to what were termed 'urban commons' was granted through the Law of Property Act 1925, and remains in force today. Some large 'rural' commons were made subject to the same right by agreement with the landowner, in the 1920s and 1930s — such as those granted by the Crown Estate for large areas in Wales.

As might be expected, there has been pressure for this situation to be changed. The Commons, Open Spaces and Footpaths Preservation Society is one of the oldest amenity bodies in Britain, with a history, as we noted in chapter 2, stretching back well over a century. Now called more simply the Open Spaces Society, it is as vigilant as ever in defending common land from the many threats that it faces. These go well beyond access issues to include road schemes, housing developments, prestige golf courses, industrial estates and much else. In some cases, such as Esher Common in Surrey, compensatory gifts of land have been negotiated when parts of a common have been lost — in this case to a motorway. But more insidiously, the present law inhibits rather than encourages cooperative management to protect the wildlife and recreational value of common land.

Commons all had to be registered under the Commons Registration Act 1965, so their extent is known. The Royal Commission on Common Land as far back as 1958 recommended

that access for quiet enjoyment on foot be granted to all such commons. More than 30 years later, nothing has been done. Once again, public access to the countryside has been accorded a very low parliamentary priority.

Twice in the past decade Dr David Clark, a Labour MP who was at the time chairman of the Open Spaces Society, tried to introduce a Bill in the House of Commons to extend the legal right of access to rural commons. On neither occasion could he gain government support or sufficient parliamentary time. Instead, the Common Land Forum was set up by the Countryside Commission in 1984 to consider all of this. It was in many ways a remarkable enterprise including as it did landowning interests, amenity bodies, ramblers, farmers and local authorities. The Forum's report, published in 1986, surprised many people — the fact that accord was reached at all was in many ways very encouraging. The report recommended that public access should be granted to all registered common land, although there were conditions attached. Stronger restrictions against de-registration of commons was another recommendation. Legislation was promised in the Conservative Party manifesto of 1987. But, up to the time of writing, nothing has happened in terms of legislative action, and, indeed, as we shall see in chapter 10, some landowning interests are orchestrating further opposition to the Forum's proposals. Meanwhile, commons continue to be enclosed, built upon, carved up for roads, and de-registered. If the current status of common land is unsatisfactory, so too is the present position regarding public access; granting access on foot to all rural commons as part and parcel of them being better managed and conserved would secure over 400,000 hectares for public enjoyment and recreation.

Byways and bridleways

Access to the countryside is not only provided by public paths. There are other types of rights of way — byways, bridleways, and the rather arcane roads used as public paths (RUPPs) — which will not be with us for very much longer. Let us take bridleways first. These are routes that equestrian traffic has the right to use. Local authorities were required to indicate on the definitive maps produced in the 1950s which routes these were. Where doubt occurred, it seems that the equestrians got the worst of it. It was simpler to have a path, which meant providing and maintaining access only for people on foot, than to have a bridleway, which clearly would have to be wider and have gates rather than stiles.

Since then, in the Countryside Act 1968, bridleways have been opened to cyclists as well as equestrians. This only happened after a spirited campaign by the Cyclists' Touring Club led to an amendment to the original Bill being proposed in the House of Lords and accepted. This has resulted in the opening up of all bridleways to cyclists — some 33,000 km in all. In addition to these bridleways the Cyclists' Touring Club made specific proposals for long-distance off-road cycling routes, but none has yet come to anything.

Byways and RUPPs are both open to vehicular traffic and also to pedestrians, equestrians and cyclists as public rights of way. Under the provisions of the Wildlife and Countryside Act 1981, local authorities were required to redesignate RUPPs — which were mainly unsurfaced roads or tracks used occasionally by motor traffic — as footpaths, bridleways, or 'byways open to all traffic'. Rambling, horseriding and cycling organisations have pressed for these routes, which in many cases provide very attractive and straightforward access into the countryside, to be reclassified as bridleways, while motoring organisations have sought to retain vehicular rights of way for trial-riding and increasingly, four-wheel-drive vehicle use. The process of reclassification, which is carried out purely on the legal evidence of use, not the use which would be most appropriate, is still going on, and is proving controversial. In many areas, routes now classified as byways are being heavily used and eroded.

Other national access perspectives

It is both pertinent and useful at this point to look at the situation regarding access to the countryside in other countries for a comparison with the access legacy of the 1949 Act. Four examples will suffice to show both the good and the bad points of what we have in England and Wales. First of all, let us consider New Zealand. Its landscape could be considered comparable to that of Britain. Indeed, the country was a British colony and its basic agricultural tradition is very similar to ours. However, the position regarding access to its countryside is very different. Not for the New Zealander the extensive network of public rights of way, the footpaths and the bridleways we take almost for granted. Access to the land, in legal terms, is very restricted. Legally speaking, New Zealanders have to ask permission of the landowner before venturing onto open country. If they do not, they are liable to prosecution for trespass. Legal access is confined to the country's national parks and its small network of official 'walkways', of which the Milford Trail is perhaps the best-known. People certainly do walk

6.9 Traffic-ridden byways
The Ridgeway path that runs from Ivinghoe to Avebury along the chalk downs is just one prehistoric way that is being ruined for the walker because of its use by cars and motorbikes.
Source: Countryside Commission

the New Zealand mountains outside these designated areas, but in law they have no right to do so. In this respect at least, it would seem that we are better off than our New Zealander cousins.

France is a large country with many hundreds of miles of unsurfaced roads and tracks which are open to the walker. It also has a very well-developed national network of walking routes (the Grandes Randonnees), which are coordinated centrally so that they link up, but are maintained and administered locally by rambling groups. Using these routes, it is possible to walk from the English Channel to the Mediterranean or from the German border to the Atlantic. Robert Louis Stevenson's famous journey through the Cevennes can be re-traced and the coast of Brittany can be walked un-interrupted. Many other local trails that still link small villages can be followed and in many areas, gites, — simple unexpensive shelters — are common. This network has been developed to ensure that both French people and visitors to the country have plenty of walking opportunities. Much of the countryside of France is cultivated, for arable crops, fruit, wine or livestock. The well-developed, well-signposted and well-coordinated network of Grandes Randonnees means that both the walker and the farmer or landowner know where they stand. It is a system that has worked well because it has been properly planned and fully understood.

However, it is in the Scandinavian countries that we perhaps come closest to the long-desired 'free access' situation for which many active recreationists in the UK have pressed for so many years. The law known as 'Allemansratt' (every man's right) says there shall be no restrictions on access to the countryside, except in the areas immediately around inhabited buildings and with certain exceptions for agricultural or military reasons. Generally speaking, the people of Scandinavia can walk, ride and camp where they choose. Everyone has the rights in law to cross another person's land, providing no undue disturbance or actual damage is caused. It works both ways: landowners can face fines if they try to obstruct public access, and the public similarly can be prosecuted for such things as leaving litter — indeed, they can even be sent to prison if the case is thought to be serious enough. Sweden, where this law is longest established, is of course a large country with a small population. Nonetheless, there appear to be relatively few problems even in the more densely populated areas. If it can work in Sweden, why can't it work here? Is it a question of our attitude to the countryside — and to landowners? Until we try the experiment, we shall never know the answer.

Finally, and closer to home, we turn to Scotland. It is not unrealistic to say that it contains much of the best walking country in the British Isles. The situation regarding access is different from England and Wales. Is the overall result better, or worse? Scotland is different simply because it has a different legal system. In 1947, when the Ramsey Committee was reporting on aspects of the countryside in Scotland, alongside Hobhouse, the wild land of that country was much more open to walkers that it had been even 20 years earlier, thanks to the efforts of the Scottish Rights of Way Society, the mountaineering clubs, and the National Trust for Scotland which had purchased some of the most important areas, such as Glencoe. Although the recommendations of the Ramsey Committee, including that of free access as of right, were not acted upon, this probably affected access very little. Access to the wilder countryside in Scotland is based upon a well-established system of mutual respect between walker and landowner. The walker, provided he takes reasonable care and respects the land, may go where he pleases, with remarkably few exceptions. These concern the stag shooting season from mid-August to mid-October and grouse shooting at a similar time of year. The income from these activities is vital to many Highland estates. Even if you regard that situation as regrettable, the employment produced is invaluable in keeping remote communities alive, so the situation is tolerated.

From the landowner's point of view, the responsible walker creates few problems and can indeed on occasion be helpful in informing estate staff where deer are congregated or where sheep are in distress. Problems only arise where the shooting periods referred to above are ignored, or where numbers rise from some unusual cause. Perhaps the establishment of long distance walking routes can be placed in the latter category. The West Highland Way, in particular, has undoubtedly brought income to the communities along its 95-mile route from Glasgow to Fort William, but it is also beginning to bring problems for the more traditional type of lone Scots walker as landowners and farmers, concerned over the greatly

6.10 Footpaths suffering from success
The Three Sisters of Glen Coe, viewed from the West Highland Way. Its scenic attractions have made it so popular, that landowners are being forced to impose restrictions. *Source*: Picktail Picture Library.

increased numbers, attempt to impose restrictions. Noticeboards banning camping have sprung up where there was previously no problem; erosion has occurred simply through increased pressure; and walkers are urged to 'keep to the path', a directive which is utter anathema to the Scottish hill gangrel.

Contrary to what some people believe, there is a law of trespass in Scotland. It is not an offence simply to be on another person's land, unless you cause damage, but you can be asked to leave, and in the case of persistent refusal, an interdict can be sought. Camping without permission is also, strictly speaking, an offence, although the only prosecutions in recent years have been against tinkers and other 'travelling folk' and not against walkers. The access situation in the wilder parts of Scotland can, then, be regarded as relatively satisfactory. In the farmed lowlands the position is not so satisfactory as there is no equivalent of the definitive map that exists in England and Wales to clarify where walkers have the right to go. Few problems arise if the walker behaves responsibly in the wilder areas, but bureaucratic machinery may impose

153

undue restrictions in the years ahead; indeed the eventual introduction of national parks to Scotland, which we discuss further in
chapter 11, may need to be treated with a great deal of caution.
The landscape of Scotland is very different from that of England
and Wales. There is much more wild, open country and much less
intensively farmed land. Even so, there are lessons that can be
learned and what they are will be considered in the final part of this
chapter.

The ramblers' heritage

A substantial part of the 1949 Act was concerned with access to the
countryside — something for which dedicated people had argued
and fought over a long period of years. Looking both back over
40 years and forward to the future, what has been achieved and
what should we hope now to achieve? Let us look at the positive
points first. The Act did enable us to place on record in a definitive
form the rights of way open to those who wish to walk, ride or
cycle through our countryside. We have seen that 'definitive' is still
not the last word. Many rights of way were undoubtedly missed
off the first editions of the definitive maps and precious few of these
have been reclaimed since. But at least the situation is a good deal
clearer now than it was pre-1949. And in truth, the system of
public rights of way that we have is the envy of many countries —
ask a walker from New Zealand or from the USA! It is fortunate
indeed that we have such vigilant amenity bodies keeping a close
surveillance on what goes on, for without them we would be much
worse off than we are.

We also have a truly excellent national series of maps showing
our rights of way. The Ordnance Survey series at both 1:50,000
and 1:25,000 scale are invaluable to the walker, and standards are
extremely high both in surveying and mapping. Maps are updated
regularly and developments in computerisation mean that detail
such as contours is now much more accurate.

We have a widely used and slowly expanding network of long
distance routes, which could not have existed prior to the Act.
Organisations such as the Ramblers' Association would argue that

the network has been developed neither fast enough nor extensively enough, but the paths we do have cover about 2,800 km of fine country and receive high levels of funding for their maintenance, even if more should be spent in places where erosion is a problem.

Perhaps the most significant development of the past 40 years has been the enormous increase in public awareness of the countryside and the parallel growth in walking as a recreation, to the point where it now far outstrips other outdoor recreation activity. Millions of people enjoy the countryside in an individual way. Most of them seek only local walks which they know well, but a significant number venture further afield. Rambling and mountaineering clubs have proliferated and paths in some areas have come under very heavy pressure as a result.

One of the less positive signs, the shortage of funds to carry out legal duties regarding public rights of way, has already been referred to. A further change has been the effective replacement of the provisions in the 1949 Act regarding public rights of way by parts of the Wildlife and Countryside Act 1981. Previously local authorities were required to update definitive maps every five years. Few, if any, were able to do so in practice. The duty now is simply to bring the map and statement up-to-date 'as soon as is reasonably practicable' and thereafter keep it under continuous review. Thankfully, many more authorities are making a determined effort to comply. But the loose phrasing means that it could be difficult, if not impossible, to enforce the duty on an authority which chose, now or in the future, to neglect this work. The onus for collecting evidence of change has also shifted and is now placed much more upon the public — in the words of the Byways and Bridleways Trust, 'a hopeless situation'. The Trust says that 'The burden being placed on the public is intolerable. Individuals have not the time, money or expertise to take action which will ensure the definitive map is correctly modified'.

Nor has the substantial part of the 1949 Act dealing with access to the open country by agreement been particularly successful. As we have seen, apart from in the Peak National Park, authorities have neglected to use these provisions, and there is every indication that they will continue to neglect them. Access by agreement was always going to be difficult: given the lack of resources and/or will amongst our public bodies, this part of the Act seems destined to continue as a failure.

As to the situation in Scotland, this shows that strict legislation to achieve a high level of access at least to wilder countryside is not necessarily needed. But pressure on the countryside of Scotland's southern neighbours is very intense and different solutions are needed. What are those solutions? With much of the rights of way network, even if defined on maps, still largely unusable; with common land, which could be used much more for quiet enjoyment, still under threat; with access agreements almost a defunct piece of legislation, and at the same time with more and more people wanting to explore the countryside, how can we best provide for them?

The Countryside Commission has attempted to address this question through a number of consultation papers and policy statements in recent years. *Enjoying the Countryside* and *Paths Routes and Trails: Policies and Priorities* have made a strong case concerning rights of way, with some success. But the answer in legislative terms seems as far away as ever. That answer can only be one that is unpopular to the landowners and which requires considerable courage to implement. There is no real reason why free access to the open country, to mountain, moorland and coast, should not be provided. Legislation has never addressed this question. From the 1949 Act through the Countryside Act 1968 to the Wildlife and Countryside Act 1981, all reference has been to legally defined rights of way and to access agreements. Future legislation such as the water privatisation proposals follow the same pattern. Reports such as Sandford's, which we discussed in chapter 5, skirted round the question. Meantime, the arguments for free access lose none of their force.

Free access, given the benefits it can bring to virtually the entire population, should be the justification for support from central government through grants or fiscal means for the management that open country needs. It is completely unreasonable in the last decade of the 20th century for a small number of landowners to expect to be able to bar the public from their land. Access must be accompanied by an expectation of good behaviour, and of an atti-

6.11 Obstructing our rights of way Even forty years after the 1949 Act, too many footpaths remain obstructed or deliberately uncleared. *Source*: Countryside Commission

tude of respect for the land and the life it supports. But that attitude will not arise unless the access is provided. Until it is, there will always be a resentment that we are denied, for no good reason, that which we could enjoy, appreciate and respect.

A desired future must be to see free access to all open countryside granted within a reasonable time-scale. That this must be a political decision will be a matter of regret to some who find the notion of the countryside as a political battleground repugnant and would readily advocate a responsible use of the rural environment in return for the right to enjoy it responsibly and freely. For the moment it has to be conceded that the 1949 Act failed to give that freedom or to demand that responsibility. It achieved a good deal, but it did not take the final great step of giving the citizens of this country free access to their own countryside. In that major respect, it was a failure. But to look back and criticise is easy. It is probably more fruitful instead to look forward and hope that in another 40 years, our descendants will look back and wonder why it took us so long to open up the mountains, moors and other open country that they enjoy — and value — in freedom.

7 Areas of outstanding natural beauty and the wider countryside

AONBs and their designation

The term 'area of outstanding natural beauty' (AONB) originated in the 1949 Act. People say it is clumsy and not objective, nothing like so evocative as 'national park', or even 'heritage coast'. Nevertheless, the need to identify and protect areas which, though of the highest visual quality, might not be suitable as national parks because of their size or lack of wildness has imaginative origins in John Dower's concept of 'other amenity areas'. As we saw in Part I of this book, these became the conservation areas of the Hobhouse and Huxley Reports before emerging in the Bill as debated in the House of Commons with a name that has remained with us ever since.

As it turned out, in the 1949 Act, AONBs were to be recognised solely as areas where the landscape could be protected. They were to have none of the administrative and financial framework of national parks which had been designed to promote positively their conservation and enjoyment objectives. Instead, the administration of AONBs was to be left to the whim of individual planning authorities, goaded if need be by the National Parks Commission. Certainly, the imaginative proposals of Hobhouse, if not Dower, for these areas had been watered down significantly during the period in which the Bill was under consideration. Gone were the requirements for an advisory committee for each area. Gone, also, was any direct reference to scientific interest and recreational value as criteria for the selection of areas. And gone was the 12-month period within which proposals should be made for designation.

With a National Parks Commission that was often regarded as weak in the early years and much preoccupied with setting up national parks, a widely accepted view that planning control could do all that was necessary for the protection of rural areas, and a natural tendency for local authorities to concentrate on urgent day to day problems, AONBs were slow to come off the drawing board. But if they were not high on the political agendas of the time, nor, in those days, was the wider countryside.

So it was that although national and local amenity societies had pressed for some time after the passing of the 1949 Act for AONB designation, it was not until the mid-1950s, when seven out of the ten national parks had been set up, that the Commission, with its minuscule staff, felt able to turn actively to a programme for this. Having reviewed the areas suggested by the Hobhouse Committee, it gave priority to the Gower Peninsula and Quantock Hills. Gower, its unspoilt coast, heathland and rich wildlife, under much pressure for recreation, but watched over by the very active Gower Society, was the first designation to be confirmed — in 1956. The Quantock Hills were also a special case. They had originally been included by the Hobhouse Committee as an offshoot of the Exmoor National Park, but later, despite their delightful landscape contrasts, they were thought insufficiently scenic for this status.

By the mid-1960s, 19 areas had been designated. These included the Cornwall AONB, whose beautiful and wild coastal section were on Dower's priority national park list, but had been regarded by the Hobhouse Committee as too fragmented for administration as such; Dorset, especially the Hardy country, from Dower's reserve list of potential national parks; and 'lungs' close to major centres of population such as Cannock Chase, the Surrey Hills and the Chilterns.

A decade later a further 13 were on the books. These included the Sussex Downs (originally recommended by the Hobhouse Committee as a national park on account of their proximity to London, and still exhilarating despite having lost much downland to the plough), and the more remote and spacious North Wessex Downs, which were on Dower's reserve list. Thereafter the pace slowed somewhat. Experience had pointed to a need for rather wider consultation, especially with farming interests, as each new area came under consideration; and, in any case, the programme

7.1 AONBs – the first round
Oxwich Dunes and Pennard Cliffs form part of the Gower, the earliest of these areas to be designated.
Source: Archie Miles

was beginning to draw to a close. One very controversial case, the North Pennines (also on Dower's reserve list), occupied a great deal of time. By the end of 1988, a total of 38 AONBs had been designated, covering nearly 13 per cent of the area of England and Wales, in addition to the nearly 10 per cent included in national parks.

Between 1973 and 1986, some 1370 km of coastline had also been defined as heritage coast, a concept stemming from Prof J.J. Steers' report in the 1940's *Coastal Preservation and Planning*, and the Countryside Commission's 1970 report *Coastal Heritage*. Most of the 41 areas so defined are in AONBs, and to a lesser extent in national parks, which is probably the reason why, with so much importance attached to the coast by Dower, and the Hobhouse and Huxley Committees, action had not been taken earlier. Although not provided for in the Act, heritage coast definition carries the same conservation objectives as AONB designation, but with more emphasis on positive management.

The present extent of AONBs is shown in figure 7.2. Together with those still due to be designated, the Tamar and Tavy Valleys, the Blackdown Hills (on which a good deal of progress has been made), the Berwyn Mountains and possibly the Nidderdale Moors, it will be seen that they vary immensely in size and landscape character. Some are well known, for example Cornwall, coastal areas in Devon, the south's chalk downland and the Cotswolds; they draw visitors from far afield. Others such as the Forest of Bowland with its magnificent gritstone fells, have a more local appeal. With notable exceptions (especially the North Pennines) they are smaller than the national parks, and tend to be in agricultural, 'lowland' Britain, in contrast to the parks' wilder, upland locations. To a degree, therefore, they are more accessible to the urban populations of the south-east then are the parks themselves. Heritage coasts, also shown in figure 7.2 tend, on the other hand, to be in scenic holiday regions.

Fourteen of the Hobhouse Committee's areas are missing from the AONB list. Two of these are instead defined as heritage coasts. The remainder include very scenic parts of central Wales, where Radnor Forest was dropped from the programme on account of the outright opposition of all the Welsh local authorities concerned; Breckland, because much of its open, species-rich landscape has been lost to forestry; and Leicestershire's Charnwood Forest, which is bisected by the M1. The New Forest, also on the list, can hardly be regarded as having been rejected; it has unique and historic status as a Royal Forest, and the privately owned estates in the south-east corner are within the South Hampshire Coast AONB. A New Forest Heritage Area Committee is now proposed, to promote the conservation of the whole Forest and its associated fringe as being comparable in importance to the national parks.

There have been four additions, however, to the Hobhouse list: Lincolnshire Wolds, a peaceful, gently undulating landscape in the county that has taken the brunt of modern agricultural development, for whose designation there was much pressure from the county council; Dedham Vale, of special cultural value as Constable country; Chichester Harbour, a potential arena of conflict between water recreation and the conservation of its remarkably varied scenery and masses of birds; and the Solway Coast, at risk formerly from caravan sites, but now sharing with Scotland a lonely beauty of firth landscape and wildlife, whose international significance may not have been fully appreciated by Hobhouse and Huxley.

Areas of Outstanding Natural Beauty and Heritage Coasts in England and Wales

as at Autumn 1989

AREAS OF OUTSTANDING NATURAL BEAUTY

	Date confirmed
Anglesey	13.11.67
Arnside & Silverdale	15.12.72
Cannock Chase	16.9.58
Chichester Harbour	4.2.64
Chilterns	16.12.65
Clwydian Range	24.7.85
Cornwall	25.11.59
Camel Estuary (Extension)	28.10.83
Cotswolds	19.8.66
Cranborne Chase & West Wiltshire Downs	28.10.83
Dedham Vale	20.5.70
(Extension)	21.8.78
Dorset	29.7.59
East Devon	20.9.63
East Hampshire	26.9.62
Forest of Bowland	10.2.64
Gower	10.12.56
High Weald	28.10.83
Howardian Hills	19.10.87
Isle of Wight	20.9.63
Isles of Scilly	18.2.76
Kent Downs	23.7.68
Lincolnshire Wolds	17.4.73
Lleyn	28.5.57
Malvern Hills	22.10.59
Mendip Hills	1.12.72
Norfolk Coast	8.4.68
North Devon	25.5.60
North Pennines	7.6.88
Northumberland Coast	21.3.58
North Wessex Downs	1.12.72
Quantock Hills	1.1.57
Shropshire Hills	11.3.59
Solway Coast	12.12.64
South Devon	2.8.60
South Hampshire Coast	18.12.67
Suffolk Coast & Heaths	4.3.70
Surrey Hills	8.5.58
Sussex Downs	7.4.66
Wye Valley	13.12.71

HERITAGE COASTS

	Date defined		
St Bees Head	2.2.89	Hartland	3.4.86
Great Orme	5.3.74	Pentire Point	3.4.86
North Anglesey	3.7.73	Trevose Head	3.4.86
Holyhead Mountain	3.7.73	St Agnes	3.4.86
Aberffraw Bay	3.7.73	Godrevy-Portreath	3.4.86
Lleyn	5.3.74	Isles of Scilly	5.12.75
Ceredigion Coast	2.12.82	Penwith	3.4.86
St Dogmaels & Moylgrove	2.7.74	The Lizard	3.4.86
		The Roseland	3.4.86
Dinas Head	2.7.74	Gribbin Head-Polperro	3.4.86
St Davids Peninsula	2.7.74	Rame Head	3.4.86
St Brides Bay	2.7.74	South Devon	4.12.86
Marloes and Dale	2.7.74	East Devon	7.6.84
South Pembrokeshire	2.7.74	West Dorset	2.2.84
Gower	5.6.73	Purbeck	4.6.81
Glamorgan	5.6.73	Tennyson	1.12.88
		Hamstead	1.12.88
		Sussex	2.4.73
		Dover-Folkestone	6.11.75
		South Foreland	6.11.75
		Suffolk	2.4.87
		North Norfolk	3.4.75
		Spurn	6.10.88
		Flamborough Headland	4.8.89
		North Yorkshire & Cleveland	7.5.81
		North Northumberland	1.2.73

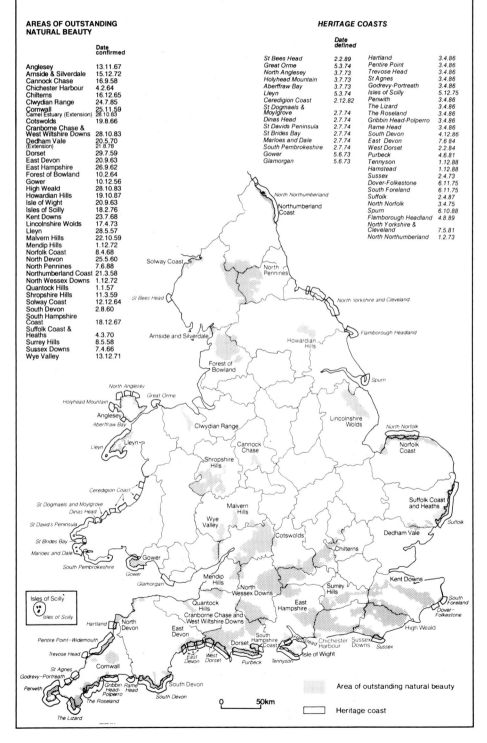

Area of outstanding natural beauty

Heritage coast

0   50km

The Commission (by now the Countryside Commission) has re-appraised its designation programme twice, reconsidering the Hobhouse Committee's areas and looking at some others, such as the Dean Valley in Hampshire and the Swale Estuary in Kent. There is much consistency between the conservation areas and the actual designations, despite the Hobhouse Committee's use of rather wider criteria than in the ensuing legislation. The Commission's assessments of landscape quality contain factors such as relief, shape, natural and semi-natural character, contrast and harmony, which are often closely related to scientific values. Thus an important connection with the Hobhouse Committee has been reintroduced. Where there have been variations in the extent or actual choice of areas, it must be remembered that landscape assessment, however systematic, inevitably involves subjective judgement, and that designation has policy implications to which local communities respond in different ways.

The Countryside Commission's policies

Early in the 1970s when the designation programme itself was first being reappraised, the Commission began to feel the need for a more fundamental review of general policy towards AONBs. A combination of factors had arisen during the previous decade. One was the growing interest in policy for the countryside as a whole, created by the 'Countryside in 1970' Conference and higher fore-casts of car ownership and leisure time. Another was the arrival of some influential new personalities at ministerial level and in the upper echelons of the Commission: Keith Joseph and Fred Willey in Whitehall, whose concern to promote wider recreational oppor-tunities had resulted in the Countryside Act 1968; also John Cripps, Chairman, and Reg Hookway, as first Principal Planning Officer and later Director of the new Commission, anxious to raise its profile, the quality of its forward thinking and technical ability.

Hitherto, AONB policy had been almost entirely a matter of development control standards, on which there was reasonable consensus. Even so, in 1961 the Commission had proposed that the 1949 Act should be amended to assist conservation projects in

7.2 AONB and heritage coasts in 1989
Source: Countryside Commission

163

AONBs. This initiative had been overshadowed, however, by the controversy over administrative organisation in the national parks. Subsequently, in 1963, discussions between the Commission and the Ministry of Housing and Local Government had even contemplated abolishing AONB designation. Instead, AONBs would be introduced through development plans, though still entitled to grants. Nothing came of this, despite the Commission welcoming it as part of a package; perhaps it was not worth the inevitable controversy with amenity groups.

During the 1960s and 1970s, as each AONB was designated, the Commission had encouraged local planning authorities to set up a joint advisory committee where appropriate, and to produce a Statement of Intent. They also urged the inclusion in development plans of more positive planning and management policies for such areas. The response was disappointing, however. Also causing concern was the opposition of farming and land-owning interests to new designations made in the mid-1970s. The consensus seemed to be drifting apart. All this, and calls from other bodies for a review, finally led the Commission to begin a major re-think of the strengths and weaknesses of AONBs.

The review started in 1978, and was intended to produce clear policies for planning, that is plan making and control, and for management. The latter would involve initiatives in the field by local authorities and other public bodies in the interest of conservation and of activities such as recreation and economic development. At the outset, the Commission published a discussion paper in which its frustration was neatly summarised: AONBs had few, if any, implications for the other government planning systems affecting the countryside. It posed several questions, including the possibility of scrapping AONBs altogether. However, it also set out for the first time a series of policy objectives. Conservation through management, as well as by development control, should be the prime consideration, and a high priority should be given to public enjoyment and local economic development so far as is consistent with this main aim. The discussion paper was favourably received at a conference called to mark the beginning of the review, as was the appointment of Kenneth Himsworth, who we noted in chapter 5 was appointed as the first Clerk to the Lake District National Park,

7.3 Countryside management in AONBs
Practical management, rather than just control, became more important in the development of these areas from the early 1970s.
Source: Gloucestershire County Council

to make a comprehensive study of how far the statutory purposes of designation had been achieved.

Himsworth reported in 1980. His report is a veritable gold-mine of information about the state of the art of AONB planning and management in the late 1970s, a basis from which it should be possible in future to make some judgements about progress since then. As a prelude to many detailed recommendations on matters such as area definition, the designation process, planning, conservation, recreation and administration, Himsworth posed key questions: for example, has designation been effective and in the public interest? Would present circumstances have been materially different if there had been no designation? His answers were guarded. Designation had resulted in some recognisable, if uneven, effect on landscape protection. It had been achieved at modest price and seemed well justified in the public interest. But nothing had been done in an AONB that could not have been done under normal planning powers, and it could not be said that things would have been very different had there been no designation. Despite some apprehension expressed about AONBs by the farming industry and forestry interests, and despite his own doubts about the provable success of designation, Himsworth gave the concept a clean bill of health and aimed his recommendations at improving it. In this, he was clearly influenced by the degree of public support expressed during his many consultations. Surely designation must have been regarded as worthwhile.

Consensus was re-emerging. On the strength of the report and its own review of the many comments favourable to AONBs received in response to its discussion paper, the Commission decided to continue with designation. In doing so, however, it acknowledged that the statutory purposes of AONBs were not always being achieved. This, it said, was due as much as anything to a lack of clear planning and management strategies, inadequate resources, and, in some cases, lack of coordination between local authorities. At the end of 1980, it therefore presented to the government a published policy statement which placed an important emphasis on planning and management, including administration and grant aid. By and large, these policies reflected the tenor of Himsworth's recommendations on matters of principle.

The Government's response came in 1982, in the form of a statement by the Secretary of State for the Environment couched in the usual cautious Whitehall language. However, it confirmed a continued commitment to safeguarding AONBs, and generally endorsed the Commission's new policies, with three important exceptions. The first of these was really a matter of emphasis: recreation should not be an objective of designation as originally proposed by the Commission, so much as a use of land which is consistent with conservation, agriculture, forestry and other rural activities. The second concerned mineral working and road construction, where slightly less demanding criteria were preferred. The third affected the Commission's proposal to extend to AONBs the agricultural notification procedures used in national parks; this was unacceptable because of the manpower implications, although there was a hint that it could be reviewed at some future time.

All this was very understandable politically, and only a comparatively minor setback. Undaunted, the Commission published in 1983 a revised policy document, taking account of the government's views. Here at last was a major pronouncement on strategy which, together with specific matters in statutory instruments and Government Circulars, has since endured as the basis of the Commission's approach to all AONB issues. The essentials were as follows.

- All existing AONBs to be retained, and a further five designated[1].
- Conservation of natural beauty to be the primary objective of designation, demands for recreation only being met as far as is consistent with this and with the needs of agriculture, forestry and other users. Account to be taken of the needs of rural industries and local communities in pursuing the main objective.
- Broadly based joint advisory committees to be encouraged in multi-authority AONBs, and for every AONB a named local authority officer with special responsibilities.
- A Statement of Intent to be encouraged for each AONB, linked to statutory development plans; and also, where appropriate, the production of management plans to help to resolve rural land use conflicts.
- For development control: a clear recognition of the national importance of conservation in AONBs, new major developments being regarded as unacceptable unless in the national interest and there being no alternative site; mineral workings and road schemes to be subject to the most rigorous examination; sympathetic treatment to be given to small-scale industries where associated with settlements; informal notification arrangements to be encouraged for farm buildings; and improvements to be made by statutory agencies in their consultations on major developments.
- The Commission to give high priority to grant aid for landscape conservation, visitor management and preparation of management plans.

AONBs and countryside planning

Although we shall discuss progress in the realisation of these policies later, we must, first of all, look at the place of AONBs in the full range of countryside planning measures that were emerging in

---

[1] Two of these, the Clwydian Range and the Howardian Hills have since been designated

167

the wake of 1949 Act. We have seen that AONBs took a second place in the Commission's priorities in the early days, despite the maxim that their landscape quality is by no means secondary to that of the national parks. Gradually, however, the Hobhouse Committee's vision of conservation areas took shape on the ground in modified form, rather low-key, and without the political support for the pattern of administrative coordination it regarded as essential. Eventually, some 35 to 40 years after the passing of the Act, AONB designation was almost complete, and a policy framework had emerged at national level for their administration and planning. Meanwhile, as we shall show later, local planning policies were also being spelt out for each area formally in structure plans, but sometimes in supplementary planning documents too, and management projects were becoming important components of conservation, especially in heritage coasts. Even now, staffing in planning authorities that deal with these areas is minimal, however, as is financial support. Grants are only awarded for specific actions, not for general administration, and the level of grant is for the most part no higher than in the wider countryside. It is now evident enough that, despite the policy and financial intent of the Commission, the planning and management of AONBs has much more in common with the ordinary countryside in which they are set than with national parks.

Meanwhile, policy for the wider countryside has not stood still, and it is worth taking a closer look at this. The relevance of the 1949 Act, never strong here, became tenuous. Indeed, for the first 15 years or so decision makers were almost entirely concerned with development provisions of the Town and Country Planning Act 1947. Although consulted on more controversial planning applications and on development plans, the National Parks Commission, with its slender resources, made little impact in the early years. Policy for the wider countryside was embodied in ad hoc measures, with little strategic framework: the vague restrictions of 'white land', which we recognised in chapter 3 as part of the 1947 Act, and the additional degrees of restraint brought about by green belts; the seemingly unrelated areas of landscape or scientific value; and high-quality agricultural land. For a variety of reasons there was a tendency for development to be steered to

7.4 Conserving our heritage coasts
Start Point in Devon is part of such an area, but these, along with AONBs, have always been managed on a shoe-string.
Source: Devon County Council

selected villages only, sometimes with very unfortunate results.

However, a new era began during the 1960s with the growing realisation that leisure and other conflicting pressures were seriously threatening a wide variety of key rural resources, needing coordination beyond the scope of traditional planning. Clearly this required strategic thinking and innovation. Fortunately, at government level, both Keith Joseph and Fred Willey were receptive as we noted above. Both were influential in the 1966 White Paper *Leisure in the Countryside*, which, although not advocating a comprehensive approach to rural policy, favoured proposals for a Countryside Commission, and for enjoyment of the wider countryside to relieve pressure on national parks and other outstandingly attractive places. Country parks, picnic sites, improved access to water and open country, footpaths and bridleways, trees and woodlands were now all on the agenda. Legislation quickly followed in the Countryside Act 1968, the main recreation provisions of which were taken up with alacrity by pioneering local authorities and landowners. This resulted in a steady increase of site-based facilities. In practical terms, the existence by 1988 of 220 country parks and 264 picnic sites speaks well for the efforts of all concerned to respond to public demand, especially at a time of growing financial constraint. Figure 7.5 reveals a pattern of facilities which, although opportunistic, tends to be clustered around major centres of population, almost entirely outside the national parks and largely outside AONBs and heritage coasts. This is as it should be, bearing in mind the intentions of those who wrote the White Paper. Thus, a deficiency in the 1949 Act had been rectified some 20 years later, the wider countryside being used to redress, strategically, the recreational imbalance that was putting designated areas at risk.

New problems began to appear in the 1970s and 1980s, however, highlighting once more shortcomings in the inter-relationship of rural policies. As early as 1972 the Commission was showing concern over the future of agricultural landscapes, whose continued erosion, accompanied by loss of wildlife habitat, was soon to become a matter of public debate. Anxiety grew during the next ten years with the knowledge that major food surpluses were occurring and that there would probably need to be radical changes in EC and UK agricultural policy, with far-reaching economic, social and physical consequences. This was not the only problem, widespread though it was. Forestry policy was having a profound impact on some upland landscapes and wildlife. Also, there was much anxiety over the condition of urban fringe areas, despite imaginative projects such as those undertaken by Groundwork Trusts, with their special fund-raising expertise. Furthermore, over large areas of countryside, pressure of population dispersal and the need for rural economic regeneration were calling into question the adequacy of long-standing rural settlement policies.

Alternative approaches to rural planning

Meanwhile, approaches to rural planning were being developed further by some local authorities. Tracts of countryside where amenity, landscape, ecology, recreation and productive farming are strongly interdependent were to become units for policy making, supplemented by management projects. As yet, all of this is in its relatively early stages, but it is soundly based on know-how from the national park initiatives referred to in chapter 5, as well as heritage coasts and experiments elsewhere in the wider countryside. One such example of this approach was in the Bollin Valley, on the southern fringe of Manchester, where there was an urgent need for

7.5 **Designated for recreation, 1989**
Source: Countryside Commission

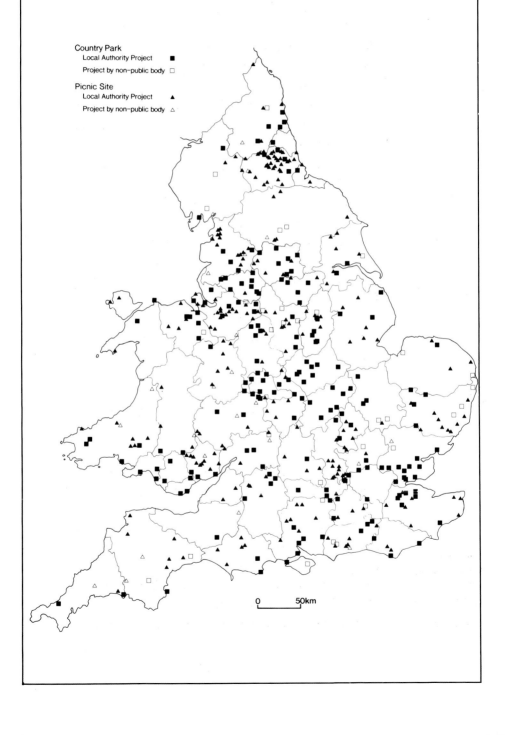

Country Parks and Picnic Sites

Country Park
- Local Authority Project ■
- Project by non-public body □

Picnic Site
- Local Authority Project ▲
- Project by non-public body △

0   50km

positive measures to reconcile recreation and farming and to prevent further landscape erosion. A project team, set up in 1972 by the local authorities and the Countryside Commission, worked closely with the many interests involved in the area to produce and put into practice a management plan, successfully enlisting local goodwill and voluntary help, and bringing together the use of public and private funds.

Another good example of the new approach can be found in Hertfordshire. Here, in 1976, the county and district councils established two countryside management areas in the urban fringe of north London. The know-how, exemplified in the need for work to be compatible with the aims for local interests, to have long-term dependability, and to develop a strong educational content, was successfully applied and extended. Gradually, in association with the London Borough of Barnet and with financial support from the Commission, the county and districts have extended the scheme and now deploy countryside managers over eight areas of the county as a whole. Each manager is responsible for about 26,000 hectares, 'enabling' conservation and access, especially rights of way, through daily contact with farmers and landowners, as needs and opportunities arise.

Hampshire has followed a rather different, though no less comprehensive course. Concerned initially at the loss of ancient woodland, the county council has collected and published detailed accounts of all main types of heritage site throughout Hampshire so that it may be made aware of incipient risks to them. As a direct result, it has completed more than 250 management agreements (mostly under the 1949 Act) to secure protection, often at a minimal cost. Interestingly, the heritage sites bear no particular relationship to the county's several AONBs.

In both counties, spending on such schemes, running into six figures including grants from the Commission and other sources, has all-party support, though more money is badly needed to tackle large projects. The scope is now widening into rural economic development, in addition to the well-developed recreation service that already exists.

This is a flexible, pragmatic and incremental activity, limited by its reliance on goodwill and cooperation, but nevertheless strategic in concept. It is not confined to these counties alone, however. The Commission has recognised its importance by 'targetting' their grants increasingly to countryside management, including ranger services, in areas of the wider countryside under the most recreational pressure, such as the urban fringe, as well as heritage coasts and selected AONBs.

Those who are involved in it would be the first to agree that more needs to be known about the issues, particularly the impact of current trends in agriculture. It is very encouraging, therefore, that the Commission resolved to address these key questions comprehensively through a Countryside Policy Review Panel, set up in 1986. The Panel reported with commendable speed, and the Commission was able to publish its response in autumn 1987. Specific government policies on agriculture and economic development were also evolving throughout this period, and it is much to the credit of the Commission that it took the initiative in lateral thinking, following it up with further papers on forestry and on planning a year later.

All three documents reinforce the case for better coordination of policy and management affecting the quality of the wider countryside, and, bland though some of the conclusions inevitably are, their strategic thrust is very welcome. Major features include: a general lowering of the intensity of farming, applying Environmentally Sensitive Areas (ESA) principles more widely,

7.6 A Hampshire heritage site
This rich unimproved water-meadow at Knoll Farm, near Fordingbridge, is protected by a management agreement made between its owner and the county council.
Source: Hampshire County Council

173

with greater emphasis on environmental care and recreational provision; a greater diversity in forestry schemes; new efforts to provide public access to countryside; a national policy for the urban fringe; and a constructive, coordinating role for county councils by means of countryside strategies for their areas. To persuade other agencies and government departments that such action is necessary will be an acid test of the Commission's standing, but the omens seem to be good at present.

Thus the context for AONB planning and management has changed almost beyond recognition since the early days of the 1949 Act. Far from being an activity aiming to conserve selected landscape, pursued largely through the use of planning powers, AONB policy is increasingly being influenced by objectives for the countryside at large, its social, economic and natural resources. The drive to provide sites for recreation to relieve pressure on sensitive locations is now giving way to the area-based approach, although it must be admitted that much of this activity is non-statutory and limited to parts of the country where the climate of opinion is receptive to the outlay in manpower and finance. Furthermore, the future may depend critically on what influence county councils can still wield after the government's promised legislation on development plans, with its implications for their role in planning. Change is in the air.

How does planning and management in individual AONBs relate to the Commission's policies and the changing context outlined above? It is to this consideration that we now turn.

Action on the ground in AONBs.

One of the Commission's policies has been to encourage joint advisory committees in multi-county areas. Of the 38 AONBs so far designated, 16 are in more than one county, five being just marginally so. There are nevertheless only eight joint committees or equivalents in multi-county areas. These are generally the larger ones, including the Cotswolds Joint Advisory Committee (five counties), the Chilterns Standing Conference (four counties) and the Wye Valley Joint Advisory Committee (three counties, straddling the national boundary between England and Wales).

These committees tend to be broadly based, as favoured by the Commission, typically a forum of planning authorities, statutory agencies and participant groups (national and local), meeting three or four times a year to consider policy and management issues. Development applications are not normally referred to them. The most successful, probably, are those with a strong participant input, but this means they may be large and unwieldy, so subdivision into smaller working groups is vital for successful operation, as with the Chiltern Woodlands Policy, for example. In some of the multi-county areas which do not have a joint committee, the preference seems to be for annual meetings with participants, convened by the planning authorities, and supplemented by inter-authority liaison groups. This is so, for example, in the Sussex Downs and the High Weald; here, local authority and participants' priorities are so widely dispersed over the attractive counties within which they lie that the effort of frequent AONB meetings is not thought to be justified.

There are a further five joint advisory committees in single-county areas. They tend to be where there are special problems requiring such organisation. Examples are the Isles of Scilly, where the Environmental Trust set up by the Duchy of Cornwall acts in this capacity; and the Quantock Hills, whose unusual problems of heathland conservation can only be tackled in a combined opera-tion between the planning authorities (especially the county coun-cil), Ministry of Agriculture, Nature Conservancy Council, National Trust and the local Commoners' Association. In areas where there is no joint committee, local planning authorities work through their normal committee organisation and participation arrangements; experience suggests that in single counties with well-tried procedures of this kind, special administrative arrange-ments could be wasteful duplication.

The Commission attaches importance to having a named local authority officer with special responsibilities for each AONB. This helps to generate an identity for the area and for measures to con-serve it, and a reference point for all involved in its day-to-day man-agement. Coverage is by no means complete, and the level of responsibility varies considerably. Some AONB officers hold full-time project-based appointments, financed temporarily with grant

175

support from the Commission; some are more senior staff on the permanent establishment of the parent departments, often hard pressed on other duties as well; some exist for part of a multi-county area only. A recent count suggests that nine AONBs have their own named officer in some way or other (a further seven work in AONB heritage coasts), but that the number is increasing, due largely to the Commission's continuing to offer initial financial assistance. As yet, there is no evidence that councils are unwilling to take over the full cost after pump-priming ceases; the method is well tried, especially in heritage coasts, and the costs are low in comparison with the total amount of expenditure that a good AONB officer can generate from a variety of sources, public and private.

AONB policy making and concerns

One of the earliest attempts at policy making for an AONB was the East Hampshire study. Aware that the traditional 'broad brush' treatment of rural areas in development plans was becoming quite inadequate in the face of trends in agriculture, forestry and countryside recreation, the study set out to explore new techniques of policy making through a multi-disciplinary team drawn from the County Council, Countryside Commission, Ministry of Agriculture, Nature Conservancy, Forestry Commission and the Ministry of Housing and Local Government. The team made a detailed study of the area's natural resources and the activities affecting them at the time and in the foreseeable future. The impact of these activities on the resources and on each other was then conjectured, and the team hammered out planning and management policies for landscape, wildlife conservation and recreation. These were to be applied according to zones derived from an evaluation of the resources and an assessment of the acceptability of various activities in them. It was all a considerable departure from the usual land use concerns of development plans.

For a variety of reasons this study was never translated into action. One shortcoming was that it had no shopping list of priorities amongst its many recommendations; another was its lack of input from politicians and participants. Nevertheless, its techniques were developed in other projects (including the New Forest Study), in the course of which they were simplified to enable issues to be more quickly identified, and the process was made more participatory.

This experience is recounted because of its relevance to the process by which policies currently being applied in a number of AONBs are made, often under the aegis of joint advisory committees or their equivalents. The techniques used in the original study sound very systematic, but within the broad objectives set by the Commission, national or regional guidance, and in structure plans, there is inevitably scope for much compromise. Where successful conservation depends largely on action for which there is no powerful statutory backing and no unified decision-making organisation, 'bargaining' is the order of the day, using such means, including political clout, finance and land ownership, as are available.

Before looking at the policies being applied on the ground in AONBs, it is useful to summarise problems arising in them which need to be tackled. Drawing on evidence from individual planning documents and from other anecdotal evidence, for their has been no systematic collection of data, it would seem there are three main areas of concern.

Firstly, about deteriorating landscape and habitats due to the following.
• Agricultural change, reported from many areas, upland and

lowland; loss of unimproved grassland, wetland, trees, hedges, walls and archeological features; the growth of scrub as a result of a decline in grazing and commoning; the neglect of small woodlands; obtrusive modern agricultural buildings, and decrepit vernacular ones.

- Mineral working, although this is only reported as a problem in a few areas.

- Recreation: not a matter of universal concern so much as an issue of extreme pressure in 'honeypot' localities, causing vegetational loss and disturbance to wildlife; and in areas with open countryside, where off-road driving and parking causes severe but localised disturbance of the same sort.

- Development of various kinds, from urban housing to hill-top aerials, affecting southern AONBs in particular, despite strong planning controls. This is usually a question of general intrusion into the landscape rather than one of design standards, although standards are still unsatisfactory in some areas, for example the remoter ones.

Secondly, there is concern about recreational opportunities. This stems from uncertainty over the level of recreation to be provided for within the overall objective of conservation. It arises in various ways.

7.8 Visual intrusions in protected landscapes
Radio relay masts are one of the most disruptive elements in AONBs, despite their special designation.
Source: Countryside Commission

- The need for balance between tourist promotion, on the one hand, and local carrying capacities, on the other, especially in southern AONBs.
- Conflict between forms of recreation: a serious problem in the more accessible AONBs, with golf courses, equestrian centres, noisy activities and water sports competing with informal recreation; and in moorland areas, with occasional conflict between game preservation and access to open country.
- The attractions of honeypots in the more popular AONBs, resulting in overcrowding of visitors, traffic and parking problems on local roads, erosion of local rights of way, and poor observance of the Country Code, especially with respect to litter.

Thirdly, there is concern about the well-being of local communities, especially in the following areas.
- The effect of tight controls over village expansion: the well-known difficulty of providing affordable housing for local people, a problem that exists in upland areas as well as in the popular residential countryside of the south.
- Fears that local economic development would be severely restricted by designation of an AONB: these have been voiced for some time and became a major issue in public inquiry held in 1985 into the North Pennines designation.

These are the raw materials of policy making. It is not a list from which one can draw earth-shaking conclusions; most of the issues are well known in the countryside at large. Furthermore, the lack of systematic monitoring in AONBs makes it impossible to say how seriously they, in particular, are affected. Nevertheless, compared with the problems revealed in early AONB studies, the list suggests a considerable growth in potential conflicts and in planners awareness of them. All of this has led to a plethora of initiatives, to which we now turn.

Local policies, local plans

Policies for individual areas are expressed through statutory development plans and increasingly through non-statutory documents.

Some policies exist only in the heads of AONB officers, or almost literally on the back of an envelope. At county structure plan level, policies for rural conservation usually say that particular care will be taken in areas of landscape importance, including AONBs. Beyond this, treatment of AONBs varies immensely.

Most plans set out general priorities for recreation in them, and for minerals and waste disposal, being land use matters for which the overriding importance of conservation needs to be clearly spelt out. Most also give environmental criteria against which building development will be judged. Some include general guidance on farm buildings, rural traffic management, and on wildlife conservation. A few more recent ones emphasise the needs of rural communities in AONBs.

However, if all of these policies tend to be in very broad terms, among the most specific is Somerset, with two and a bit AONBs, as well as the ecologically important Somerset Levels. Here, the plan deals with all of these topics and also the protection of archeological features and woodlands, making frequent references to the special needs of each AONB. By contrast, Kent, Surrey and Hampshire, counties with important AONBs and much experience in them, focus their guidance almost exclusively on county-wide aspects of conservation. There may be important implications in this for future AONB policy, and we return to the point later.

There is only one statutory local plan for a whole AONB, produced in 1986 jointly by Somerset and Avon County Councils for the Mendip Hills. This is of interest, since it combines the land use advantages of a statutory development plan with guidance on a whole range of measures normally found only in informal management programmes. The keynote is persuasion: to balance farming and conservation and to guide forms of recreation into more satisfactory patterns of activity. The plan has a zonal basis, as in East Hampshire, and a four-year costed programme for recreation, interpretation, environmental improvement, conservation and access.

The Mendip Local Plan is a bold experiment, valuable in this particular area. The Beaulieu Estate Plan, adopted by the authorities for part of the South Hampshire Coast AONB, is another, covering a complex set of issues, including intense recreational pressure. On the whole, however, it is doubtful whether the formal status of a local plan is necessary for most AONB purposes; something more flexible, procedurally, may be better.

This is probably why Statements of Intent are favoured by the Commission. Several AONBs now have them, but there is little of consequence in some of the earlier ones. The Statement for the Forest of Bowland (1985) is a shining example, however, and a credit to the Advisory Committee's detailed knowledge of the area, and its policy and management needs, especially for 'soft' landscape. This, like other more recent examples, has produced joint finance for a project officer and still acts as a basis for his very successful work programme. It has some similarities to the several management plans now in existence, from vintage ones such as Dedham Vale (1968) and the Chilterns (1971, by the Chilterns Standing Conference), to later productions including Wye Valley (1980), Chichester Harbour (1983), Gower (1988), Quantock Hills (currently in draft), and, in a more specialised vein, South Hampshire Coast (1983).

7.9 Producing plans for protection
The Beaulieu estate plan is a fully integrated part of the South Hampshire Coast AONB.
Source: National Motor Museum

It is through management plans that some of the most successful AONB conservation work has been done. They are broadly comparable to the national park plans, without the corporate approach to implementation that a national park authority can provide. Management plans are particularly valuable in areas with problems that cannot be tackled through normal planning measures. Take, for example, the sheer weight of conflicting recreation pressures in the Wye Valley (comparable to those of a national park), in Chichester Harbour and parts of the Mendip Hills; the very sensitive ecological, social and economic issue of commons management to conserve heathland in the heart of the Quantock Hills and Gower; the need to maintain the woodlands so characteristic of the Chilterns; to re-create the landscape of the Constable country, ravaged by Dutch elm disease and at further risk from drainage schemes; or to conserve wildlife habitats of national importance on the coastal marshes each side of the West Solent in Hampshire and the Isle of Wight. They are essentially action plans, needing a driving force from the public, private or voluntary sector, in the absence of a coordinating agency, and generous funding to bring them to fruition. Regular review (annually, as in the Cotswolds, for example), is essential, to keep up momentum and to adjust to change, especially in the availability of finance.

Before illustrating how these plans are being implemented, it is necessary to ask whether the problems described earlier as the raw material of policy making are, indeed, the ones that are being tack-

7.10 Visitor pressure in an AONB
Symond's Yat rock provides many with a magnificent panorama of the Wye valley AONB, but creates considerable recreation management problems.
Source: Gloucestershire County Council

led. By and large, this is the intention. The plans' strengths lie in the way in which they have adapted the Commission's priorities, for example, on recreation and on mineral working, to a host of different local situations. Their weaknesses reflect the limitations of the role of planning authorities in farming matters. To advocate persuasion and management agreements is all very well, but until the most recent changes in British and EC agricultural policy, the financial dice have been fairly heavily loaded against them. Indeed, only a few have dared to go beyond the legitimate question of siting farm buildings to consider in policy terms the impact of farming practice on the environment, let alone questions of set-aside and extensification. Equally, only the more recent plans try to establish a constructive relationship between conservation and local economic development; several agencies are involved in this, and there is much to learn about the ways in which cooperation can produce benefits.

Creative management and implementation

The term implementation is used here to imply creative management in support of the policies applying in an area, as distinct from the often reactive process of day-to-day development control. The existence of a management plan is normally a prerequisite, as are resources of staff time and specific funds. Out of the 38 designated AONBs, ten have management plans of various kinds. As we have already suggested, about the same number have the constant attention of a named officer. At least 14 have a warden or ranger service, but just a few have a readily identifiable budget. (These are supported to a greater or lesser degree by grant from the Commission. In some areas, for example, Cornwall, including the heritage coast and the ESA, the total amount from the public purse is far from negligible, though small by comparison with national parks.)

Experience suggests that the factors which make for success in implementation, and the difficulties encountered, can be summarised on the following lines. Firstly, commitment to the job. In the Wye Valley, despite differences of political persuasion amongst the main local authorities, the joint committee have geared themselves up over several years to an ongoing work programme with an annual cost of more than £100,000 funded jointly with the Commission. The main aims are to carry out landscape conservation projects and to provide facilities for the area's two million visitors each year. Led by an officer's working party, this has been done through a team of paid and voluntary wardens and, until recently, Manpower Services Commission task forces, working in conjunction with the Nature Conservancy Council, tourist boards and voluntary bodies, such as the Woodland Trust and the Royal Society for the Protection of Birds. Their projects include woodland management, eyesore removal, making a spine footpath, tree planting, interpretation, and major improvements at areas where visitor and conservation conflicts are at their most acute, notably Tintern and Symonds Yat. This is an undoubted success story, although those involved would be among the first to acknowledge shortcomings; for example, that the management plan has been over-ambitious and needs re-focussing against a background of somewhat patchy monitoring.

This example also illustrates the importance of commitment from bodies other than local authorities and from landowners. The National Trust and the Nature Conservancy Council, for example, own or manage extensive parts of some AONBs, especially coastal ones; their contribution to management in Gower, in particular, has been a major factor in the conservation of this very popular coastal area, with capital expenditure and additional wardening. Equally, the roles of the Rural Development Commission and the Agricultural Development and Advisory Service are likely to be of critical importance in areas such as the North Pennines, where there is a need to coordinate the local rural development programme with conservation projects and the advice given to farmers. When there is no such coming together of priorities, this does not necessarily mean that one party or another is wrong, but it is possible that a county-wide strategy, rather than one which concentrates on designated areas, might provide a more useful base for consolidation of effort.

The resource of a full-time local authority team is also most valuable, both for its own output and for the commitment it can generate. We have already referred to the employment of project

7.11 Working for conservation In the 1980s MSC job creation and work experience schemes offered opportunities for a variety of conservation works such as this clearance scheme at Over Ponds nature reserve, Gloucestershire. *Source*: Gloucestershire Trust for Nature Conservation

officers. In East Sussex, for example, the heritage coast management scheme was extended into the adjoining AONB countryside in 1982, with additional grant aid from the Commission. Led by a project team of two, the annual budget in 1987 was £42,000, with an extra £100,000 worth of MSC labour. Their activities cover maintenance of footpaths, litter clearance, developing an environmental records system, general conservation work including pond restoration, and, with some 70 volunteer rangers, recreation guidance and interpretation. They also help to establish new ventures, such as the ESA mechanism, a federated ranger service, and the Seven Sisters voluntary marine conservation area. The project has since been extended once more, with further support from the Commission, to enhance the enjoyment of the whole county, including the Downs and the High Weald AONBs. Similar work is carried out in the West Sussex part of the Downs.

Project officers such as these have a highly opportunistic role, with considerable autonomy to promote action on the ground and to influence others. Evidence from Sussex Downs, the Forest of Bowland, Dedham Vale, the Clwydian Range and heritage coasts, to name but some, suggests that the role has undoubtedly been successful. It is at its best in dealing with small-scale projects, nevertheless, and the contribution of the former MSC programmes has been a key factor in achievement; unfortunately, the pace may now slow down. Opportunism usually works best 'from the bottom up', and there is clearly a risk that a project officer's own objectives could get out of step with wider strategic considerations. Much depends on the individual and on ability to communicate; even comparatively minor jobs need delicate and time-consuming negotiations. A particular problem arises because the Commission's grant for such appointments is for a limited term only. This is sensible, all in all, but the need to secure new funding can add to the never-ending demands on a project officer's time.

Secondly, success in implementation can depend on the resource of land open to the public. Providing for public enjoyment and channelling pressures into manageable areas is an important complement to conservation measures in the more popular AONBs. The Surrey Hills are a case in point, the county council having for long had a policy of obtaining land for informal recreation, through public and private ownership. More than 7,700 hectares are open, 1,740 in 14 sites owned by the council, about 810 by means of five access agreements (under the 1949 Act) negotiated with landowners, the remainder being provided by the Forestry Commission and the National Trust. In total this amounts to some 19 per cent of the designated area, much of which is linked through the North Downs Way and to local footpath systems. Cannock Chase is another instance, where Staffordshire County Council was one of the first to turn its mind to positive action in an AONB and has created a very successful country park. Both of these examples, and others such as Hampshire's protective purchase of land on the South Hampshire Coast (now a nature reserve) and in East Hampshire (where the county council and the Forestry Commission run one of the leading country parks), are much to be commended. The measures were born of necessity perhaps, in the wider interest of conservation in these very popular areas. Unfortunately, even with a grant from the Countryside Commission, it would not be easy for local authorities to repeat them in these days of increasing land costs and restraint over public spending, other than on a very small scale. The responsibility will fall increasingly on private owners.

Thirdly, development control is a key factor in successful implementation. Despite some inconclusive evidence from research studies, Himsworth noted a deep and widespread opinion that designation has had its effect on development. He quoted historical successes such as the laying of underground electricity grid lines in Wye Valley and the North Wessex Downs, re-routing of major roads in Suffolk and at Arnside and Silverdale, and the bringing to an end of quarrying in the Malvern Hills. He also noted what are regarded as failures, including mineral developments and a nuclear power plant allowed in the national interest.

One could add to a list of this kind. Credits, for instance: the award-winning integration of major oilfield development on the Isle of Purbeck in Dorset; successful resistance to holiday camps and recreation complexes in some other coastal areas; setting up voluntary consultation schemes for farm buildings at Dedham Vale, the Chilterns and Lincolnshire Wolds; consultation with the Forestry Commission in all areas. Debits, too: among these might be included an artificial ski slope on the edge, and an extensive pig farm, which did not require planning permission, in the middle of the Mendip Hills; the Department of Transport motorway line which may cut deeply through a prominent chalk hill in East Hampshire; and other proposals deemed to be in the national interest, such as a further nuclear power plant in Suffolk and a civil

7.12 Countryside cosmetics
Trees successfully screen the pumping stations at the oil development, Wytch Farm, Dorset.
Source: British Petroleum

aviation radar station in the North Pennines.

The Commission has been very active in support of local authorities where its 1983 policies have a bearing on major issues like these. The chances of success depend on the attitude of the proposers, not all of whom are thought to be sufficiently aware of the purpose of AONB designation, and on differing interpretations of where the national interest lies. When it comes to the normal day-to-day control of development, however, Himsworth's implied conclusion is that in AONBs this has been a success story.

AONBs: retrospect and prospect

Supposing the 1949 Act had made no provision for AONBs, what would now be the condition of these areas? At least their landscapes would have been protected in development plans, on the same lines as areas of local landscape value. Some, by no means all, would probably have acquired special non-statutory definition similar to heritage coasts, recognising their national importance. It is questionable whether many would have been able to withstand the more intense pressures for major projects of the kind that have been successfully resisted by virtue of designation. There would also have been fewer chances of promoting concerted action for their conservation; the will and the money would have been subject to many other competing claims of seemingly equal merit.

Even though Himsworth found that nothing had been done in AONBs which could not have been carried out under other legislation, the mere fact of designation and ministerial ratification has surely been influential in ordering priorities. Examples of the kind quoted earlier illustrate the measure of achievement directly attributable to the Act. It can also be argued that designation has given a sense of identity, acting as a local catalyst of community pride in an area and further encouraging its conservation.

Thus it is likely that, had there been no provision in the Act, some of the best English and Welsh landscapes outside national parks would have deteriorated further than they have done in any case. This is not to say for one minute that there is cause for complacency. Not all AONBs have received the local initiatives that our examples record. Even some of those that have may be at risk in the totality of local spending priorities, depending crucially for their success on the continued drive of one or two key personalities, political or professional.

On a wider front, too, the Act itself has an Achilles Heel. AONBs tend to be in agricultural, lowland Britain, and some contain significant amounts of higher grade land. It is likely, therefore, that their superb landscapes are as much at risk from agricultural change as 'ordinary' countryside, yet they mostly get no special protection. The effect of this on the Sussex Downs and on their often claimed potential as a national park is well known; other examples can be quoted, especially in chalk and limestone terrain. Agriculture was not an issue 40 years ago and could not reasonably have been foreseen as one. Now, however, in a greatly changed market and support system, the need for agriculture to be guided towards environmental gains is the biggest challenge facing AONB conservation.

The impact of agricultural change in the countryside at large is foremost among the reasons why some major local authorities and the Commission are exploring the possibility of an integrated approach to rural conservation. At present their powers of persuasion in this are limited, but at least a few counties are making impressive attempts. The national park authorities are also applying more widely the experience gained in Environmentally Sensitive Areas. Such action requires scarce resources of money and expertise, and, as we have seen, landscape value is not the only criterion to be considered in choosing priorities. It could therefore be argued that the importance attached to AONBs in the range of countryside designations diverts attention from more pressing needs. Might a system of selection that reflected the whole range of countryside resources (an aim towards which Hobhouse was working) have had more relevance?

To pose such a question is to move dangerously outside the confines of this chapter into wider questions of rural policy and organisation. Even the more limited issue of the future of AONBs is a very sensitive one. There is no doubt that designation has been valuable. Furthermore, Himsworth's report, the Commission's

189

review and the subsequent official statements all go to suggest that it commands much popular support. So, more recently, does the opposition to boundary changes which sought to exclude parts of existing areas. AONBS, regarded by some as Cinderellas in the household of countryside designation, look like being here to stay. Indeed, their close policy connections with the wider countryside suggest that their guardianship should remain under local government, rather than be hived off to special administrative bodies, as has been suggested from time to time. Assuming that their number is finite in qualitative terms, what action is necessary to adapt them to the changing context?

On the evidence of this chapter, one could argue that the priority assumed by designation as an AONB needs to be reconsidered. Is there a case for reducing this in areas that are relatively well provided for, in order to give more attention to tracts of the wider countryside which are experiencing major problems, such as the urban fringe, some stretches of coast, or places where set-aside will be extensive; and increasing it in AONBs where little has been done or where resources are otherwise at risk? This is more or less what the Commission is seeking to do, knowing that it cannot hope to fund countryside management to the extent it would wish in an ideal world. So are some local authorities, within their own areas. Should they consider doing so more widely through their regional organisations? Perhaps such 'targetting', nationally, regionally and locally, is a trend that ought to be strongly encouraged, whether through funding as at present, or on any new basis developed from the ESA experience. So, too, should efforts to tap more resources, local and national, for this purpose, in partnership with those of the public sector.

This question of external balance, important as it is, nevertheless, should not be allowed to overshadow the need for study of matters internal to AONB conservation, including concerns listed earlier in this chapter. Many options have to be looked at. One thing is quite clear, however: if any reconsideration of AONB policy is to reach objective conclusions, we urgently need to know far more about what is happening to the natural and historical heritage of these precious areas, and to have this recorded and monitored systematically.

Nature conservation 8

The birth of the Nature Conservancy

Sir Arthur Tansley was not only one of Britain's great men of nature conservation and an ecologist of distinction, but also a key figure in events leading up to the 1949 Act, as we noted in chapter 1. He remained so throughout the early years of its implementation until his death in 1955. In the mid-1940s he had endorsed suggestions that the government should take formal responsibility for the conservation of native wildlife, both plant and animal. He stressed the impossibility of discharging such an obligation without countrywide research on fundamental ecological problems to make possible the scientific management of nature reserves and other areas. He favoured the amalgamation of the Biological Service that would be needed for such research with the authority responsible for controlling nature reserves, whether national or local, since the reserves would be indispensible places for a considerable part, although by no means the whole, of the work of research. He concluded in favour of constituting a new Ecological Research Council, in parallel with the Agriculture and Medical Research Councils, employing research officers and maintaining a central office to act as a clearing house for ecological information.

As we saw in chapter 3 these recommendations were favoured by the Huxley Committee which also recommended the establishment of a series of ecological research institutes, four of which should be in England and Wales and one in Scotland. Its proposals, together with those of the Ritchie Committee for Scotland, were to feed through White Papers directly into the National Parks and Access to Countryside Act 1949. The Act certainly represented the fruits of the work and dreams of Tansley, Max Nicholson and others, since it offered an official service with the twin tasks of expanding and expediting ecological research for the benefit of conservation and acquiring and maintaining a national series of nature reserves. Indeed, earlier recommendations for a Biological Service and a Nature Conservation Board were to be brought together within a single body — the Nature Conservancy.

The manner in which the 1949 Act provided for national parks and a National Parks Commission and addressed questions of access, was, as we have seen, controversial and aroused strong emotions, but reaction to the inception of the Nature Conservancy with its very considerable authority seemed to cause little adverse comment by comparison. The proposals for nature reserves amounted to just over 28,000 hectares of land most of which was of little economic value and would, it was estimated, cost about £500,000 to acquire. Although the Nature Conservancy was to be given very considerable authority that extended over Scotland as well as England and Wales, its functions were not seen to conflict with these of existing bodies, notably the planning authorities, and, as we saw in chapter 4, the scientific conservation clauses of the Bill referring to nature conservation went through parliament very smoothly. The Nature Conservancy became an incorporate body with a Royal Charter to enable it to discharge its statutory powers and functions under the Act, and was directly responsible to a Committee of the Privy Council. It was established, in essence, as a Research Council.

The Nature Conservancy was thus the Government's chosen instrument to implement the nature conservation clauses in the 1949 Act. The way in which the Conservancy was expected to function is best described by quoting from a paper, *The Nature Conservancy*, published in 1950 by the Committee of the Privy Council for Agricultural Research and Nature Conservation to which the Nature Conservancy was responsible. To begin with, its basic functions would be:

> 'To provide scientific advice on the conservation and
> control of the national flora and fauna of Great
> Britain; to establish, maintain and manage nature
> reserves in Great Britain, including the maintenance
> of physical features of scientific interest; and to
> organise and development research and scientific ser-
> vices related thereto'.

The Conservancy's responsibilities would include both the conduct of research by its own staff and the promotion of research by the making of grants for specified work to be undertaken by universities, other research bodies, or individual members. The scientific work of the Conservancy was to be wide in scope, bringing in the specialised knowledge derived from a number of different lines of inquiry. Many problems would demand the coordinated approach of various specialists working as a team, and facilities for observational work in the field and laboratory would need to be provided. This combination of field and laboratory work was expected to lead to important advances in fundamental biological knowledge which would throw light on the principles of conservation and help to complete the foundations upon which to base authoritative 'scientific advice on the conservation and control of the natural flora and fauna of Great Britain'.

Declaring national nature reserves

The Committee of the Privy Council's document went on to say that the Nature Conservancy had provisionally scheduled about 150 places in England and Wales as national nature reserves (NNR). Of these 70 to 80 areas of biological and physiographical importance were in England and Wales, about 30 in Scotland and

8.1 Scientific research for conservation A scientist recording the habitat of sand lizards at Studland Heath national nature reserve. *Source*: Nature Conservancy Council

there were some 40 features of special geological importance (originally called Geological Monuments). It was the Conservancy's intention to declare them as NNRs under the 1949 Act as soon as they had been surveyed and delimited. A Public Declaration was required that an area of land was to be managed as a nature reserve before it could be so managed and by-laws made.

NNRs were stated as being selected for one or a combination of the following reasons: because they are good representative samples of the various types of natural and semi-natural vegetation existing in this country; because they include the habitats of particular groups of plants or animals which should be conserved; or because they display biological, physiographical, or geological features of special value to science and education. In the words of the Act, they were to be managed:

> 'For the purpose (a) of providing, under suitable conditions and control, special opportunities for the study of, and research into, matters relating to the fauna and flora of Great Britain and the physical conditions in which they live, and for the study of geological and physiographical features of special interest in the area, or (b) of preserving flora, fauna or geological or physiographical features of special interest in the area, or for both those purposes'.

The Conservancy was able to enter into agreement with the owners, lessees and occupiers 'of any land, being land as to which it appears to the Conservancy expedient in the national interest that it should be managed as a nature reserve, for securing that it shall be so managed'.

Agreements made under the Act in this way would run with the land. If the Conservancy was satisfied that it was unable to conclude such an agreement on terms appearing to it to be reasonable, it could acquire the land compulsorily. However, the Conservancy was expected to avoid compulsory purchase except as a last resort.

The Nature Conservancy was empowered to make by-laws for the protection of NNRs and it could also control the killing of birds within such an area surrounding and adjoining a reserve as appeared to it appropriate for its protection. This last provision was seen to be necessary because the destruction of birds in the vicinity could seriously affect the bird population of a reserve. The declaration of a reserve conferred no public right of way, but Conservancy policy was expected to encourage the use and enjoyment of reserves by all who were genuinely interested in nature and would adhere to a simple code of behaviour.

In addition to NNRs, the 1949 Act allowed a county council, borough council or (in agreement with the county council and Nature Conservancy), a county district council to provide and manage a nature reserve on any land in its area where it seemed to that council expedient that it should in the interests of the locality. Most of the provisions of the Act, *mutatis mutandis*, applied to these local nature reserves as well as to NNRs. The local authorities were to exercise these functions in consultation with the Nature Conservancy.

As for the management of reserves in general, it was recognised that by far the greater proportion of the land in this country still occupied by communities of native plants and animals had been affected by human activities, of which drainage, grazing, burning and cutting were the most important. The native vegetation that was so affected was termed 'semi-natural' vegetation. A nature reserve made on such land — as most of them were expected to be — would require either a continuation of the present regime, or the finding of a satisfactory substitute to maintain the conditions for which the reserve was created. It would therefore be essential actively to manage most reserves.

If the Nature Conservancy's first objective was to preserve as nature reserves good samples of the various types of natural and semi-natural vegetation with accompanying animals, as well as the status of rare and interesting groups of species, the Committee of the Privy Council's document nevertheless recognised the impossibility of protecting by this means more than a small fraction of the land which showed features of great biological, geological and physiological interest. Nature reserves alone could not provide for the general conservation of flora and fauna. To meet these additional needs, Section 23 of the 1949 Act gave the Nature Conservancy the duty to notify the local planning authorities concerned of any other places or sites of special scientific interest (SSSIs). This was in line with the Huxley Committee's suggestions, which in turn had been based on the work done by a sub-committee of the Society for the Protection of Nature Reserves. The Nature Reserves Investigation Committee, as it was called, had in 1942 recommended hundreds of such sites worthy of consideration which could not be included in any list of NNRs and geological monuments.

It was not expected that in the general development of the country all areas of special scientific interest should be kept unchanged by local planning authorities, but such notification would ensure that the arguments in favour of a development scheme outweighed the contrary arguments produced on scientific grounds. The Nature Conservancy would seek to persuade competent authorities of the importance of scientific interests and encourage the general conservation of flora, fauna and features of geological importance over wider areas by all concerned. Although agriculture and afforestation had not been brought under planning control, the Nature Conservancy would establish liaison with the Forestry Commission and agricultural departments. It would also establish good links with the National Parks Commission because areas of outstanding natural beauty and national nature reserves often coincided in whole or in part.

The lines along which the 1949 Act was expected to be implemented by the Nature Conservancy were thus very clearly laid down by the Privy Council soon after the Act was passed, and provide a clear basis on which the effectiveness of the Act can be assessed.

National nature reserves and their management

Its Royal Charter enabled the Nature Conservancy 'to purchase, take on lease or otherwise acquire any lands, tenements or hereditaments within the United Kingdom not exceeding in the whole the annual value of £50,000 to be determined according to the value thereof at the time when the same are respectively acquired'. What that sum was based on is not clear, but the Conservancy lost no time and acquired its first nature reserve at Beinn Eighe in Wester Ross in Scotland, a magnificent area of 4,212 hectares of

8.2 Land purchase for nature conservation Beinn Eighe in Wester Ross in Scotland was the first such national nature reserve. *Source*: Nature Conservancy Council

relict Caledonian pine forest, birchwoods, bog, moorland and mountain. This was followed by Yarner Wood of 130 hectares in Devon. The first NNR in Wales was declared in 1955. It was stated in that year that the Conservancy hoped to complete the declaration of national nature reserves in about four years.

Under the 1949 Act, no national nature reserve could be declared without the Conservancy acquiring a legal interest in the land as owner and occupier but, contrary to expectations (for the Huxley Committee believed it necessary to own key sites to protect wildlife), ownership was not proving the main method by which reserves were protected. Although the leasing of land became important in Wales, it was less so in England and was used very little in Scotland. Instead, most of the area of NNRs were declared and managed under nature reserve agreements made under the 1949 Act between the Conservancy and the owner or occupier, to whom an agreed sum of money, usually nominal in the early years, was paid as a lump sum or annually.

Under Section 15 of the Countryside Act 1968, this ability to make agreements was extended to land which was not for the time being managed as a nature reserve, but which formed part of an area of special interest by reason of its flora, fauna or geological or physiographical features, ie an SSSI. Section 15 agreements were

8.3 Management agreements over time
Both the number and area of management agreements has grown considerably in the 1980s.
Source: Nature Conservancy Council

little used in the years immediately after 1968, because of financial stringencies, but after the Wildlife and Countryside Act 1981 they were to become a much more important method of conserving nature. The stimulus given to Section 15 management agreements by the financial provisions of the 1981 Act is clearly shown in figure 8.3. As to the costs, these proved exacting, rising from £25,000 in 1980, to more than £4.5m in 1988.

Management Agreements under S15 of the 1968 Act in force at 31 March

		NUMBER	AREA (ha)		
	England	25	1,002		
1980	Scotland	12	1,177		
	Wales	6	49		
	Total for GB	43	2,228		

		NUMBER	AREA (ha)	COST	COST/ HECTARE
	England	42	1,238	£34,104	£27.54
1981	Scotland	14	1,262	£ 1,451	£ 1.15
	Wales	14	77	£ 3,523	£45.75
	Total for GB	70	2,577	£39,078	£15.16

		NUMBER	AREA (ha)	COST	COST/ HECTARE
	England	134	4,726	£763,641	£161.58
1985	Scotland	57	5,346	£161,364	£ 30,18
	Wales	29	305	£ 23,688	£ 77.66
	Total for GB	220	10,377	£948,693	£ 91.42

		NUMBER	AREA (ha)	COST	COST/ HECTARE
	England	736	15,687	£2,652,000	£169.01
1988	Scotland	204	19,652	£1,600,000	£ 81.42
	Wales	113	3,108	£ 304,000	£ 97.81
	Total for GB	1,053	38,447	£4,556,000	£118.50

By the mid-1960s it was becoming increasingly difficult to view proposals for additional national nature reserves within the broader context of a common scale of values throughout Britain. The areas listed earlier by various committees had been worked through and more extensive and detailed surveys frequently threw up sites that until then were not well known. Comparative studies were undertaken — for example a survey of all woodlands over four hectares was initiated initially in East Anglia in 1966 and then extended over Britain, but in the late 1960s these habitat-based studies were brought together in what became known as the Nature Conservation Review (NCR). The review, led by Derek Ratcliffe, sought to describe the range of ecological variation in Britain as a basis for assessing how adequately this variation was represented in NNRs and to determine future acquisition policy and priorities. The NCR was published in 1977 in two parts.

The review of geological and physiographical sites from the earlier lists, made before and at the time of the 1949 Act, had continued in parallel with the work on biological sites, and some geological sites had been declared as NNRs. However, the assessment of geological sites met exactly the same problems as had the assessment of biological sites, and in 1978, as soon as resources permitted, the Nature Consevancy launched the Geological Conservation Review to complement the (biological) NCR. Its purpose was to identify and notify those localities whose conservation was essential for the continuation of geological education and research.

The acquisition of national nature reserves continued steadily after the 1949 Act. In 1961 the 100th NNR was acquired, giving a total area for all NNRs of nearly 77,000 hectares. This was out of a target of 140 NNRs covering just over 100,000 hectares, a target that exceeded expectations at the Bill stage of the 1949 Act, but was in accord with the Privy Council estimates in 1950. The progress of acquisition of NNRs is shown in figure 8.4. The total in 1988 represented 0.72 per cent of the area of land and inland water in Great Britain.

The acquisition of reserves was but the first stage in their protection, and the Nature Conservancy sought to manage them both for research and for their conservation needs. The shortage of

8.4 Growth in national nature reserves
Numbers still continue to increase forty years after the 1949 Act.
Source: Nature Conservancy Council

Number and area of NNRs

		NUMBER	AREA OWNED BY NNC (ha)	AREA LEASED BY NNC (ha)	AREA MANAGED UNDER AN NRA (ha)	TOTAL (ha)
1956	England	32	5,042	1,768	3,162	9,972 (30%)
	Scotland	10	6,447	191	14,920	21,558 (64%)
	Wales	5	8	907	1,009	1,924 (6%)
	Total for GB	47	11,497 (34%)	2,866 (9%)	19,091 (57%)	33,454 (100%)

		NUMBER	AREA OWNED BY NC (ha)	AREA LEASED BY NC (ha)	AREA MANAGED BY NC UNDER NRA (ha)	TOTAL (ha)
1960	England	43	5,159	1,898	4,398	11,455 (20%)
	Scotland	24	19,673	1,815	19,714	41,202 (73%)
	Wales	17	815	1,318	1,459	3,592 (7%)
	Total for GB	84	25,647 (46%)	5,031 (9%)	25,571 (45%)	56,249 (100%)

		NUMBER	AREA OWNED BY NC (ha)	AREA LEASED BY NC (ha)	AREA MANAGED BY NC UNDER NRA (ha)	TOTAL (ha)
1965	England	56	5,987	5,407	7,320	18,714 (34%)
	Scotland	31	19,678	2,122	8,489	30,289 (55%)
	Wales	26	1,000	1,867	2,837	5,704 (11%)
	Total for GB	113	26,665 (49%)	9,396 (57%)	18,646 (34%)	54,707 (100%)

		NUMBER	AREA OWNED BY NC (ha)	AREA LEASED BY NC (ha)	AREA MANAGED BY NC UNDER NRA (ha)	TOTAL (ha)
1970	England	63	6,287	8,495	10,027	24,809 (23%)
	Scotland	38	20,843	2,141	51,971	74,958 (69%)
	Wales	29	1,265	4,027	3,189	8,481 (7%)
	Total for GB	130	28,395 (26%)	14,663 (14%)	65,187 (60%)	108,245 (100%)

Figures in brackets denote % by area.

		NUMBER	AREA OWNED BY NC (ha)	AREA LEASED BY NC (ha)	AREA MANAGED BY NC UNDER NRA (ha)	TOTAL (ha)
1975	England	70	6,676	9,374	10,607	26,657 (23%)
	Scotland	41	22,278	1,994	54,456	78,728 (69%)
	Wales	29	1,398	4,176	3,555	9,129 (8%)
	Total for GB	140	30,352 (26%)	15,544 (14%)	68,618 (60%)	114,514 (100%)

		NUMBER	AREA OWNED BY NC (ha)	AREA LEASED BY NC (ha)	AREA MANAGED BY NC UNDER NRA (ha)	TOTAL (ha)
1980	England	82	7,368	9,729	11,577	28,674 (23%)
	Scotland	53	24,087	3,057	67,013	94,157 (71%)
	Wales	31	1,878	4,202	3,644	9,724 (7%)
	Total for GB	166	33,333 (25%)	16,988 (13%)	82,234 (62%)	132,555 (100%)

		NUMBER	AREA OWNED BY NC (ha)	AREA LEASED BY NC (ha)	AREA MANAGED BY NC UNDER NRA (ha)	TOTAL (ha)
1985	England	97	10,649	14,373	13,145	38,167 (25)
	Scotland	62	24,287	2,299	73,864	100,450 (67%)
	Wales	36	3,082	5,453	3,113	11,648 (8%)
	Total for GB	195	39,918 (26%)	22,125 (14%)	90,122 (60%)	150,265 (100%)

		NUMBER	AREA OWNED BY NC (ha)	AREA LEASED BY NC (ha)	AREA MANAGED BY NCC UNDER NRA (ha)	DEC TOTAL UNDER S25 (ha)	
1988	England	120	11,848	15,278	13,604	542	41,272 (25%)
	Scotland	67	32,227	2,984	76,751	77	112,039 (68%)
	Wales	44	3,184	5,585	3,217	186	12,172 (7%)
						805	
	Total for GB	231	47,259 (29%)	23,847 (14%)	93,572 (57%)		165,483 (100%)

Figures in brackets denote % by area.

money, however, meant that most reserves were put on a care and maintenance basis with more detailed management concentrated in a few reserves such as Yarner Wood, Woodwalton Fen and Beinn Eighe. Indeed from its earliest years the Nature Conservancy was concerned about its very limited finances, which were described as 'throttling' the site acquisition programme and 'crippling' the management programme. The acquisition of reserves was always well ahead of the production of management plans for them, and the best percentage achieved was in 1961 when 50 of the then total of 91 NNRs had management plans.

The Conservancy was very determined that its research and experimental management on national nature reserves should provide a basis for advice to other local users and practical examples of good land management. In 1958, the Conservancy acquired the island of Rhum. It was intended that Rhum would fulfill the same kind of role for upland management as Rothamstead Research Station had done for the lowlands. Large-scale trials would be set up to discover the reasons for soil erosion and deterioration of the vegetation cover, and methods by which badly devastated habitats and the fertility of the land could be restored. The ultimate goals were cropping systems and afforestation schemes that would provide both a higher return and greater protection for the soils and vegetation.

If the 1949 Act made no provision for marine nature reserves, such provisions were built into the Wildlife and Countryside Act 1981. A shortlist of possible sites based on consultations with universities, marine institutions and others was drawn up. The waters surrounding the Scilly Isles were expected to be the first marine nature reserve to be declared, but in the event this distinction fell to the seas around Lundy Island in the Bristol Channel on 21 November 1986. The formal consultation was circulated to more than 130 government departments, agencies and individuals, following a prolonged series of deliberations over years with scores of people.

Local nature reserves and their role

Both the Huxley and Ritchie Committees had called on the

Government to introduce legislation to widen the involvement of local authorities in the provision of nature reserves, views which were enthusiastically endorsed by the Nature Reserves Investigation Committee. The power to provide, and to secure, the provision of nature reserves was given to local authorities under Section 21 of the 1949 Act. By 1950, various committees and bodies had identified a total of more than 500 areas for local nature reserve (LNR) status, most of which were selected on scientific grounds, but in some cases there was reference also to their educational potential. The first LNR was Aberlady Bay in East Lothian, Scotland, which was declared on 14 July 1952, and was followed a fortnight later by Gibraltar Point in Lincolnshire. Aberlady Bay was also the site of an important test case; it was established here that the Nature Conservancy could make bye-laws applicable to the foreshore, a power which until then had been much disputed. By 1960 there were seven LNRs and declaration continued steadily as figure 8.5 shows.

8.5 Other nature reserves
These provide a second and wider line of defence beyond national nature reserves. *Source*: Nature Conservancy Council

Nature Reserves
Local

		NUMBER	AREA (ha)			NUMBER	AREA (ha)
	England	40	4896		England	133	9137
1973	Scotland	2	291	1988	Scotland	6	2688
	Wales	2	8		Wales	16	3384
	Total for GB	44	5195		Total for GB	154	15209

Non-statutory

		NUMBER	AREA (ha)
	England	1791	72,577
1988	Scotland	164	83,671
	Wales	239	21,860
	Total for GB	2194	178,108

The Nature Conservancy concluded early in its work that it was unnecessary to convert into statutory NNRs areas that were successfully managed as informal, independent nature reserves by public and other bodies or individuals. Some of the voluntary conservation bodies were, in their earliest years, not intending to own or manage land. For example, the Society for the Promotion of Nature Reserves (SPNR) was formed in 1912 to stimulate the National Trust into acquiring more properties of interest to naturalists. But because, in the view of the SPNR, acquisitions and management by the National Trust did not meet the standards they expected, the Society became involved in land holding and management. Woodwalton Fen was given to the Essex Naturalists Trust because the National Trust, the originally intended recipients, had refused to become responsible for it. The Norfolk Naturalists Trust was started in 1926 to take over Cley Marshes when the National Trust refused to accept the property. By 1941 it had acquired seven nature reserves. The Yorkshire Naturalists Trust was formed in 1946 and the Lincolnshire Naturalists Trust in 1948. One of the first priorities of the latter was to persuade the then Lindsey County Council, which owned Gibraltar Point, to declare it as an LNR. Thereafter there was a steady stream of counties or groups of counties forming trusts until all counties in Britain were covered with what are now called wildlife trusts; these have acquired and managed their own nature reserves. An excellent grass-roots network of conservation volunteers has thus been provided, a point we take up again in chapter 9.

The SPNR and the early county trusts found that the costs of management were very high and a policy of laissez-faire was adopted on many reserves, partly through a belief that this was the best form of management, but partly also through economic necessity. However the policy was often unsuccessful. For example, the changes taking place in Woodwalton Fen through lack of management were reducing its biological value, so in 1954 the Fen was leased to the Conservancy, which immediately undertook urgent work on monitoring and controlling water levels.

With time not only did the number and area of nature reserves held by the voluntary bodies increase but also standards of management rose. Today the nature reserves held by county trusts, the

National Trust, the RSPB, the Woodland Trust and so on, complement the national nature reserve series and are a priceless asset to
nature conservation (figure 8.5). Non-statutory nature reserves
now cover 0.77 per cent of the area of land and inland water in
Great Britain compared with the 165,483 hectares or 0.72 per cent
held by the Nature Conservancy Council in statutory reserves.

Designating sites of special scientific interest

The Nature Conservancy, soon after its formation, began schedul-
ing the sites prepared by the Nature Reserves Investigation
Committee which ranged in size from half a hectare or so to thousands of hectares. It placed much importance on supplying the
local planning authorities with county schedules, as required by the
1949 Act. Once assembled it considered that these schedules
would serve as a foundation of sound information on places of scientific value. Many of the sites identified for wildlife in 1942 had
been damaged or destroyed as a result of changes in land-use and
management and the new Act offered hope that this scale of
damage could be reduced very substantially.

There was no legal obligation to notify owners and occupiers of
the site of special scientifc interest (SSSI), designation, but from
the earliest days the Conservancy sought to do this. However, the
rate at which owners and occupiers were informed could not keep
pace with notifications to the local planning authorities. The Town
and Country Planning Act 1947 had laid down an exacting
timetable compelling counties to proceed with their development
plans, and the planning authorities looked to the Conservancy to
carry out the survey and notification of SSSIs very quickly. This led
to a lag in notifying owners and occupiers. Nevertheless, by early
1953, 1,098 sites in England had been notified to 58 planning
authorities, 41 sites in Scotland to seven planning authorities, and
21 in Wales to one planning authority.

It was intended to revise the SSSI schedules every five years and
such revisions added to the burden of work of the under-resourced
Nature Conservancy. These revisions brought home the continuing damage to SSSIs, mainly as the result of agricultural and

8.6 Protecting habitats from development
Gedney Drove in Lincolnshire – one example of where a coastal SSSI has been successful in resisting development.
Source: University of Cambridge Aerial Photography Unit

forestry activities that were not subject to planning control. In 1960, out of a total of 474 SSSIs in southern and eastern counties of England, 15 were given up as destroyed and 29 were damaged and had to be reduced in extent. In 1980, a random sample of 15 per cent of biological SSSIs showed that 13 per cent of the total had suffered significant damage to the biological interest. Some of this damage was from permitted development, although there were occasional cases where development was refused in the interests of nature conservation, such as at Gedney Drove in Lincolnshire.

8.7 Designating SSSIs
Although initially slow, most SSSIs have been re-designated under the Wildlife and Countryside Act, 1981.
Source: Nature Conservancy Council

The accelerating rate of destruction of wildlife habitats, and the need for strengthened legislation to enable the government to comply with the European Birds Directive, led to the bringing forward of the Wildlife and Countryside Bill. The Act as passed in 1981 very considerably modified the SSSI provisions, for until it became law SSSI and NNR were mutually exclusive designations. But after the Act a national nature reserve could be an SSSI; indeed the SSSI designation gives the longer term protection to NNRs that were leased or managed under an NRA. Notification proce-

Area (ha) of SSSI on 31 March

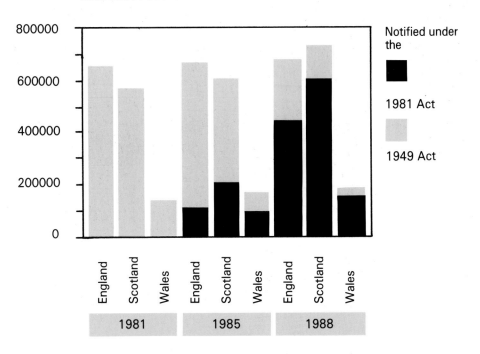

Number of SSSI on 31 March

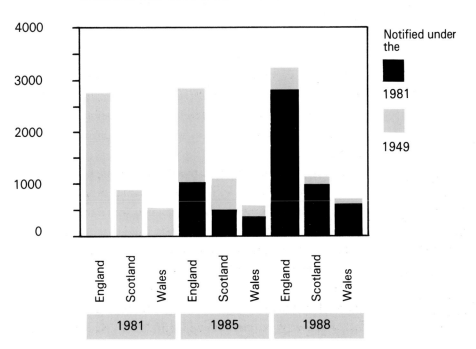

dures were also elaborated. The Nature Conservancy Council, as it had then become, had to notify the local planning authorities as before, also the Secretary of State and each owner and occupier. Notification was in the form of a description of the special interest of the site and its extent, with a map and a list of those operations which, if carried out, could damage the special interest. SSSIs were now to be formally entered into the appropriate land registers, so that the SSSI designation would be known to any new owner. The provisions of the 1981 Act for SSSIs would only apply to any SSSI if it was re-notified under the Act.

The progress of re-notification and notification of SSSIs under the 1981 Act started very slowly, and is shown in figure 8.7. Initially renotification took place in an atmosphere of mistrust and misunderstanding. Suspicion and opposition were widespread and were moderated only after long and frequent consultations, and especially the signing of management agreements as an indication of government's and the Nature Conservancy Council's good intentions.

In the years immediately after the 1981 Act, damage to SSSIs continued, but the rate of damage has now slowed. Section 29 orders under the 1981 Act, that is Orders made by the Secretary of State to allow more time for negotiation, were sparingly used and there were 17 such orders in force during the period 1 April 1987 to 31 March 1988. It is expected that when re-notification is completed there will be about 6,000 SSSIs. Meantime, the area of SSSIs as at 31 March 1988 represents 6.9 per cent of the area of land and inland water in Great Britain (figure 8.7).

Scientific conservation: research and advice

Research and nature conservation, as exemplified by the purposes for which national nature reserves were created under the 1949 Act, were, as we know, united in the Nature Conservancy, since it was considered that the need for research, its priorities and urgency would be brought out by managing, and advising on the management of, natural areas. But the relationship between the Conservancy and the ecological institutes that were to be developed was left vague. Members of the Huxley Committee thought it would be wrong for the Biological Service (as it was then thought of) to dictate the research to be undertaken. Not least amongst these was Charles Elton, who said that the most productive research groups were those where individuals were given 'the utmost freedom to try improving ideas' and to engage in field experiments. Tansley also wanted freedom from 'utilitarian compulsion' and was convinced that 'the highest type of research, which has been productive of the most fundamental discoveries, is essentially the work of individual minds, freely dealing with their chosen material'. The contrary view was that there should be more central control of research in Britain to ensure that scientists contributed more fully to the life and needs of society.

The Nature Conservancy followed, as might be expected, the Tansley viewpoint, and its scientists were given considerable freedom within broad fields of study. The staff of scientists was built up as resources permitted and over the first ten years or so scientists formed about one-third or more of the total staff. The first research station to be established was at Merlewood in the south of the Lake District, which was considered to be well situated for work in England, Scotland and Wales and a good centre for the uplands. Furzebrook in Dorset soon followed, especially chosen for work on lowland heaths. By 1972 the Conservancy had estab-

8.8 A lowland habitat research station Furzebrook in Dorset was one of the research centres specially set up by the Nature Conservancy in the early 1950s. *Source*: Institute of Terrestrial Ecology

209

lished eight research stations, as well as some more specialised research units for biometrics, grouse and moorland ecology, and climatology. The research in the Conservancy was overseen by a Scientific Policy Committee which contained many eminent scientists.

In 1952, nearly 50 per cent of the Conservancy budget was spent on scientific work and it was stated that 'with sources of information about rocks, soils, physiography, climate, vegetation and fauna and with their freedom from bias as between one or other economic use, the Conservancy can bring together the many important contributions of particular specialists and interests as a sound and well-balanced technical basis for decisions about land-use'.

Monkswood Experimental Station was opened in 1963 with three research groups, one of which was formed to research on wildlife in relation to the use of toxic chemicals. There had been concern over the use of herbicide on roadside verges since the early 1950s, but the increasing use of chemicals in agriculture and the resulting higher mortality of wildlife, especially birds, together with Rachel Carson's book *Silent Spring*, triggered off a wave of concern which strengthened the Conservancy's existing activities.

In 1966 the Conservancy was incorporated as a Committee and component body of the Natural Environment Research Council (NERC) and its research staff were reorganised into eight habitat teams. Research, however, continued to be primarily related to conservation management and advisory work. The relationship between the NERC and the Conservancy was never happy and in 1972 it was proposed to split the latter into two parts; the research staff and stations would remain within NERC and form the new Institute of Terrestrial Ecology, and the staff concerned with conservation management and advice and other statutory functions would become the Nature Conservancy Council. The idea became a reality with the passing of the Nature Conservancy Council Act in 1973. The definitive account of those troubled times has yet to be written, but whatever the background, the proposal to split research from practical conservation, as it existed in the Conservancy, was greeted with widespread dismay and was a setback to the intentions of the 1949 Act.

Nature conservation research was by no means undertaken solely by the Conservancy as work was also done by universities and other research bodies funded substantially by the Conservancy, just as the 1949 Act has foreseen. As early as 1952 the Conservancy funded 33 research studentships. In 1970 a total of £438,247 was spent on research grants, including 92 research studentships and 24 advanced course studentships. By 1988, although expenditure on research and advanced course studentships had dropped as a result of the split of the Nature Conservancy, the amount spent on research contracts amounted to £3,505,530. Support was also given in 1960 to the development of the first post-graduate course in nature conservation at University College London. For many years students on this course have been supported by the Nature Conservancy and its successor, the Nature Conservancy Council, and particularly close links were established with Monkswood Experimental Station. Ecology and related courses were also supported at the University of Aberdeen and of Edinburgh, as well as at University Colleges at Bangor and Wye.

As early as 1943, it was stated that the proposed nature reserves would be of little value unless wildlife was given greater protection throughout the countryside. The provision of advice to help provide this greater protection was a function of the 1949 Act and strengthened under the Nature Conservancy Council Act 1973, which also gave the new Nature Conservancy Council the duty, in the discharge of its functions, to 'take account as appropriate of actual or possible ecological changes'. Some examples will show how the functions of providing advice and disseminating information were carried out.

The use of pesticides and herbicides in the countryside grew rapidly in the wake of post-war agricultural expansion and the Conservancy found it increasingly difficult to furnish appropriate advice in relation to wildlife. In 1960 the Conservancy set up a unit under Dr Norman Moore to investigate the effects of toxic chemicals on wildlife. One of its earliest actions was to call for a ban on aldrin, dieldrin and heptachlor, following the spring cereal sowing in 1961 which resulted in heavy and widespread casualities to birds and animals. The government responded by banning these chemicals at the time of spring sowing only. Dr Moore's unit was greatly expanded in the new Monkswood Experimental Station and the Nature Conservancy Council has continued to have a major advisory role on pesticides in relation to wildlife to this day.

In 1967 the Torrey Canyon spilled 100,000 tons of crude oil in the English Channel which affected the coast of south-west England and north-west France. About 1.75 million gallons of emulsifier-solvent was used to reduce the extent and intensity of oil pollution at sea and on the beaches. The impact of the oil, and also the chemicals used to disperse the oil, was very severe on birds, fish

8.9 Oil spill and environmental damage
The Torrey Canyon disaster of 1967 devastated the wildlife of the western approaches to the English Channel.
Source: Associated Press

and shellfish. It was estimated that about 20,000 guillemots died, the equivalent of the breeding population between the Isle of Wight and Cardigan Bay, and about 5,000 razorbills, equivalent to about one-third of the breeding population in the same area. The Nature Conservancy Council continues to be involved in the mechanisms designed to minimise the effects of any oil spill.

More recently, as a result of the initiative shown by the British Minister of Agriculture, the EC agreed a scheme in which member states are permitted to give grants to encourage farmers in areas designated 'environmentally sensitive' to continue traditional farming practices. The Nature Conservancy Council and the Countryside Commission, after study and consultation, were able jointly to advise the Minister of Agriculture on 19 locations to form the first Environmentally Sensitive Areas.

Not all of the advice was through committees or directly to individuals or organisations and much advice is given through pub-lications. Meetings, conferences and exhibitions remain the other means of providing advice. National Nature Week and the three 'Countryside in 1970' conferences in 1963, 1965 and 1970 brought together many people from different walks of life, one of the results of which was agreement that a wider and stronger Countryside Commission should be developed out of the National Parks Commission in England and Wales. It was also suggested that a new Countryside Commission was needed in Scotland.

However, a recent major source of advice has been through the development of the Farming and Wildlife Advisory Groups. These were set up and managed by local farmers and other land users, with financial and other support from the Countryside Commission, the Nature Conservancy Council and the Ministry of Agriculture, Fisheries and Food, and are an important means of bringing together countryside people in a local context to discuss conservation matters and to provide practical advice.

Designated nature conservation areas: an appraisal

The provisions of the 1949 Act in relation to the declaration of national nature reserves have been an undoubted success. The lists provided in the 1940s were built on and expanded, and the total in 1988 of 231 NNRs distributed between England, Scotland and Wales with an area of 165,483 hectares testifies to that success. In addition to this there are 2,194 non-statutory nature reserves with an area of 178,108 hectares and 154 local nature reserves with an area of 15,209 hectares. In combination these three types of nature reserve now cover about 1.5 per cent of the land and inland water area of Britain. The statutory and non-statutory reserves complement each other and will probably prove to be one of the finest achievements of the 1949 Act and a gift for which future generations will be most grateful. The catalyst which made this development possible was the Nature Conservancy and its successor, after the 1973 Act, the Nature Conservancy Council. The combination of science and practice embodied in the Nature Conservancy, energetically directed and led, was a winning formula and the envy of many other countries in the world. Here the major contribution to nature conservation made by Max Nicholson must be acknowledged. His involvement spans well over four decades, starting in the years leading up to the 1949 Act, including his 14 years as Director General of the Nature Conservancy, after Arthur Tansley, and his conservation activities continue to this day. His vision, enthusiasm and drive have done more than any other to implement the provisions and intentions of the 1949 Act and to make nature conservation an important factor in land-use decisions. The incorporation of the Nature Conservancy into the Natural Environment Research Council and the subsequent splitting off of the research branch slowed some areas of progress, but a crucial clause in the Nature Conservancy Council Act 1973, which gave the Council power to initiate and carry out such research as was directly related to their functions, allowed the research/practice combination to continue, although in a much modified form.

The ability, under the 1949 Act, to declare nature reserves under a variety of mechanisms was also a far-sighted provision. Ownership had been expected to be the main mechanism for acquiring nature reserves, and although it is important and accounts for some one-quarter to one-third of nature reserves by area, it has been complemented by leasing mechanisms and, more important, by the ability to negotiate nature reserve agreements with owners and occupiers.

The management of the national nature reserves did not fulfill the high hopes held out that experience in NNRs would be useful in a wider land-use demonstration role. This was due, in part, to the scarcity of resources for the management of these reserves throughout the history of the Nature Conservancy and its successor, and also to the fact, which was soon recognised, that the problems were exceedingly complex and needed time as well as money to resolve. There are plenty of local successes in maintaining the variety of conditions and wildlife in a reserve, but there are also failures for reasons which are not clear and which are not always connected with a shortage of money. It also became more and more difficult to carry out destructive types of research on national nature reserves because of a conflict with conservation objectives. A good example was the attempt to elucidate the relationship between populations of oyster catchers and the commercial take of cockles in South Wales. Increasingly nature reserves were acquired for their value for the conservation of biological and physical features and less and less for their research potential, which was earlier, as the Privy Council had stated in 1950, the principal reason for acquiring them. This switch in emphasis is seen also in the expenditure figures. In 1960 about 20 per cent of the budget of the Nature Conservancy was spent on NNRs and about 50 per cent on scientific research. Twenty years later the Nature Conservancy Council expenditure was about 40 per cent on reserves and 20 per cent on research. The cost comparisons are not exact but provide an indication of priorities.

It is difficult to give a simple 'yes' or 'no' if asked if the provisions of the 1949 Act in respect of SSSIs were successful. With regard to the actual notification of SSSIs the answer must be 'yes' with a total number of 5,000 SSSIs (under the terms of both the 1949 and the 1981 Acts) which is likely to rise to 6,000, and a total area of more than 1.5 million hectares or 6 per cent of the area of land and inland water in Britain. The reason for not giving an unqualified 'yes' is because the 1949 Act did not go far enough.

E.J. Salisbury, a noted botanist, had said as early as 1929 that one-sixth of all the plants recorded in England had become rare or extinct in one or more counties owing largely to the impact of land drainage. The Nature Reserves Investigation Committee had, in 1944, described farming as the most serious threat to wild plants and animals. But such views were by no means shared by all, as we noted in chapter 3. The highly influential Tansley, writing in 1944, said that it seemed 'scarcely probable that the extension of agriculture will go much further, for the limits of profitable agriculture must have been reached in most places'. Again in 1945

> '...the great extension of agriculture during the war has not, on the whole, diminished the beauty of the countryside — rather the contrary is true... In places, no doubt, heath has been destroyed and farmland drained and ploughed, and some of the changes have been deeply regretted by the naturalist and lover of nature. But the total loss has not been very severe, and is offset by the gain in agricultural area'.

The requirement in the 1949 Act was to notify the local planning authority of areas of special interest. These planning authorities could only act in relation to the planning laws, and farming and silvicultural operations did not constitute forms of 'development' under the 1949 Act and as we know, they were exempt from the provisions of the Town and Country Planning Act of 1947. Notifications of SSSIs were quite ineffective for controlling fundamental changes on sites arising from agricultural or forestry operations and it was such operations that became the main causes of biological change.

A result of the exemption was that one government body scheduled a site and sought to protect it with public funds while another used public funds to destroy it, and both the Ministry of Agriculture and the Forestry Commission claimed that improvement grants could not be withheld if reclamation was technically feasible. No mechanism was available for taking an overview of land-use which would seek to balance the needs of different interests.

Ten years after the 1949 Act, the Nature Conservancy drew attention to the value of the SSSI notification as a protection against statutory development, but also its total inadequacy against agricultural and forestry developments. The need to improve plan-

216

8.10 The consequences of draining farm-land
Two pictures illustrating the landscape of a river – before changes resulting from drainage and after. Drainage problems of this kind were recognised even before the 1949 Act.
Source: Temple Smith

ning procedures in relation to those activities was recognised, but it was not until 1981 that the improvements were made. The Countryside Acts of 1967 for Scotland and 1968 for England had laid on 'every minister, government department and public body a responsibility to have regard to the desirability of conserving flora and fauna'. Yet government departments still gave grants to drain land, plough up old meadows, afforest semi-natural upland areas and so on. The EEC's Directives on *Mountain and Hill Farming and Farming in Certain Less-Favoured Areas* were also elements of the Common Agricultural Policy that worked against nature conservation. Until the Wildlife and Countryside Act 1981 strengthened the protection given to SSSIs and even afterwards, sites of high conservation value continued to be eroded or lost.

A further difficulty arises because the SSSI mechanism is better adapted for use in the lowlands than in the uplands. The boundaries and special interest of an oak wood in a sea of cereals are more easily perceived by an owner and occupier than, what to them might appear to be, an arbitrary selection of a part of an expanse of moorland. It must also be said that in the latter case it often is a matter of opinion where the boundaries of an SSSI should lie exactly. This difficulty did not matter much under the 1949 Act, but is a matter of consequence under the 1981 Act which gave bite to the SSSI designation.

The Cow Green reservoir story provides an example of the problems arising from lack of a detailed knowledge of a site. The special interest of Upper Teesdale, which included Cow Green, was recognised by its designation as an SSSI before there was a proposal to build a reservoir in the area. The initial response of a team from the British Ecological Society was that the reservoir should be built

8.11 SSSI uncertainties Contradictory evidence about the ecological value of the Cow Green site on the upper Tees River during an inquiry into its planned use as a reservoir, reinforced the need for adequate habitat appraisal. *Source*: Countryside Commission

elsewhere, but if it had to be in Upper Teesdale, then the Cow Green site would cause the least damage to the SSSI. Eventually the water authority proposed to build the reservoir at Cow Green, by which time further botanical surveys had revealed the floristic richness of that particular part of the SSSI. The Nature Conservancy and other conservation bodies objected and much play was made in the subsequent public inquiry of the Conservancy's uncertainty and apparent change of view. Similar incidents have happened since, but it is hoped that continuing surveys will reduce their occurrence.

Changing priorities in scientific conservation

The 1949 Act was particularly concerned with the protection of sites and hence habitats, and less so with species. Species legislation goes back over many years in respect of birds and there have been a series of Acts over the years concerned with deer, badgers, seals, plants and so on. The Conservation of Seals Act 1970, introduced by Lord Cranbrook, was a landmark in nature conservation legislation. It recognised that an animal had different attributes depending on the viewpoint. A seal is an animal that deserves to be conserved in its own right; it is a resource which can be harvested on a sustainable basis for its meat and fur; it is also a pest to salmon fisheries and needs to be controlled. Provisions within the 1970 Act accommodate each of these viewpoints. But it was the Wildlife and Countryside Act 1981 that put the conservation of rare and endangered species on a much more systematic basis and made provisions for five-yearly reviews of the lists of protected species.

It has been explained earlier how the use of NNRs for research and practical demonstration did not live up to expectations at the time of the 1949 Act. In general, although the Nature Conservancy and Nature Conservancy Council have carried out research on many subjects related to nature conservation, often to a very high standard, the outcome of some of the research has not been as pertinent to the management of nature reserves and general land use issues as it was expected to be. Monitoring has not been carried out on a sufficiently systematic basis to be as effective as it could have been. Lack of resources is partly to blame, as is the necessity to respond to immediate pressures; for example, the re-notification of SSSIs. It was expected that a longer-term research strategy could have been carried out by the Research Councils, but the advent of the Rothshild customer/contractor relationship, followed soon after by a reduction in the resources available to the NERC and others, has meant that short-term aims now predominate at the expense of the longer-term research needed in land-use matters. The break-up of the Nature Conservancy also coincided with the introduction of the Rothschild customer/contractor principle, an expensive, bureaucratic and unsuccessful replacement for the direct relationship which then existed between the customers, or the field staff of the Nature Conservancy, and the contractors, or the research staff of the Nature Conservancy, universities and others. A close working relationship was replaced by a longer, less effective chain with increased administrative costs and a smaller proportion of money spent on actual research.

The provision of advice and the dissemination of information have been markedly successful in terms of the provisions of the 1949 Act. A glance at the 1988 annual report of the Nature Conservancy Council will show how much time is spent on advice in its various forms: to ministers and government bodies; statutory agencies; committees of one sort or another, including parliamentary committees; in relation to development of many sorts; to private companies and individuals; to voluntary bodies; in agriculture and forestry; internationally in relation to conventions and agreements; and in relation to bills before parliament. Indeed there is hardly a sphere of activity now in which advice on nature conservation is not sought and proferred. However, at the time of the 1949 Act, the advisory capacity of voluntary bodies, such as the Royal Society for the Protection of Birds and the Royal Society for Nature Conservation, was very limited and often not sufficiently firmly based. Since then the voluntary bodies have become much more professional and authoritative and are now the leading source of information on a variety of subjects concerned with nature conservation.

New challenges for nature conservation

The Scott Committee noted in 1942 that 'even were there no economic, social or strategic reasons for the maintenance of agriculture, the cheapest way, indeed the only way, of preserving the countryside in anything like its traditional aspect would be to farm it'. Also 'The countryside cannot be preserved.... it must be farmed if it is to retain those features which give its distinctive charm and character'. These words are as true today as when they were written. The problem is to marry together the productive aspects of farming and forestry and other enterprises, such as water and energy supply and industrial development, with their nature conservation possibilities and responsibilities.

Most developments create problems for nature conservation. Modern farming, the afforestation of marginal land, the effects of fertilisers and agricultural effluents on water supplies, atmospheric pollution, the very rapid growth in marine fish farming, the continuing encroachment on the countryside by industrial development, and the development of estuaries are some of these. But there are other developments whose effect on nature conservation is less easy to foresee. The destruction of the ozone layer, the 'greenhouse' effect and the climatic changes to which they may give rise are matters for speculation at this stage. The extension of

8.12 Agricultural pollution and water quality
An algal mat in this Somerset dyke has been caused by excess nitrates in fertiliser run-off.
Source: Philip Steele

the use of biological control, including viruses for agriculture and other pests, offer enormous possibilities for better targeted and cleaner technologies and hence advantages to nature conservation. But there are also dangers that cannot clearly be foreseen and accurately evaluated.

However, these developments and the difficulties for conservation that they may bring are technical problems which, at least in theory, can be solved technically with a sufficient input of intellectual and other resources and adequate controls. What is more difficult to achieve is the introduction of a conservation ethic into the activities of all users of land and other natural resources. Financial inducements and schemes such as Environmentally Sensitive Areas and 'set aside' of agricultural land are helpful mechanisms, but they need to be put into the context of what is right for the whole variety of natural resources and not just for the production of barley, beef or wood pulp. A legislative framework is necessary to show people what constraints are put upon them, but a legislative framework for the land and all that depends on the land, which is not rooted in ethical considerations, becomes a bureaucratic restraint rather than an encouraging opportunity.

A problem of the 1949 Act and the Wildlife and Countryside Act 1981 is that legislation has run ahead of many people's ideas of what is necessary for the general good of the land. The development of a much more broadly based conservation ethic requires people to know and understand the full range of issues involved, so that they can contribute to conservation and, if necessary, be rewarded for activities in the national interest. Such rewards may be financial, but perhaps more important is the esteem in which people are held by their peers. Farming has become as successful as it undoubtedly is in terms of agricultural production because farmers have been told it is in the national interest to produce more food. They have been rewarded for their skills and industry, both financially and by peer esteem, and their positive attitude to food production has been fostered and supported by a single-minded well-financed Ministry, itself encouraged by an effective lobby in the National Farmers' Union.

The attitude to nature conservation has been much more ambivalent, both on the part of government and land occupiers.

222

Where difficulties arise a compromise is usually sought. But compromise in this context always entails a loss to nature conservation and a gain to whatever form of development is under consideration. It is a mis-use of words to call a reduction in area of a proposed afforestation of an SSSI a 'loss' to forestry; whatever the size of the area planted it is a gain, and it is the nature conservation interest that loses. Like land, the stocks of natural features, both biological and physical, are limited and development too often leads to the attrition of the resources of the natural environment on which we all ultimately depend.

'Sustainable development' is becoming something of a catch-phrase and a glib panacea for all environmental ills. Individual and specific developments can be made sustainable at least within the time spans which we use, although sustainable development is not easy to achieve, for example, in tropical forests. To say that a development is sustainable is not to say that development can be sustained indefinitely. There are biological and physical limits to growth in our use of resources and in the number of people using these resources. Without an appreciation of these limitations nature conservation can only be a holding operation, not a long-term goal, and no amount of legislation will overcome the inherent problems.

There are difficulties enough in resolving current problems in nature conservation in Britain, but these problems will be compounded by two developments, namely the delegation of more planning responsibilities to local authorities and the increasing degree of legislative direction and control emanating from Brussels. In relation to the first, it seems likely to be concluded that the exclusion from planning control of agriculture and forestry is no longer justified. If this were to happen then the zoning of land for nature conservation would also be controlled. Notification of SSSIs and the declaration of NNRs would be considered as a major land-use change, either potential or actual, and would be subject to planning processes. SSSI notification is done after an 'opinion' is formed, based on scientific evidence, so it would be for the planning authority to take a view on this opinion in relation to other land-use possibilities. Planning authorities now take a view on whether one development application is superior to another, or whether, indeed, any development should take place, and they could equally take a view on 'special interest' even if they may need to be staffed rather differently.

Bringing nature conservation designations under planning control — and such a decision only makes sense if its main competitors for land, agriculture and forestry also come under planning control — would bring a degree of flexibility into the notification process, but it would remove the post-notification flexibility that now exists. Decisions on future use and compromises would be made before notification, and, after an area has been 'zoned' for nature conservation, which requires freedom from development, it is inconceivable that such development would be allowed. The present system appears to be the more satisfactory in terms of flexibility and of ensuring sound land use, but the extension of planning control seems likely before long.

Britain's activities in the field of nature conservation and its procedures and practices in relation to the protection of habitats and species, both in nature reserves and in the wider countryside, are far from perfect, but generally compare well with those of other countries. How our practices will be affected by the development of the European Community remains to be seen. If a levelling up of safeguards were to take place under Community guidance, it would improve the quality of our air, our freshwater and the seas immediately around us, but we would need to be able to maintain our site and species protection provisions.

PART III

9 *The conservation legacy of the Act*

Returning to the pressure groups

So far in this volume we have traced, in Part I, the pressures for the National Parks and Access to the Countryside Act 1949, together with its passage through parliament. In Part II we have presented views about how the provisions of the Act have been implemented. The main successes and failures of the statute have been identified, largely from the view of influential people who have been working for some considerable time inside the system that the Act created. But what of the pressure groups that were instrumental in bringing the Act about? What do they think of the Act 40 years on? It is a most fitting way to conclude this book by seeking these very views. To this end, we have returned to a number of these organisations, which still remain active today, to talk about the principal legacies of the Act and to seek their opinions about the future of those aspects of the countryside that the Act was designed to address.

Their views, of course, are unconstrained by the statutory duties and official policies by which governmental or quasi- governmental organisations are bound. They derive from deeply held convictions about the ways in which our countryside might most appropriately be protected. They are also expressed in the context of pressure group agendas that are entirely self-determined and for which national parks, access and the countryside have varying degrees of centrality. We have thus discussed the issues raised in this book in this spirit and have weighed the criticisms of these groups in a blend of personal views and official positions in these final three chapters.

To begin with, we interviewed Kate Ashbrook, of the Open Spaces Society, which, as the Commons, Footpaths and Open Spaces Preservation Society, was founded in 1865 from an upper class Liberal caucus intent on protecting the commons of Victorian

Britain for the public at large. It was perhaps the least working class of the pressure groups lobbying for recreation in the 1940s and, as we shall see in chapter 11, did not endear itself to the recreation fraternity as a whole when its general secretary, Sir Lawrence Chubb, severely disadvantaged ramblers through his modifications to the provisions of the Access to Mountains Act 1939. Next, we went to talk to Stuart Housden, of the Royal Society for the Protection of Birds; founded in 1889 for the reasons we outlined in chapter 1, it rapidly broadened its aims to protect birds in general. The Society had an important role to play in the run up to the 1949 Act in, quite unusually, championing the causes of both scientific conservation and the public enjoyment of nature. From here, we interviewed Laurence Harwood, the Regional Director of the North West Region of the National Trust, the Victorian origins of which we also examined in detail in chapter 1 and which had an important role to play in the formation of the Standing Committee on National Parks. This was certainly a most influential consortium, in the years leading up to the Act, as we saw, again at the beginning of this book.

We then interviewed Tim Sands of the Royal Society for Nature Conservation. Formed in 1912 as the Society for the Promotion of Nature Reserves, it did much to encourage the establishment and proper management of nature reserves in its early years before championing the cause of the national nature reserve and sites of special scientific interest provisions of the 1949 Act. Fiona Reynolds, of the Council for the Protection of Rural England, came next. This was formed in 1926 as the Council for the Preservation of Rural England to promote legislation to this end. Like the National Trust, the Council for the Preservation of Rural England had a central role to play in the activities of the Standing Committee on National Parks. We then interviewed Chris Hall for the Ramblers' Association, which was formed in 1935, as we saw in Part I of this book, to co-ordinate the role of ramblers' clubs in bringing pressure to bear for new legislation. We went also to see Amanda Nobbs, of the Council for National Parks, which was formed in 1936 as the Standing Committee on National Parks, the organisation central to the pressures for the 1949 legislation.

Clearly, the continued existence of these organisations today is testimony to the fact that the 1949 Act has not turned out to be a universal panacea for the conservation of, and access to, the countryside. But we have also sought the views of two environmental organisations very much a product of the 1960s and 1970s. In interviewing Bryan Lymbery, of UK 2000, and Frances Vernon, of Friends of the Earth, we have been keen to gain a perspective of the 1949 Act from organisations the *raison d'etre* of which is different from that of the others. In recording the views of all of these pressure groups we examine, in this chapter, the conservation legacy of the Act. We noted in chapter 1 that this conservation heritage actually meant many different things to different people and that there was no such thing as a single conservation movement. Here, we assess opinions about both the amenity conservation and scientific conservation elements of the Act's provisions, and examine the tensions between them. In chapter 10 we evaluate the attitudes of these groups to what a number of them would consider to be the residual provisions of the Act — recreation and the wider countryside. Finally, in chapter 11, we report on their views of both the future in the areas of concern of the 1949 Act and of the role that each of these organisations might play in shaping that future.

National parks: organisation and funding

In the 1949 Act, all national parks were to have autonomous boards but, as we saw in chapter 5, the largely successful opposition of many of the county councils made them optional subsequently. All but the Lake District and the Peak District have simply remained county council committees, even after the 1974 local government reorganisation. Has this difference led to disparities in the way that the parks operate? Generally, there is a feeling among the pressure groups that the degree of independence from the county councils afforded by the Act to the Lake District and the Peak District has given both of these Parks a clearer identity and vision of what national parks ought to be. It has been here, and in the Peak District in particular, that some of the most important innovations in national park planning have taken place. In other parks, development and management are felt often to be much more at the whim of the constituent county councils. In Devon, for example, Dartmoor National Park had to get permission from the county council before it was allowed to appear at the public inquiry in opposition to the Okehampton bypass. The Peaks and the Lakes can operate much more swiftly and surely in these circumstances.

Other parks are also felt to be more subject to the influences of local landowning interests than the Lakes and the Peaks, a characteristic that pervades much of the legacy of the Act. County committees, all of which have landowning interests represented upon them, have to interrelate with each other. National park boards are more autonomous. But differences between parks may not be entirely due to organisational structure. There is a view expressed by the Royal Society for the Protection of Birds, that the differences are as much to do with their location and the potential of their land. For example, the ploughing on Exmoor, and the afforestation in Northumberland National Park (17 per cent of the park has been afforested since it was designated) are due as much to their natural characteristics and their location, as to their organisational structure. For the future, there is a common view that

9.1 Constraints in controlling development
Before opposing the Okehampton bypass, Dartmoor National Park had to seek the consent of the county council. Too many national parks lack sufficient planning autonomy.
Source: Dartmoor National Park

229

national parks should become more comparable in organisational terms, and that this might be accelerated by the proposals in the new White Paper, *The Future of Development Plans*. This is a point we return to in chapter 11.

If the organisational arrangements for national parks were weakened in the passage of the 1949 Bill, so too were their financial provisions. There has been ever since, a considerable difference in the amount of money going to each park even on a size or per visitor basis. The two joint boards — the Lake District and the Peak District — have always done relatively well, compared with the other parks, because they have not had to fight their corner for funding allocations within a county council structure. Parks such as Exmoor and the Pembrokeshire Coast have been particularly poorly financed since the passing of the Act.

Overall, it is felt that there is far too little money going into the national parks. Less is being allocated by the Treasury than had been envisaged at the time of the Act; at the same time the parks are becoming more popular than had ever been imagined. The National Trust, for example, often finds that it can get more finance from government for projects outside national parks than inside them, such is the poverty of the allocation of park funds. It is the Trust that makes the forceful point, too, about the relative levels of expenditure disposed to parks. In 1989, the government allocated £15.5 annually to our ten national parks. In comparison, it supported one opera house — the Royal Opera House, Covent Garden — to the tune of £13.5 million a year — hardly a subsidy to the poor! More curiously we have a national defence policy aimed at protecting the valued things of British life. National parks, central to this valued heritage, however, attract annually only 8 per cent of the £190 million it costs to build **one** nuclear submarine. We are paying insurance premiums larger than the value we place on the heritage itself.

National parks: a national or local resource?

One of the most difficult concepts pertaining to national parks in the 1949 Act was that, although they are situated in specific localities and the land is largely owned by private individuals, they were designed to serve the national rather than just the local interest. How they were actually to do this was always left a little vague, but one administrative mechanism was that one-third of all members of national park committees or boards were to be appointed 'in the national interest'. Over the past 40 years, has this mechanism been sufficient to ensure that a national interest is taken into account in the planning of national parks?

The majority of the pressure groups feels that neither this mechanism nor the serving of the national interest more generally has been very successful in national park development. In the early years, there was some success in getting the national/local interest about right in some parks because 'strong' appointments were made of individuals who had long been part of the movement for parks. The appointment of Sylvia Sayer on Dartmoor, and Gerald Haythornthwaite in the Peak District were very important for getting national parks off on the right foot, and giving them a good name. These were strong personalities who were prepared to fight their corner against more parochial interests. Indeed, both had campaigned before the Act was passed to see that national interests would not be quickly drowned in a sea of local self-interest. Credit should go to the Standing Committee on National Parks, now the Council for National Parks, for these appointments, since they did much lobbying to put them in place, a point we return to in the final chapter.

Aside from the influence of these notable pioneers, it is generally felt that localism has remained a pervasive force amongst most national park committee and board members. National appointees are simply in too much of a minority to overrule local interests, and in most parks, both the chairman and vice-chairman of the committee or board are local members. This further suppresses the national voice. At the core of this localism, of course, is again the representation of landowning interests in the parks, but it may also be significant that locally elected members on committees and boards are often answerable to a local electorate, which is often one with which they are a very intimate. This often makes them very entrenched, because their accountability is more immediate than that of the national appointees. Invariably, perhaps, the local community has the most powerful influence over decisions because it is the one that is most commonly considered. We must not overlook the fact, though, that even 'locally elected' members frequently do not actually live in the parks themselves but are indirectly appointed, for example by county councils.

Although this localism has been prevalent since the inception of the parks, into the 1970s one man did tip the balance a little. Malcolm MacEwen, a member of the Exmoor Society and the Exmoor National Park Committee, was nationally very vocal about what he saw as the ravages of the local farming interests in the Park. His was an unusual position, because although he was a nationally appointed member of the Park Committee, he lived inside the Park. He effectively blew the whistle on the worst of local farming autonomy, and almost single-handedly influenced changes in government thinking, and eventually legislation in the form of the Wildlife and Countryside Act 1981, in relation to the protection of landscapes against agricultural practices. His idea of local representation was perhaps a little different from that which dominated in the Park at the time.

Whatever the long-term advantages or disadvantages of localism in national park decision making into the late 1980s, the championing of local causes in national parks has again become popular. It is now a commonly held view that local people in national parks are becoming rapidly displaced by second-home owners, large-scale tourist developments and so on, and that this will be to the detriment of the physical appearance and cultural ambience of parks. Any 'national' interest in national parks will only be successfully served through first of all gaining local involvement, sustenance and commitment. In the late 1980s, this ethos is manifest particularly in the development of local housing needs policies in all of the parks as part of a national movement for rural localism.

So the dominance of local interests in national parks seems, from the view of the pressure groups, to be almost inevitable. This is perhaps not surprising in a system where the ownership of the land in such parks remains in private hands. Only where the land of national parks is in the ownership of the state, as in the USA, as we saw in chapter 1, will national interests truly prevail. The only real recourse to national interest in parks is through the planning

9.2 Local housing needs in a national park Housing for local people, as in this example from the Peak National Park, is just one way in which park authorities serve the local communities. *Source*: Peak National Park

appeals system in connection with development proposals. Here, though, the parks are in a very similar position to the rest of the countryside. But even though the development planning framework is similar for all parts of the countryside, is it implemented any more stringently in national parks?

Development pressures in national parks

Of course, one of the means of controlling the quality of the landscape in national parks under the 1949 Act was through the development control process, the mechanisms for which were set up in the Town and Country Planning Act of two years before, as we noted in chapter 3. This process was particularly important for the national parks because planning decisions had to be taken, in the spirit of the 1949 Act, in accordance with both the national and the local interests that we have discussed above. Planning criteria, therefore, were slightly different from elsewhere — the landscape was to be conserved and the national interest was also to be considered. But have development policies in the parks really pursued these criteria to good effect? The pressure groups have concerns in this area, too.

Most groups feel that the national interest criterion, is open to some abuse when new developments in national parks are being considered. There is the danger that nationally significant developments may be irrelevent to the locality and at the same time be damaging to the landscape of the park yet, strictly, be in the national interest. For all proposed developments, therefore, it is important to examine both national and local interests really closely, and explore the possibility of alternative development locations outside the parks, before new developments, and then only if consistent with development plans, take place. One of the most worrying areas of development in parks has always been that of quite alien projects of considerable scale. Major government or quasi-government schemes have often been the source of disquiet, but now an additional matter for concern is development relating to the tourist industry. While all such schemes tend to be proposed as being in the national interest, they actually often owe nothing to their national park setting, and give very little indeed to the local community. The Council for National Parks has, through the recent spate of tourist complex public inquiries, successfully ensured that 'national need' is no longer a criterion in considering their development. In fact such tourism proposals often appear simply to be trying to cash in on the fact that parks have been kept

9.3 Tourist development in national parks
Time-share enterprises, as at Langdale, are one of a number of tourism initiatives that cause planning problems for national park authorities.
Source: Langdale Estate

beautiful for the past 40 years. Certainly leisure proposals have been put forward by national or multi-national leisure organisations that have no local roots at all. The Council for National Parks is aware of over three dozen of these currently being proposed in parks. Planning decisions made concerning these ultimately might be decided on appeal, which takes the decision out of the hands of the park altogether.

In addition, large developments have taken place in national parks, such as the Fylingdales early warning system and its successor, which is soon to be built on the North York Moors, and the military training areas on Dartmoor, with special military development rights that can overrule national park policies. Very large civil developments too, such as the Okehampton bypass on Dartmoor, have been permitted through parliamentary bills, where the views of the national park authority can be overruled easily. Increasingly, there is uncertainty over the outcome particularly of appeals decisions, because, in the view of a number of pressure groups, the criteria being used by the Secretary of State for the Environment are becoming less clear, and his decision-making rationale is increasingly Quixotic. An appeal determined by the Secretary of State himself is almost twice as likely to be upheld as an appeal determined by one of his Inspectors.

Yet again, part of the problem associated with the lack of control over development in national parks has been attributed to the prevailing land tenure in the parks, and all of the vested interests that this implies. Despite these many problems there is still a degree of optimism that the operation of the planning system in the parks has probably had an influence, stemming the tide of development that might have otherwise taken place with a weaker system of control.

Undoubtedly it is the case, too, that not all developments in parks seen today as damaging to the environment, will remain so forever. The Fylingdales early-warning system has a sense of majesty and now familiarity to many visitors to the North York Moors National Park. Some will feel a measure of sadness when it is dismantled, to be replaced by its successor. The new development, certainly, has met with much public opposition, but no doubt when its useful life is over, there will be some regret at its disappearance. At Millers' Dale in Derbyshire, to provide another example, there was organised environmental protest when the viaduct was built in the 19th century, but an even greater organised protest in 1979 when it was pulled down.

Although the Town and Country Planning Act 1947 did provide the mechanisms for protection in national parks against most types of development, it allowed, as we know, exemptions from such control of much of agriculture and forestry. Although this was perhaps understandable in a post-war economy keen to boost domestic food and timber production, it did allow these two sectors relatively free rein over production patterns even in national parks, irrespective of their landscape impact. This lack of control over agriculture and forestry causes great dismay to most of the pressure groups, although it is felt that the development control mechanisms that pertain to built developments might not be the most appropriate with which to control agriculture and forestry. These controls are considered rather negative, but also would be often inoperable against more subtle forms of landscape change brought about, for example, by stocking densities and changes in crop types.

It is generally accepted that current agricultural production incentives, even outside the price support mechanism, have had a devastating impact on the environment. Grant-aid for farm

9.4 Defence or offence?
The new replacement for the Fylingdales early warning system in the North York Moors National Park, may prove as controversial as the 'golf balls' that preceded it.
Source: North York Moors National Park

improvement until the late 1980s almost totally ignored landscape impacts, and to counter this at least in part, the National Trust on its holdings in the Lake District has built specific environmental objectives into the management plans for specific areas. National parks thus need both carrots and sticks in agricultural and forestry control, and importantly these should not be tied to output levels. Have more recent arrangements in the parks gone some way towards achieving this kind of situation? It is felt that the requirement, under the Wildlife and Countryside Act 1981, for farmers to notify the national park authority of the intention to undertake potentially damaging operations, has nominally given the authorities some powers over landscape control, but this is widely considered to be tokenism. Such notifications, for example, are proving quite costly, since failure to reach agreement about the development of such operations can lead to a management agreement where the park must pay compensation for the farmer to desist from damaging operations. Not only can this be expensive but also there is, some feel, a hint of blackmail in the whole process. Incentives need to be centred around positive husbandry, aimed at producing wholesome food and a beautiful countryside, rather than simply doing nothing.

Individual parks have more recently undertaken specific initiatives to engender a conservation ethos in farming practices. We have already noted in chapter 5, for example, the pioneering agricultural grants championed by the Peak National Park in their integrated rural development experiments in the villages of Longnor and Monyash. Other parks have innovated too. In the Broads, a national park in all but name, the grazing marshes scheme was influential in the development of the Environmentally Sensitive Areas designation. In the North York Moors National Park, the authority has a specific scheme that allows grant-aid to farmers for positive conservation works, thus embracing environmental objectives. While this type of initiative has been met with a degree of excitement amongst the pressure groups, there is still a feeling that it allows the Ministry of Agriculture, although a contributor to this scheme, to avoid directly its conservation obligations, and in particular to minimise its expenditure on landscape conservation. The Agriculture Act 1986 gives explicit environmental objectives to the

Ministry, but to date, nearly all of the expenditure that it has undertaken in this category has been, in fact, on animal sewage disposal systems — hardly, it is felt, what was meant by the provisions of the Act.

Tensions between amenity and scientific conservation

One of the unique characteristics of the 1949 Act was that it created a clear distinction between both the provisions and organisations associated with amenity conservation on the one hand and scientific conservation on the other. We examined the reasons for this duality quite closely in chapters 1 and 2. The amenity conservationists were essentially concerned to develop the quality of the landscape and, as a result, the potential of access and human enjoyment associated with it. The scientific conservationists were much more concerned with the inherent scientific worth of the fauna and flora of the countryside. Is this duality, virtually unique to Britain, still a useful one today?

The pressure groups feel that this distinction has had some uses over the first 40 years of the Act, because it has allowed the conservation movement to develop a very broad base, both politically and in terms of implementation. Today it is felt that there is a good deal of coexistence between the two in the management of the countryside, but less in terms of organisational structure. Such tensions as do exist are, according to at least some of the groups, largely due to the elitism of the scientific fraternity. Certainly, the interdependence of landscape and nature conservation appears to be an increasingly important part of planning for conservation. On the ground, good management plans for scientific conservation invariably lead to harmonious landscapes, too. The Royal Society for Nature Conservation feels that, indeed, landscape values can be defined successfully by recourse to scientific criteria.

A note of caution is sounded in the context of the nature conservation versus landscape conservation debate, by UK 2000. This is that if only these two types of conservation are considered, there is a danger that the conservation of buildings in the countryside will not be given proper priority. There were hardly any specific provisions in the 1949 Act to ensure that the built heritage remained conserved, other than as part of the landscape as a whole. Some organisations do pursue this type of conservation as a primary objective — the Civic Trust, the Victorian Society, the Georgian Society and so forth — but it is still a residual conservation priority for the countryside as a whole, except perhaps on estates and farms owned by the National Trust. This is slowly changing, however. The pioneering work of the Peak District National Park, with its concern for buildings as part of the wider environment, is now being followed by other national parks. The Yorkshire Dales National Park Authority, for example, is devising strong conservation policies for its field barns, and there is an explicit allocation in the national park supplementary grants now being identified for buildings conservation.

In organisational terms, the advantages of having the Countryside Commission in charge of landscape conservation and

9.5 Grants for buildings renovation
Field barns like this one in Swaledale are now a high priority for national park authorities.
Source: Peter Gaskell

the Nature Conservancy Council in charge of nature conservation are considered to be few. True, this structure does allow, as some pressure groups would claim, more voices with which to lobby government, but this has the danger of creating two differing views of conservation that could cancel each other out. The Nature Conservancy Council already suffers from this duality in respect of its scientific work. The separation of the Nature Conservancy Council from the Institute of Terrestrial Ecology in 1973, that we discussed in chapter 8, has simply served to make less clear the responsibilities for scientific work in relation to conservation, particularly because since that time the Nature Conservancy Council has set up its own scientific arm. The differences between the Countryside Commission and the Nature Conservancy Council in terms of their ownership of land — the latter does the former does not — is also widely considered to be counterproductive.

Generally there is a feeling that if the Countryside Commission and the Nature Conservancy Council could in some way merge, this would be of advantage to conservation overall in Britain. Fears are expressed, however, that such a merger would be practically difficult because of the landowning differences between the two, but it would also lead to a power struggle for the conservation priorities in government policies. In this case the countryside recreation functions, already a residual to conservation as we shall see in chapter 10, would be further marginalised. It is felt by the Royal Society for the Protection of Birds, too, that such a merger might lead to the loss of the Countryside Commission's greater propensity to speak out against government policy or to promote bold new initiatives than that of the Nature Conservancy Council.

In addition to these problems, the landscape/nature conservation division will become increasingly anachronistic as we move towards the free movement of capital goods and services in the European Community in 1992. This distinctive organisational structure will be at variance with the whole of the rest of Europe, and most of the pressure groups feel that it is inevitable that the government will have to introduce a single environmental protection agency at least by the turn of the century. This would relieve the Department of the Environment's increasingly untenable position under which it is having to act as both gamekeeper and poacher as a department in control of both development and environmental protection. UK 2000 feels that this debate about the merging or otherwise of conservation responsibilities is again in danger of masking a broader issue relating to the custodianship of the countryside. More functions than conservation need to be integrated in organisational terms if the welfare of the countryside is to be optimised. The social, economic and cultural functions, as well as those of recreation and conservation, have to be considered in a single decision-making framework, otherwise the 'popularity' of conservation will overshadow the welfare of the rural community.

One of the more intriguing aspects of the passage of the 1949 Bill through parliament, which we have commented on in chapter 4 and again in chapters 6 and 8, is that the amenity conservation and recreation clauses were the subject of much public debate, but the scientific aspects of the Bill received hardly any attention at all, and were indeed passed through parliament almost on the nod. This is felt by our organisations to be very much because there was such little understanding of any aspect of science in parliament at the time of the Bill. Despite this seemingly 'conspiratorial' approach to the passage of the provisions for scientific conservation, the Royal Society for the Protection of Birds, at least, feels that the allocation of designated scientific areas as a result of the Act — particularly sites of special scientific interest and national nature reserves — was both prophetically and comprehensively well done.

This lack of confidence to speak on scientific matters in parliamentary legislative debate, it is felt by the Royal Society for Nature Conservation, simply would not happen today. The public, whether it does or not, thinks that it has a wide knowledge of all matters relating to the natural environment, and that parliament has a responsibility to debate these fully. There was thus a strong contrast in the passing of the scientific provisions of the 1949 Act, and those relating to species protection in the Wildlife and Countryside Act 1981. These were widely debated and amended, particularly in the House of Lords, with much lobbying from a range of interest groups.

Nature conservation and public access

We have seen in chapters 4 and 8 that the principal thrust of the scientific conservation provisions of the 1949 Act was for research and experiment, rather than primarily for the enhancement of the public enjoyment of nature. At one extreme, arguments were developed that proposed the exclusion of the public from nature

9.6 Conservation as education Interpretation is now seen to have an important role in balancing conservation and recreation objectives. *Source*: Countryside Commission

conservation sites altogether. At the other, pressure for public access to all such areas was mobilised. In the late 1980s, this balance between exclusion for the pursuit of scientific objectives and public access has never been totally resolved. Indeed, many of the pressure groups feel that such an issue simply cannot be generalised about, but individual sites must be considered on their own merits. Nevertheless, all the groups did have a view on the propriety of such exclusion. In the majority of cases, it is felt that the exclusion of the public from areas of nature conservation value should be avoided wherever possible. At least two reasons are articulated for this. Firstly, it is felt that people have to learn about nature conservation so that its public worth might more fully be understood. This can only be done by allowing access wherever possible. Secondly, developing public support for nature conservation is a necessary prerequisite for political support (and therefore more resources) and both of these types of support would be enhanced by the development of access provisions on nature conservation sites.

Some organisations, such as the Royal Society for the Protection of Birds and the Royal Society for Nature Conservation, do feel that there is an inherent value in conserving nature for its own sake, irrespective of public consumption, but even in these organisations the size and growth of their membership, which is invariably interested in observing nature in some way, is testimony to the importance of public access for them. Friends of the Earth feel that even if the public were excluded more frequently from sites that are disposed to scientific research, there is no inherent reason why botanists working on the site would do any less damage than the public! At the core of this issue of exclusion from areas of scientific conservation is some understanding of actually how much damage is done by public access. The fear of environmental damage by recreationists is still pretty much a presumption, and there has been surprisingly little research undertaken in this area. Until such work has been executed, it is hard to develop a very strong case for the exclusion of the public.

All organisations agree that, at the extreme, the exclusion of the public from very fragile natural habitats can be justified. Some exclusion is, in fact, necessary for the UK to meet international wildlife standards and obligations, and, without exclusion, there is always a danger that people will destroy the very things that they have come to see. Great care has to be taken, however, that such cases are not used as convenient excuses for exclusion when it is not really necessary. The key to balancing access and exclusion is universally heralded as good management. Generally, scientific conservationists are felt to be getting better at managing people, and their methods of interpretation are becoming more sensitive. There is less emphasis on a 'prohibitive' approach to management (based on steering people and excluding them), and more of encouragement and guidance.

In this respect, the restoration of Cockshoot Broad in the Norfolk Broads is considered a particularly good example of the coexistence of scientific conservation and public access. Here, a walkway and a hide from which the public can observe wildlife unobtrusively have been set up, and by this mechanism a large volume of visitors can be tolerated. This is not always so, however. A case is also cited of the Moorland Association, an organisation we shall return to in the next chapter, which was formed, in part at least, to resist the access proposals onto grouse moorland put forward by the Common Land Forum. The Association has argued that the public should have only very restricted access to grouse moors, because of the need to protect the grouse habitat. It is commonly felt, however, that such restrictions

9.7 Marrying conservation and public access Cockshoot Broad has been developed as a conservation area with specific objectives for public enjoyment. *Source*: Countryside Commission

in access are desired not so much for reasons of scientific conservation but more so that the public will be less intrusive when the grouse are being shot!

It is the view of the pressure groups, then, that public access should be allowed whenever possible to areas of scientific worth in the countryside, and that potential conflicts arising from such access should be tempered whenever possible by good and sympathetic management practices. But what of access provisions more generally in the 1949 Act? It is to these that we turn first in chapter 10.

10 *Access and the wider countryside : a story of neglect?*

Recreation and public policy

We have seen in chapters 4 and 9 that, partly as a result of lack of challenge in parliament, the provisions for scientific conservation in the 1949 Act were passed with very little debate. Indeed, they were modified hardly at all by either public pressures or entrenched landowing interests. This was not so for the provisions for access and the wider countryside, the legacies of which we turn to in this chapter. They were very much compromised by a range of interests to the extent that, according to many of the pressure groups, they were emasculated. Central to this process of debate, which we have examined in chapter 9 in the narrow context of scientific conservation and exclusion, was the relative priorities that were to be accorded to recreation and conservation as policy objectives. It is to these that we turn first.

One of the themes that has surfaced throughout this book as the legacy of the 1949 Act, is that relatively greater priority is given to conservation compared with recreation in many aspects of rural policy. Does this historical prioritisation of conservation still have a validity in the late 1980s? Not surprisingly, there are mixed views about this in the different pressure groups. In the organisations concerned with implementing action on the ground, for example, the Royal Society for Nature Conservation, the conservation primacy is very important. Indeed, they are worried about the development of the Norfolk Broads as a new 'national park', and the privatisation of the water industry, which we examine more closely in chapter 11, precisely because this conservation priority is not explicit enough. For the Council for National Parks, too, there must be a conservation priority because unless conservation is put first, there will be nothing left to enjoy. Caution must be expressed, however, that such a conservation priority is not used as a means of unnecessarily restricting access. Indeed quiet access on foot is rarely in conflict with conservation, apart from in a small number of particularly popular places where erosion can occur. The relevance of the conservation priority has a much clearer focus in the context of more active recreation pursuits.

For other organisations, the conservation priority is less defensible now than it was at the time of the 1949 Act. This is because the demand for rural leisure is so much greater in 1989 and recreation has the power to develop economies more effectively than conservation. In turn, economies with more vitality often have a greater contribution to make to conservation developments. It is felt by many groups that the separation of the Nature Conservancy Council from the Countryside Commission that we discussed in chapter 9 simply serves to confuse this recreation/conservation priority. Other organisations, such as the Open Spaces Society, see the 'joint consumption' characteristics of recreation and conservation as being so strong, that to prioritise one over the other is actually meaningless. The Royal Society for the Protection of Birds, too, finds the roles of the two statutory bodies increasingly hard to separate. The Open Spaces Society feels that within the Countryside Commission the conservation priority is actually wrong, since it leads to some Commission expenditure, for example in supporting the Farming and Wildlife Advisory Groups, that rightly should be the responsibility of other organisations altogether, in this case the Ministry of Agriculture, Fisheries and Food.

Irrespective of any relative importance of conservation compared to recreation, all of the pressure groups feel that the right of access to the countryside on the part of the public at large is of paramount importance as a principle of freedom. There should therefore be a clear public policy priority to provide for the opportunity for countryside recreation, and all landowners should share in this responsibility. This is often not the case, as the Wychwood example that we cited in chapter 6 clearly demonstrates. Public policy mechanisms could be used to engender this spirit among landowners, for example their liability against injury to those taking part in customary access could be curtailed. In tandem with

10.1 Public access to private land
Restrictions in access to the Wychwood Forest (see illus. 6.3) have now been eased by the introduction of this footpath following negotiations with the land owner. *Source*: John Blunden

this highly prized notion of the principle of access, the Council for National Parks feels more pragmatically that access provides the strongest argument for the public subsidisation of the countryside environment.

In this respect, the most urgent aspects of public policy requiring legislation are widely felt to be the spheres of access to common land and public rights of way. The outstanding problem here is the failure of the Common Land Forum's recommendations to reach the statute book in late 1989. Central to this failure have been the perennial disputes between the landowner and the access lobby. Although the Common Land Forum had representation from the Country Landowners' Association on it, a caucus of grouse moorland owners has been vehement in its opposition to the Forum's proposals for unrestricted access to open country, and formed the Moorland Association in 1986, in part to oppose these proposals. We noted one of its scientific arguments for the restriction of public access to grouse moors at the end of chapter 9. Conciliatory committees have been set up by the Countryside Commission between this Association, the gamekeepers and the Open Spaces Society, and the Ramblers' Association, but still agreement has not been reached about the extent of access to common land, where grouse are being shot. In the course of these negotiations, it was confirmed that the Open Spaces Society's grant-aid from the Countryside Commission would not be renewed, because of its opposition to the Countryside Commission's recommendations for grouse moors, and its constant criticism of large landowners (including the National Trust) over access. Little, it seems, has changed in the access/landowners conflict, since 1949.

Rights of way on definitive maps are also as much of a problem as ever. Even the president of the Council for the Protection of Rural England (and producer of the film *Chariots of Fire*), David Puttnam, went to a public inquiry in 1988, to re-route a footpath and a bridleway from his land, having already provided alternative routes. This was found to be admissible, but it has led to arguments between the Open Spaces Society who were opposed to the diversion and the Wiltshire area of the Rambler's Association who were not. Rights of way disputes are thus still as much a part of our lives forty years after the 1949 Act as they were in the 19th century, even though the reasons behind them — such as an increasing ability to live in the countryside and agricultural intensification — may be different. Even concerted policy attempts to try to resolve these issues of rights of way once and for all seem to have met with little success. Thus the Countryside Commission's 'Enjoying the countryside' policy initiative (which came to pass itself, so some pressure groups have argued, only through much external lobbying and not just out of a sense of conviction on the part of the Commission), aimed to have all rights of way in England and Wales clearly identified and marked by the year 2000. Unfortunately, this initiative has been frustrated because pleas to the Department of the Environment for the resources to achieve such an objective have met with no positive response.

10.2 Charging for access

The idea of sharing the owner's amenity rights, for a fee, is not a new one!

Source: Punch

"OWNER UP" IN THE LAKE DISTRICT.

"Here y'are, Sir! Finest Waterfall in England! Sixpence a head, if *you* please! Owner don't allow nobody to look at his Waterfall for nothing!"

"Looking at that there Mounting was you, Sir? Then you're a-trespassing! I've orders from the Owner to stop anyone from looking at his Mounting."

"Hi! you Sir! Come off that grass, will you! I'm the Owner of this property, and I'll trouble you to walk in the middle of the road!"

"Here, I say, none of that! Owner's orders is no one's to disturb his Flies. You just leave 'em alone, will ye?"

A final concern in the area of recreation policy generally relates to the problems of recreation pressure, and the use of some form of rationing mechanism to regulate it. Ideas for such mechanisms from the pressure groups include visitor taxes in areas of greater demand (popular with some of the pressure groups but very unpopular with others), such as currently pertain in parts of Austria and Switzerland. As well as being able to levy these on overnight visitors, they could also be generated with the use of visitor car licences. These could be sold annually for certain of the most popular areas, with appropriate exemptions for local people. These proposals would allow the levying of much-needed revenues from visitor control. Direct revenue raising is becoming increasingly inadequate as a means of maintaining the most desirable environments. The National Trust, for example, has had to launch a Lake District maintenance appeal — for more than £2 million over the next five years — which is to be used to fund an environmental workforce. To achieve this fundraising, the Trust has 'roving recruiters' who get ramblers to sign direct debits out on the fells! However, the Trust is very aware that its present level of membership may be close to the limit beyond which new members may be difficult, if not impossible, to find.

The failure of access agreements

At the core of the policy problem for countryside recreation, then, lies the reticence of the landowner to relinquish his possession of exclusive and exclusionary rights to land. One specific mechanism aimed at easing this problem was included in the 1949 Act. This was the access agreement, by which a national park authority could negotiate for areas of access with a landowner, in exchange for cash payments and management assistance. These provisions, as we have seen in chapters 5 and 6, have only really been used in one national park — the Peak District. The pressure groups have views on why this has been so.

Most commonly, groups feel that the failure of access agreements has been due firstly, to a lack of resources, and, secondly, yet again to the influence of the landowner. In the case of resources, there is commonly felt to be too few resources in most parks outside the Peak District and the Lake District, both for negotiating agreements and for the staff to administer them, a point we noted in chapter 9. The landowners' influence is felt to be the most significant, however, since generally landowners do not wish to enter into such agreements. The Council for the Protection of Rural England and the Ramblers' Association feel there have been other, perhaps more subtle, reasons for their limited use. Access agreement provisions were drafted in direct response to the mass trespass of Kinder Scout in the (now) Peak National Park that we described in chapter 2. These provisions were designed for large tracts of open moorland close to large centres of population, and although they were enshrined in national legislation, they were only really pertinent to the Peak District. It was therefore perhaps inevitable that the agreements should be subsequently used mainly in the Peak District. Over time, the access agreement has become a less useful mechanism for dealing with the principal problems of parks (such as agricultural intensification), since it was never designed for such purposes, so it has fallen into disuse.

Changes in developments in recreation provision in national parks also have led to their disuse. Over time, access has tended to be negotiated on a much smaller scale and individual basis than was required for access agreements, and these negotiations have been inevitably much more concerned with linear routes, such as footpaths, than whole areas. The Council for National Parks feels that, irrespective of the failure of access agreements, national parks have been able to do very little indeed to secure land for the nation as a whole through land acquisition. This, rather perversely, is perhaps not a bad thing in the current political climate, because such land would now be in danger of being privatised, with the result that even less public control might be vested in it than currently has been negotiated. The whole philosophy behind access agreements is questioned by some who feel that paying at all for access to open country is unjust.

Recreation : social class and types of provision

One of the issues that we discussed in some detail in chapter 2 in particular, in the lead up to the 1949 Act, was the class involvement in the pressures for legislation. For recreation in particular, these were driven certainly in the North of England to a significant degree by working class Labour clubs and organisations. Yet into the 1950s and beyond, this working class pioneering spirit seemed to give way to the use of countryside by a more middle class and less active population. Was there really a shift in the class structure of those keen to participate in countryside recreation?

Most organisations feel that countryside recreation is now dominated by the middle class, partly because the population as a whole now considers itself more middle class than before the war. Passive recreation has made use of the motor car, and this almost defines a minimum level of affluence for participation. Working class interest has been engendered where specifically targeted public recreation transport experiments have been introduced, for

example, on Dartmoor and in the Peak National Park. Overall, though, as leisure options become greater and more diverse, and as leisure time increases for everyone, it becomes harder to say with any degree of certainty what the dominant class profiles of any particular type of recreation are.

One of the consequences in this growth in 'middle class' participation is that recreation problems are now much more geographically widespread than they were in the 1940s, because access to the motor car allows people to penetrate the countryside more deeply and in a more dispersed way. Prior to the Second World War, there may well have been as many ramblers in the countryside, but they were more concentrated since they were dependent on local bus routes for where they walked. Whatever conclusions might be drawn about the class structure of countryside recreation, most organisations feel that there is still a public policy responsibility to promote social recreation. This is because it is commonly felt that non-participation in countryside recreation is much more a result of deprivation than of preference. Social policies that locate recreation facilities close to towns, or target ethnic minorities, for example, are therefore valid, but the Council for the Protection of Rural England concedes that properly targeted equity policies are likely to be quite expensive. Overall, there is a view that countryside recreation should be promoted for all of the population, and opportunities made available that allow as many of them to participate as possible.

The 1949 Act sought to identify different types of recreation in the countryside. As well as introducing national parks, it was con-

10.3 Recreational transport for the public
The 'Transmoorland' summer bus service across Dartmoor has brought many walkers into the national park.
Source: Dartmoor National Park

253

cerned to clarify the position of access to parts of open country, negotiated access areas, and rights of way. Has the usefulness of this delineation of types of recreation really stood the test of time? It is commonly felt that the recreation resources defined by the 1949 Act have been more enduring than, for example, those specific recreation sites — country parks and picnic sites — designated under the Countryside Act 1968. Country parks, in particular, are considered to have had limited success: the vast majority of people prefer to recreate in the open countryside, and indeed it is very much this broader type of recreation that should be encouraged.

In this respect, public rights of way will always be the cornerstone of countryside recreation, but here, apart from the problems of delineating them that we have already discussed, confusions are emerging because the Countryside Commission is seeking to classify them differently. They are proposing, as we noted in chapter 6, four categories of path, and although they have a commitment to opening up all paths, this categorisation is leading some county councils to pursue the development of some types to the detriment of others in a hierarchical way. In Suffolk, for example, priority is now given to the development of recreation routes, at the expense of local paths for the local population. There seems little logic in this, when all paths should be opened up.

Part of the problem of the provisions of the 1949 Act is that many of the more active types of countryside recreation today, such as hang-gliding, windsurfing and parascending, were not even envisaged in 1949, and therefore statutory provision for them could not be developed. These activities, together with the growth in education and training pursuits, represent some of the most concentrated pressures for countryside recreation, particularly in national parks today, even though walking is still the most popular pursuit, and its popularity is still growing. It is commonly felt, too, that irrespective of the provisions made for countryside recreation, their exploitation will only be as good as the management regime they enjoy. For national parks specifically, there are pressures to develop recreation activities that owe little to their setting in a high-quality landscape. It is important to resist this strongly, or the intrinsic value of the parks will soon disappear. Outside the parks, the problem of identifying public rights of way is the biggest man-

agement problem. As the Ramblers' Association confirms, these are often simply not waymarked, or landowners obscure their identity. Potentially this is extremely important in terms of the overall supply of recreation resources, since a recent Countryside Commission survey has shown that 88 per cent of the public will not go where a public right of way is not obvious on the ground.

One of the biggest challenges for the management of countryside recreation facilities lies in its unobtrusiveness. Good countryside recreation management, the National Trust maintains, should be essentially invisible. If it is good, therefore, it is difficult to find funding for it, because the results of the expenditure cannot be seen. To compound matters, bad management is noticeable and is therefore commonly criticised. This essentially one-sided disposition of recreation management makes it an inherently difficult activity to execute and resource properly. Overall our pressure groups see problems in the implementation of many of the recreation provisions of the 1949 Act. Recreation is still a residual to conservation in public policy terms, and many recreation policies are thwarted by this. A lack of political will and the interests of landowners conspire to inhibit the development of effective recreation policies, and even where such policies, for example access agreements, have been developed, their use has been restricted. Uncertainties over the most appropriate types of provision to develop, and the inherent problems of recreation management, further conspire to place recreation way down the list of countryside priorities. But have provisions for the wider countryside, and areas of outstanding natural beauty in particular, fared any better? It is to this issue that we now turn.

Areas of outstanding natural beauty

Areas of outstanding natural beauty have become in many ways the poor relation of national parks, even though in the 1949 Act itself, as we noted in chapter 7, no landscape quality distinction was made between the two. Simply by virtue of their existence, some of the pressure groups feel that they are bound to have an impact on development policies and programmes within them. To an extent, too, the designation influences the propensity of developers to desist from putting in planning applications. In many respects, though, AONBs face the same problems in being able to control development as national parks. We have discussed the views of the pressure groups in this respect in chapter 9. It is again the vagaries of the appeals procedure that make development in AONBs so unpredictable. More so than national parks, though, AONBs are felt to be more variable across the country in terms of the stringency with which development is controlled within them. Their success is felt to be very much at the mercy of the constituent planning authority. Certainly, where AONBs have management committees somewhat akin to national parks committees, it is felt that these lead to a greater degree of cohesion in planning policies.

Much of the ineffectual nature of this AONB designation is felt to be due to the lack of special powers outside of development control. High-quality landscapes cannot be really properly managed with tools that offer only permission or prohibition, with no positive incentives. There are not even rudimentary controls over agriculture or forestry as in national parks. Without these, it is impossible to distinguish an AONB from any other area in terms of its agricultural practice. The Royal Society for Nature Conservation notes that the designation has relatively little impact

Conservation and Recreation in England and Wales

as at Autumn 1989

National park and The Broads

Area of outstanding natural beauty

Heritage coast

National trail

North Northumberland

NORTHUMBERLAND

Northumberland Coast

Solway Coast

North Pennines

NORTH YORK MOORS

North Yorkshire and Cleveland

LAKE DISTRICT

Cleveland Way

YORKSHIRE DALES

Arnside and Silverdale

Howardian Hills

Wolds Way

Flamborough Headland

Forest of Bowland

Pennine Way

Spurn

North Anglesey

Great Orme

Holyhead Mountain

Anglesey

Aberffraw Bay

Lleyn

Lleyn

SNOWDONIA

Offa's Dyke Path

PEAK DISTRICT

Clwydian Range

Cannock Chase

Lincolnshire Wolds

North Norfolk

Norfolk Coast

Shropshire Hills

Peddars Way and Norfolk Coast Path

THE BROADS

Ceredigion Coast

St Dogmaels and Moylgrove

Dinas Head

St David's Peninsula

Pembrokeshire Coast Path

BRECON BEACONS

Malvern Hills

Wye Valley

Suffolk Coast and Heaths

Suffolk

St Brides Bay

PEMBROKESHIRE COAST

Cotswolds

Dedham Vale

Marloes and Dale

Gower

Ridgeway

Chilterns

South Pembrokeshire

Gower

Glamorgan

Mendip Hills

North Wessex Downs

Surrey Hills

Kent Downs

North Downs Way

Isles of Scilly

Isles of Scilly

South West Coast Path

Quantock Hills

Cranborne Chase and West Wiltshire Downs

East Hampshire

South Foreland

Dover–Folkestone

EXMOOR

North Devon

NEW FOREST

High Weald

Hartland

East Devon

DARTMOOR

South Hampshire Coast

Chichester Harbour

Sussex Downs

South Downs Way

Sussex

Pentire Point–Widemouth

Dorset

Trevose Head

East Devon

West Dorset

Purbeck

Isle of Wight

Tennyson

St Agnes

Cornwall

Godrevy–Portreath

Penwith

Gribbin Head–Polperro

Rame Head

South West Coast Path

South Devon

0   50km

The Roseland

South Devon

The Lizard

on nature conservation. What is really needed for AONBs, it is felt, are more positive management powers — such as statutory plans — as were given to national parks nearly 20 years ago in the reorganisation of local government. Certainly, there have been some positive management initiatives in AONBs, as we saw in chapter 7, but these have not been part of any national directive and have been almost totally dependent on the enthusiasms and skills of particular individuals. Project officers and voluntary effort still provide the bulk of the positive developments in AONB management.

On a more optimistic note, some moves are emerging aimed at strengthening the development planning base of AONBs. Mention has already been made of the comprehensive local plan produced for the Mendip Hills, and in other areas sympathetic design guides are in operation that are trying to steer the quality of development as well as its quantity. These initiatives are playing to the main strengths of AONBs, which, it is felt, need to develop a strong sense of the regional and cultural identity of the area, with the full involvement of local people. Finally, some groups feel that the AONB is an uneasy designation that almost falls between the two stools of national parks on the one hand and the wider, nondesignated countryside on the other. Most AONBs are environmentally suited to national parks designations. This is an issue that is actively being discussed by the people of the North Pennines, for example. There, as we noted in chapter 7, the latest AONB has been designated. Although a long protracted procedure, now that it is in place, some pressure groups claim that there is a view amongst the population that they should 'go all the way' to national park status. Certainly, such a development would do more to stem the cynical proposals of the Central Electricity Generating Board, which, in the wake of the AONB designation, has proposed the building of a wind generation farm in the middle of the area. Perhaps the prevailing view about the AONB designation is best summed up by the Council for the Protection of Rural England:

> 'Areas of outstanding natural beauty actually mean very little, but we're awfully glad that we've got them'.

The principles of designation

If national parks have limitations in their powers, and AONBs are often ineffectual at conserving the environment, what do the pressure groups think about the whole concept of designating parts of the countryside for environmental purposes — a kind of rural land zoning? It is acknowledged that the original notion of countryside designations was evolved for the 1949 Act at a time when the exploitation of the countryside as a whole was envisaged as being much more sustainable than it has turned out to be. There was, therefore, no premeditated notion of using designations to downgrade the rest of the countryside. But, of course, the development of the agriculture and forestry industries in particular has led, it is felt, to this residualisation of non-designated areas. Much of this problem derives from governments being successively taken by surprise by the impacts of agriculture, and countryside legislation, particularly in the Countryside Act 1968, and the Wildlife and Countryside Act 1981, being very much a question of too little too late to do anything really significant about agriculture. Because designated areas have often had slightly greater powers to resist agricultural change, it has been the wider countryside that has faced the most damaging effects.

Outside agriculture, though, the non-designated countryside has also suffered somewhat from the development process. There have been, for example, some 'shadow' effects in development terms, in countryside just outside designated areas. To compensate for no development in Dartmoor National Park, for example, linear developments along the A38, just outside the Park all the way from Plymouth to Exeter, have been quite considerable since the time of the designation of the Park. In the Peak National Park, too, part of the Park boundary is actually defined by sections of the edge of the large Tunstead limestone quarry. In optimistic vein, the development of countryside designations provides us with a store for the future of examples of how the countryside might be better managed. Good precedents and measures of good practice do exist in the way that our national parks, sites of special scientific interest and more recently environmentally sensitive areas, for example, have been developed, and it is in these and in their man-

10.6 Beyond the bounds? Developments just outside national parks can dominate the experience within them, as is the case with Tunstead quarry, close by the Peak National Park. *Source*: Peak National Park

agement that we must provide lessons for the wider countryside.

Despite this vulnerability of the wider countryside to development, views have been expressed by the pressure groups that, more fundamentally, the core of sympathetic husbandry still lies in the wider countryside. We are reminded again that all of the valued landscapes of the countryside, as well as the ravaged ones, have come about as the result of agricultural practice. The dry stone walls and copses that are characteristic of much of upland Britain are essentially agricultural rather than environmental artefacts. Many large estates, too, as opposed to commercial farms, still have much to offer in terms of good husbandry practices that enhance rather than endanger landscape values, a view sustained by the National Trust and particularly practised in the Lake District, where it is the major landowner. Overall, there is still much to be learned, both good and bad, even from the provisions for recreation and the wider countryside contained in the 1949 Act. The fact that many cautionary tales are still to be told about damages to, and injustices in, the countryside certainly provides a justification for the continued existence of all of the pressure groups into the future. And it is to their own visions of this future that we now turn.

Epigrams and epitaphs

11

Towards 1992

> No; the world will not break,
> Time will not stop.
> Do not for the dregs mistake
> The first bitter drop.
>
> When first the collar galls
> Tired horses know
> Stable's not near. Still falls
> The whip. There's far to go.

> CS Lewis, Epigrams and Epitaphs no 12,
> In *Poems*, Geoffrey Bles, London, 1964

The continued sustenance of all of the pressure groups that we have spoken to lies in the fact that, as far as conservation of the countryside for public enjoyment is concerned, there is indeed far to go to ensure an environmental quality that can be guaranteed for future generations. The Thatcher government's desire to implement a 'full repairing lease' on the environment will take much effort on the part of many. In this final chapter of the book we look into the future and single out just a few issues that provide a concern for the continued environmental maintenance of our countryside. We also take a brief introspective glimpse at the pressure groups themselves to see how they might have played their hands differently during the 40 years since the passing of the 1949 Act, what their principal achievements have been and what role they will play into the future in safeguarding our rural heritage.

Of central and most immediate concern to the pressure groups is the prospect of the free movement of capital, goods and services provided by the European Community in 1992, bringing with it greater integration with our continental partners. There is some optimism that, because the 'green' movement is fairly significant in a number of Community states, this might make greater headway in Britain, although not as part of the direct political process until we, like the rest of the Community, adopt proportional representation. It is felt that currently Britain is environmentally minimalist and has economic policies that prefer to clean up environmental problems after they have happened, rather than prevent them in the first place. This green movement is concerned with global environmental issues. Top of the agenda, and we can already see this happening, are policies to ameliorate the depletion of the ozone layer, the 'greenhouse' effect, and more stringent pollution controls. Despite the development of these kinds of policies, two organisations feel that governments in a more fully integrated European Community would not necessarily make any link between such environmental policies and the countryside. In the midst of the 'greening' of the British government, for example, the Nature Conservancy Council has suffered cut-backs in its grant-aid allocations. Resolving the perennial access problems that we have discussed in chapter 10 will also probably have little to do with the greening of politics. The Royal Society for Nature Conservation, for example, feels that its biggest challenge for the 1990s is to ensure that nature conservation and wildlife priorities are not lost in the global environmental conservation debate. They, just as European governments are likely to, see the global environment and the countryside as quite distinct.

One of the principal concerns is that the whole of the drive to 1992 is to improve European economies rather than environments. This could be particularly damaging for the countryside. The European Commission is set to spend twice the amount that it does at present on publicly funded infrastructure works by 1992. Relative to this, expenditure on and policies for environmental controls are minimal. Initiatives such as the proposed new Habitats Directive are generally welcomed as European-wide policies, and 1992 will mean that such directives are likely to be more closely enforced. Again concern is expressed, though, that the British government has played little part in actively seeking to broaden the Directive to issues of wider interest in the countryside than habitats alone. Indeed, the government may decide to resist its implementation in the UK by recourse to the European Court. In administrative terms, there is some optimism that organisations across Europe (such as national park authorities) might federate to increase the strength of the countryside lobby. More pessimistically, though, the Royal Society for Nature Conservation is concerned about the likely increase in illegal trade in wildlife species, with no customs control inside the Community.

RIBOUREL
PREMIER CONSTRUCTEUR FRANÇAIS POUR LES LOISIRS

Leisure Properties for Sale in France Summer-Autumn 1989

11.1 A place in the sun?
The growing popularity of second homes in France may well relieve pressure on the British countryside in the 1990s.
Source: Mills and Co.

A more integrated European Community inevitably also raises concerns over the future of agricultural policy. The Council for the Protection of Rural England expresses deep concern about a 1989 speech made by Baroness Trumpington, then an agriculture Minister, in relation to 1992. In the spring of 1989 she was suggesting to British farmers that they had to become more competitive with their counterparts in France and Germany, and this would mean becoming yet more intensive and efficient. This seems somewhat perverse in the light of so many European-inspired policies aimed at solving food over-production problems. European environmental policies should be fine-tuned to take regional differences into account. Certainly, identical policies for the northern and southern parts of the Community would be an unacceptably crude solution. For example, environmental works will never be carried out by the poorer farmers in Greece, Spain, Southern Italy and Portugal, unless the incentives to do so are financially more attractive than those of food production. In northern countries, however, there are many more opportunities for diversification. There is also a view that access pressures on the British countryside might be reduced with closer European cooperation. There is an already observable tendency for people in southern Britain to buy second homes in rural France, and increasingly, people are orientating themselves towards a European countryside blessed with warmer weather, as a destination in their leisure time, possibly at the expense of rural areas in the remote parts of Britain.

National parks, agriculture and the environment

It is fitting in the 40th year of the existence of national parks, that there is a new air of excitement about their future not just in England and Wales but also in Scotland. The Countryside Commission for Scotland was asked by the Scottish Office to undertake a feasibility study of the development of national parks in Scotland, and to report by the end of 1989. An open discussion panel is sitting through 1989 and the Council for National Parks feels that the Scottish Office is keen to introduce such designations quite soon to develop the 'green' profile of the government.

Recent experiences in England and Wales, however, have led to an unusual alliance of interests promoting the idea of Scottish parks. Certainly there is a strong caucus seeking to protect valuable landscape areas, but there are also several development interests that would like to see them, too, since there is increasing recognition that the national park designation improves the marketability of leisure and related facilities. Outside these two groups, though, it is the local population that really holds the key to the success of the development of new national parks. Without a favourable attitude on their part, the implementation of the designation certainly will be difficult. In some cases, too, Scottish land law, particularly in respect of crofters rights, might make the designation of national parks legally tortuous.

Within the pressure groups the commonest concern is with future development pressures that are likely to face the parks. In the wake of our closer relationship with the European Community, regional aid is likely to remain buoyant for our remoter rural areas and because of this, more pressure for development in our national parks, than in perhaps less remote areas of countryside that do not attract the same degree of economic support, seems likely. Partly as a result of this situation, a Private Bill has been drafted by the Lake District Special Planning Board to afford greater protection for the Lake District National Park. It may be promoted in 1990. This draft bill includes measures to protect upland farming and to ease problems for those local people seeking to buy houses, but it also contains specific measures to curb and manage visitor pressures, to limit the development of noisy enterprises, and in particular to strengthen planning powers in the Park. Perhaps with the introduction of the new development planning system proposed in the January 1989 White Paper *The Future of Development Plans,* which we discuss later in this chapter, under which much more autonomy will be given to national parks, these provisions will be extended beyond just the Lake District.

For the future, all of the pressure groups see the principal challenge to be that of making agriculture more sympathetic to the environment. The introduction of Environmentally Sensitive Areas and set-aside schemes has not appeased many of the pressure groups. The notion of ESAs should now be considerably extended to allow the development of 'traditional' farming systems as the dominant practice in agriculture. This will be particularly important in upland Britain, where agriculture makes such a small contribution to output anyway. In these areas, all subsidies should be reoriented towards environmental maintenance and enhancement rather than production. The National Trust, for example, has begun to develop this kind of notion, as we noted in chapter 9, by producing management plans with environmental objectives for specific areas and then seeking to incorporate them into farm agreements with new tenants.

While pressure groups would like to see the principles behind ESAs more generalised, the principles behind the set-aside scheme are heavily, if not universally, criticised. The Council for the Protection of Rural England, for example, feels that because it is not land that is causing over-production problems in agriculture in the first place, set-aside is wholly wrong, economically, financially and for the British countryside. Others see that its principal flaw is that there has simply been too little positive guidance to farmers about what to do with the non-productive land. The Countryside Premium — a positive management system, with 'top-up' payments for farmers launched by the Countryside Commission in early 1989, might improve this. However, when introduced, it covered only seven counties in eastern England. The Open Spaces Society feels that some set-aside land should be given common land status.

As well as having an impact on the environment, changes in agriculture may well influence access to the countryside. The Rambler's Association feels that the leadership of both the National Farmers' Union and the Country Landowners' Association are taking access more seriously in the new-found climate of diversification. Possibly as a result of the Countryside Commission's 'Enjoying the countryside' policy initiatives, which we discussed in chapter 10, there is a little more attention being paid by farmers to keeping footpaths over their land open. This would have been impossible at the end of the 1980s without the introduction, in 1949, of the definitive map concept. Although there may be some increases in access as a result of changes in agriculture, the prevailing view is pessimistic. The vast increase in the areas of arable land over the past 15 years, driven by the European Community's Common Agricultural Policy, has caused countless public rights of way to be ploughed up, cropped, or unofficially diverted. Prospectively, things do not seem much better. Many forms of diversification, even in the name of recreation, may not improve access opportunities. Golf courses, deer farming and 'horseyculture', for example, may be in potential conflict with general access and will require appropriate management techniques to ensure their compatibility.

Finally, if appropriate policies are forthcoming, agricultural diversification may allow more environmental jobs to be created. Environmental work is considerably more labour-intensive than agriculture, and we should be creative in developing a broad-based conservation and recreation management workforce. Such a workforce is both necessary and legitimate, particularly if taken in the context of the Prime Ministerial 'full repairing lease' statement. It is essential that such a workforce is locally based and operates in small individual units, however, to maximise the commitment to the environment.

Water privatisation

Since the 1949 Act, the organisational structure of the water industry has been particularly volatile, with significant changes occurring every ten years or so up to 1972, when the ten regional water authorities were created. Local authorities and other countryside agencies have had to cope with these organisational adjustments in their frequent dealings with the water sector about access and the environment, but now the most significant change of all is to take place. The water industry is to be privatised. Not surprisingly, the impacts of this on the countryside preoccupy many of the pressure groups in 1989, and their principal concerns relate to the increased pressures for development and, particularly, the possible restrictions in public access arising out of the private land holdings that will be created. New clauses were added to the Water Bill in April and May 1989 by the Secretary of State for the Environment, to set up a framework for co-operation between the water companies and national parks, and to ensure a continuing 'right to roam' on the 200,000 hectares of land to be privatised; also to provide an opportunity for safeguards on land in national parks that is sold by water companies after privatisation. Despite these proposals, many organisations remain sceptical.

During discussions of the water legislation in parliament, the Lake District National Park has been given particular consideration. Here, the North West Water Authority owns some 5,000 hectares of land around Thirlmere, and more than 10,000 hectares around Haweswater, much of which is open land with good public access. In private hands, there was concern that this access could be severely restricted (or possibly closed altogether) or at the other extreme, exploited commercially, with time-share chalets and so forth. Fears were expressed that customary access would not be allowed to continue and would be prohibited altogether or charged for. In these two areas, Thirlmere and Haweswater, in particular, the Secretary of State tabled an amendment in March 1989 following pressure from the Ramblers' Association and the Open Spaces Society to safeguard the access provisons in the private water bills, which, at the end of the last century, gave a right to roam land around Thirlmere and Haweswater. In other areas the Secretary of State has proposed that the water companies would be required to notify the national park authority of 'any significant action affecting landscape, conservation and land management matters'. They will be obliged to take the views of the park managers into account and would be under a duty to protect the beauty and amenity of the countryside.

But these are only notifications, similar to the ones proposed for farmers who intended 'improving' moorland, that we discussed in chapters 5 and 9. Some are unhappy about the uncertainty of this procedure. Others feel that it creates three-tier landscapes for water privatisation — water authority land in national parks considered to be special, water authority land in national parks not considered special, and water authority land outside parks. The effect of this is to demote part of the land inside the parks and the land outside the parks, and put it at greater risk. There is some concern, too, over what will happen to the powers of compulsory land purchase of water authorities, once they are privatised. But the privatisation of water is not the only radical new government proposal in the late 1980s that will have significant impacts on the environment. Substantial reforms are also underway to the town and country planning process.

Deregulating planning

Not surprisingly, the new proposals for the reform of the land use planning system that have been proposed in the Government's White Paper of early 1989 — *The Future of Development Plans* — give cause for concern. There is concern, too, that this Paper is only a prelude to more wide-ranging reforms to the planning system, to bring it closer to an operation based on market principles. It is widely known that work is going on in a number of right-wing research organisations, such as the Institute of Economic Affairs, to this end.

In terms of the proposals for reform, one general worry is that the new planning system will be geared to the requirements and the development pressures of the south-east. Any national system that is born from the requirements of only one region is bound to

11.2 Access and privatisation
During the passage of the water privatisation legislation through parliament, much concern was expressed about the loss of access in areas like Haweswater. *Source*: Countryside Commission

lead to the development of inappropriate policies for other areas. Such a south-east-driven set of policies will have little appropriateness for application in national parks, for example the White Paper, among other things, aims to get rid of the two-tier planning system by abolishing structure plans, and introducing a single development plan to be devised by district authorities. This causes concern because many countryside issues are dealt with best at a county level. Recreation and nature conservation, for example, are likely to be given less consideration by district authorities because they simply do not have the expertise. The 'county statements' proposed in the White Paper are considered ineffectual because they will have no statutory force. As a result, countryside matters might increasingly be referred to central government. For the countryside in particular, therefore, the principle of the devolution of power to the districts might lead to the opposite effect — an increasing centralisation of decision making.

In addition to this lack of expertise in districts in relation to countryside matters, the devolution of power to districts will reduce the scale of planning. Many feel that much of the county scale of planning will be lost, and certainly there will be more local authorities with which countryside quangos must liaise. This will slow down all consultations, and therefore decisions, about the countryside. Districts are also less experienced at longer term strategic planning, and this particular element of the planning process is very important for the countryside.

There are also concerns about elements of the existing planning system. Principal amongst these is the growth in the use of planning gain to secure developments that might not otherwise have taken place. This entails the developers offering some 'public benefit' in exchange for planning permission, but some feel that this is rather too close to bribery. Certainly, developments such as housing in the countryside for the less well off are being procured under this system, but overall there are many more intrusive developments in the countryside as a result, particularly in the south-east.

Other developments in the planning system meet with more favour. The introduction of environmental impact assessment on large developments is broadly welcomed as a European initiative, although the Royal Society for the Protection of Birds in particular feels that the provisions of EIAs have been watered down considerably before application in the UK. There is also some optimism that more realistic controls over large-scale agricultural and forestry developments may result. Again, the Royal Society for the Protection of Birds feels in this respect that we could learn a lot from Denmark, which has comprehensive protection for semi-natural habitats that requires planning permission for any change of use. There are zones, for example, where the use of fertilisers is forbidden, and others where payment is actually made to encourage wildlife.

Finally, there is a view expressed by UK 2000 that, properly managed, the liberalisation of the planning system could actually be good for both the economy and the environment of the countryside. Certainly, the restrictions on development in the countryside stemming from the Town and Country Planning Act 1947 would not be so strong, and this would allow more innovative uses, for example, of existing buildings in rural areas, which in turn could facilitate the stimulation of a more non-agricultural rural economy. Managed in the right way, this could help improve the environment too. Simply deregulating planning, however, certainly will not bring about these innovations.

11.3 Rural land-use zoning
In Denmark comprehensive protection for the countryside is afforded by a wide range of environmental controls.
Source: Keith Turner

Pressure groups: into the 1990s

We have seen in the first part of this chapter that the pressure groups have a range of views on what the future holds for the countryside and the environment more generally. But what of these pressure groups themselves? Their continued existence is, of course, sustained because there is still an important role to play in protecting the countryside and for facilitating its public enjoyment. Indeed, 40 years after the 1949 Act, despite many successes championed by these groups, the pressures on our countryside, from development, from agriculture, from pollution and so on, are in many ways greater and more immediate than they were in 1949. In the face of such pressures it is vitally important that there is a collection of voices outside of government to work with enthusiasm and passion in the sustenance of our cherished countryside. It is essential too, for reasons of independence and autonomy, that these groups should be voluntary, relieved of statutory duties and free to pursue their own priorities and interests often in a partial but inevitably well-informed way.

Without any statutory public accountability, the voluntary sector always has to be mindful of public views on countryside issues. Some groups feel that there is still much to be done in fully embracing the public interest. Research by the Countryside Commission has shown that, for example, there are more than 20 million people who have an active interest in the countryside to the extent that they go walking in it more than once a year. Yet the membership of the Ramblers' Association, the largest countryside recreation organisation, is only 70,000 and that of the Council for the Protection of Rural England only about 40,000. Clearly, there is room here for increasing the membership of at least some countryside pressure groups and, indeed, such memberships generally are rising. That of the Royal Society for the Protection of Birds is increasing, at the start of 1989, by about 1,000 per week, and it is aiming to double its membership within five years to over a million. The memberships of the Ramblers' Association and the Council for the Protection of Rural England are also increasing, but more modestly. In broader environmental terms, *The Times* conducted

a survey of the membership levels of conservation and environmental organisations for World Environment Day in June 1989
and found a total membership in excess of 4 million

But pressure groups, of course, are not in existence solely to be
popular. They do not purport to represent a wider public as government and its agencies must. This gives them a singularity in the
way in which they can pursue their self-determined goals, and this
pursuit has professionalised hugely over the past ten years, often
much more so than professional and public bodies concerned with
the environment. Their powers of lobbying have improved considerably, and their access to government often surpasses that of many
governmental organisations. Their self-determination invariably
leads to some tensions in their relationships with each other. This
is perhaps inevitable between people who feel deeply about issues.
At the extreme there is sometimes competition between different
voluntary organisations each anxious to press home its views to
government, but by and large they go to considerable lengths
within the spirit of the way they work, to establish consultative and
liaison mechanisms. A good example of this is in relation to the
privatisation of water that we discussed earlier in the chapter. In
this case, the Royal Society for the Protection of Birds and the
Council for the Protection of Rural England have joined forces to
produce their document *Liquid Assets*. In working on issues raised
by the channel tunnel rail link, too, the Council for the Protection
of Rural England has joined forces with the Kent Wildlife Trust to
oppose the environmental impacts of the route.

But if these are the kinds of issues for the future of the pressure
groups, how have they fared during these 40 intervening years
since the passing of the Act? The groups have not stopped short
of being self-critical of some of their developments. To begin with,
the 1950s and 1960s represented a real trough for most pressure
groups, possibly because, with the euphoria in the wake of the
1949 Act, a little complacency set in, but more importantly,
because many of the most influential of the pressure group activists
left to become part of the establishment that was to implement the
Act. As we have seen in the first part of chapter 9, the Standing
Committee on National Parks, now the Council for National
Parks, for example, worked long and hard to ensure that the right

11.4 Voluntary effort for recreation
The maintenance of footpaths owes much to the efforts of unpaid enthusiasts, such as wardens along the Cotswold Way.
Source: Gloucestershire County Council

sort of people were appointed to national park authorities. Personalities such as Clough Williams-Ellis and Patrick Abercrombie, for example, whose roles before the Act we charted in chapter 3, became directly involved in setting up the town and country planning system.

This kind of cycle of activity is reflected also in the paths of individual pressure groups. The Ramblers' Association, for example, found itself concerned about the growth in leisure in the countryside, which was becoming increasingly apparent during the Macmillan era. It chose to keep its head down and concentrate on sharpening the provisions of the 1949 Act, particularly in terms of improving the development of the definitive map of pathways. It was keen to disassociate itself from the popularist car-based walker who, it felt, did not take rambling seriously enough, but in so doing missed out on many potential recruits and a resultant professionalisation which that would have allowed. The attitude of the Ramblers' Association has changed very much into the 1980s. Whereas the dominant membership used to be drawn from the urban population, much more attention is being given to recruiting in the countryside itself. This allows the scale of pressure and of their own management activities to be more localised and proactive. There are now more than 300 local Ramblers' Association groups, most based either in or within reach of their walking county. Invariably, they are good at keeping paths open, lobbying the local highways authority and discussing footpath issues with elected council members. There is still quite a job of work to be done, however, in persuading new members about their rights in the countryside. They exhibit the common public tendency to be too conciliatory about the paths that they do not regularly use themselves. But such work is all part of developing a broader base of membership.

The historical shortcomings of the Open Spaces Society were apparent much earlier than those of the Ramblers' Association. In chapter 2, we noted that much of the failure of the Access to Mountains Bill 1939 was related to the negotiations undertaken with landowners by the then Secretary for the Open Spaces Society, Sir Lawrence Chubb. Although at the time he was seeking a conciliatory position between ramblers and landowners, he is now generally felt to have sold the Open Spaces Society down the river, by making trespass a criminal offence for the first time. He was

11.5 Voluntary effort for conservation The county Wildlife Trusts provide a critical role in environmental improvements. *Source*: Gloucestershire Trust for Nature Conservation

some 40 years as general secretary of the Society, and in retrospect, this was probably rather too long. Certainly in the late 1980s, the Open Spaces Society is careful not to make the same mistake by giving in to the demands of the Moorland Association over common land, an issue that we charted in the first part of chapter 10.

In general terms, the pressure groups concerned with scientific conservation have had a busy time since the passing of the Act. Because the Act enabled the Nature Conservancy (Council) to notify land for its scientific interest, organisations such as the Royal Society for Nature Conservation and the Royal Society for the Protection of Birds have been able to become much more involved in the active management of such areas and the monitoring of their use by others. In tandem with the Nature Conservancy Council, the Royal Society for the Protection of Birds has been able to harness a great breadth of amateur interest in scientific conservation, with good professional back-up. The Royal Society for Nature Conservation, as the umberella organisation for the county Wildlife Trusts, has been able to develop a grass roots network of more than 200,000 people which it can keep very well informed about changes in government policy. In return, these trusts can keep a watching brief on the implementation of policies at a county level and can be vocal in ensuring their environmental efficacy.

Both the Royal Society for the Protection of Birds and the Royal Society for Nature Conservation now feel that their lobbying role should become more important than it has been in the past, as the urgency for species and wildlife conservation becomes more apparent. The Royal Society for Nature Conservation, in particular, recognises that it can learn a lot from the more refined lobbying skills of other organisations, such as the Council for the Protection of Rural England, which has been less concerned directly with the management of land. In the Royal Society for Nature Conservation's favour, networks such as that of the county Wildlife Trusts will become increasingly important as a source of opinions with which to lobby for new policies and proposals in relation to species and wildlife protection.

And finally, what of the group that did more to bring about the national park provisions of 1949 Act than any other, the Standing

Committee on National Parks, now the Council for National Parks? The fight for national park values continues as far as it is concerned. It does feel that its presence as lobby group in parliament has helped to keep national parks central in the priorities of government and has contributed to the development of a clear set of guiding principles within which national parks operate. At a more practical level, its constant opposition to inappropriate development applications in national parks at public inquiries has assisted in the sustenance of high-quality landscapes, but on a much smaller scale, it has done a great deal of work in encouraging local initiatives in national parks, particularly in relation to small farm schemes and sustainable development. It is able, in a number of different ways, to make the whip fall in the service of the provisions and spirit of the National Parks and Access to the Countryside Act 1949. But still there is far to go.....

Further Reading

Chapter 1. The development of the conservation movement

Undoubtedly, the most comprehensive volume relating to the whole development of national parks in England and Wales is Gordon Cherry's *National Parks and Recreation in the Countryside*. It is volume two of the Peacetime History series, *Environmental Planning 1939-1969* (HMSO, 1975) and is the one on which all of the contributors to this volume have drawn. Its first three chapters in particular examine in detail the policies, pressures and personalities involved, in both conservation and recreation terms, in the run up to the 1949 Act.

More specifically relating to both nature and landscape conservation, John Sheail has written two very detailed and analytical volumes relating to the history of conservation. *Nature in Trust: the History of Nature Conservation in Britain* (Blackie, Glasgow, 1976) and *Rural Conservation in Inter-war Britain* (Clarendon Press, Oxford, 1981) discuss not only the influences of the conservation interests in the developments leading up to the 1949 legislation, but also more generally the British conservation ethos in its many forms, and its influence on the political process. The historical development of conservation is also clearly and simply expounded in the first part of Bryn Green's *Countryside Conservation* (George Allen and Unwin, London, 1981, The Resource Management Series, No.3), to which we have made reference in this chapter in explaining different types of conservation value. In the same series, chapter 2 and Part II of Philip Lowe and Jane Goyder's book *Environmental Groups in Politics* (George Allen and Unwin, 1983, No.6) provides an insight into some of the relationships of the conservation movement to the political process, and includes a portrait of the development of the National Trust.

A good sketch of the development of the Standing Committee on National Parks (now the Council for National Parks) is to be found in their own publication *50 Years for National Parks* (Council for National Parks, London, 1986). Returning specifically to the national parks context, Part I of Ann and Malcolm MacEwen's *National Parks: Conservation or Cosmetics?* (George Allen and Unwin, London, 1982, The Resource Management Series, No. 5) provides a succinct history of the role of conservation movements in the build up to the 1949 Act.

Chapter 2. Public pressures for countryside recreation

As well as Anne and Malcolm MacEwen's *National Parks: Conservation or Cosmetics?* they have also produced *Greenprints for the Countryside?: the Story of Britain's National Parks* (George Allen and Unwin, London, 1987). The first chapter in this briefly summarises the recreation as well as the conservation influences leading up to the Act. For a most comprehensive account of the evolving pressures for improved access to the countryside from the Industrial Revolution to the 1949 Act and beyond, however, you should try to get hold of a copy of Howard Hill's *Freedom to Roam: the Struggle for Access to Britain's Moors and Mountains* (Moorland Publishing, Ashbourne, Derbyshire, 1980). Sadly, this is no longer in print, but it is available in many public libraries.

A much shorter account that is particularly good at distinguishing separate class involvement in various access organisations is to be found in Peter Donnelly's article 'The paradox of parks: politics of recreational land use before and after the mass trespasses', which is published in *Leisure Studies*, Volume 5 (2), 1986, pages 211-231 and is cited in this chapter. Some good accounts also have been written about specific periods in the fight for access. Ernest Baker's *The Forbidden Land: A plea for public access to mountains, moors and other waste lands in Great Britain* (Witherby, London, 1924) provides a stirling and impassioned plea for public access to Britain's wildlands at a time when public opposition to landowning interests was gaining real momentum. Understandably, this is no longer in print either. A lively and illuminating account of the Kinder Scout Trespass is given in Benny Rothman's *The 1932 Kinder Trespass: a personal view of the Kinder Scout mass trespass* (Willow Publishing, Altrincham, 1982), with many contemporary and current illustrations.

With so much good animated writing about the fight for access now out of print, it is good news to have a new volume on the subject published in 1989 by one of the key personalities of the movement. Tom Stephenson's *Forbidden Land: the Struggle for Access to Mountain and Moorland* (Manchester University Press/Ramblers' Association, Manchester, 1989) is edited by Anne Holt and is destined to take over from *Freedom to Roam* as required reading for students of the access movement.

Chapter 3. The response of the establishment: reports in profusion

Gordon Cherry's and Anne and Malcolm MacEwen's books all provide good accounts of how the recreation and conservation pressures of the early part of the 20th century were developed into formal responses by government. A succinct survey of the conservation measures and responses can be found in Alan Woods' *Countryside Conservation: The Development of Policy from 1880 to 1980* (Gloucestershire Papers in Local and Rural Planning, Gloucestershire College of Arts and Technology, Issue 24, July 1984). Again Howard Hill (see 2 above) is informative, particularly in chapters 6 to 8 about the formal responses from government to the recreation lobby.

The significance of Barlow, Scott and Uthwatt to the post-war programme of reconstruction can be found in many standard planning texts of which J.B. Cullingworth's *Town and Country Planning in Britain* (10th revised edition, Unwin Hyman, London, 1988) is one of the best. If you are keen to steep yourself in the detail of the whole of the process and the personalities involved, then another book by J.B. Cullingworth in the same Peacetime History series as Gordon Cherry's, *Reconstruction and Land Use Planning, 1939-1947* (HMSO, London, 1975), is the definitive work.

Finally, there are, of course, the seminal reports which pre-ceeded the preparation of the National Parks and Access to the Countryside Bill. First amongst these was John Dower's *National Parks in England and Wales* (HMSO, London, Cmd. 6628 (Session 1944-45), 1945). Leading out of this were the two major reports of the committees chaired by Sir Arthur Hobhouse and Julian Huxley. These were respectively the report of the *National Parks Committee* (England and Wales) (HMSO, London Cmd. 7121 (Session 1946-47), 1947) and the *Report of the Wildlife Conservation Special Committee Conservation of Nature in England and Wales* (HMSO, London, Cmd. 7122 (Session 1946-47), 1947). No more needs to be said about these as their signif-icance is self-evident from chapter 3.

If you are interested in following-up views on the relative importance of recreation and conservation in all of the reports of relevance to the Act, and indeed the Act itself, there are two good papers in a Countryside Recreation Research Advisory Group Conference Report entitled *CRRAG Conference 1978. Countryside for All? A Review of the Use that People Make of the Countryside for Recreation* (Janssen Services, London, 1978, CCP 117). The papers are by Michael Dower: 'The promise — for whom have we aimed to provide and how was it achieved?', and Marion Shoard, 'Access: can present opportunities be widened?' The development of recreation and conservation priorities specifi-cally in the context of areas of outstanding natural beauty is well rehearsed in an historical account by Margaret Anderson entitled *Historical Perspectives on the Role for AONBs: Recreation or Preservation?* Occasional Paper 3, Department of Environmental Studies and Countryside Planning, Wye College, University of London, March 1981.

Chapter 4.   The Bill reaches parliament

Gordon Cherry's *National Parks and Recreation in the Countryside* has already been mentioned in section 1 above. Its chapter 5 is the only alternative published source of information that adequately covers the story of the preparation of the 1949 Act inside Whitehall, as well as attempts by interest groups to influence its content. Its heavy emphasis on environmental planning means that it ought to be read in conjunction with parts of chapter 8 of John Sheail's *Nature in Trust* (also referred to above), which focusses on aspects of the Act relating to nature conservation.

Like the editors of this volume, both Cherry and Sheail have used original Cabinet, Treasury and Ministry papers. Of all the material available, the files numbered 334 and 335 and stored under the catalogue number HLG 29 at the Public Record Office are the most important. They contain the Ministry of Town and Country Planning memos and correspondence, both inside and outside Whitehall, relating to the preparation of the Bill and its passage through parliament.

However, the narratives of Cherry and Sheail are partial. They do not deal with the parliamentary processes that shaped the Bill as presented to the Commons for its first reading into the Act that was given the Royal Assent. For the full flavour of the parliamentary debates and the extent to which these are other intra-governmental factors lead to its amendment, it is necessary to read the relevant volumes of *Hansard*. Versions of the Bill in its latest form appeared from HMSO shortly after the conclusion of each parliamentary stage. Thus, for example, following the conclusion of the Third Reading in the Commons on 19 July 1949, HMSO had published a fresh text of the Bill on 22 July.

Although *Hansard* was used in chapter 4 to prepare a picture of the Bill passing through parliament, it was laced with the firsthand experience of a doyen of the ramblers' movement, Tom Stephenson. *Forbidden Land* (see 2 above) offers a racy account, which is good on the personalities involved, but one which concentrates on access matters.

For a view of the role of the Civil Service as part of the parliamentary process, there is nothing available in published form that relates to the 1949 Act. Evelyn Sharp, a key figure in Lewis Silkin's department later wrote a volume in the New Whitehall Series (number 14) entitled *The Ministry of Housing and Local Government* (George Allen and Unwin Ltd, London, 1969). Since this ministry succeeded the old Ministry of Town and Country Planning, the book does offer a brief picture of the National Parks and Access to the Countryside Bill and the events leading to its realisation as an Act, as well as dealing with its subsequent operation. The latter section, if brief, is worth reading. But for all Sharp's experience as an 'insider', there is little about the relationship between civil servants and politicians. For a general picture of this Peter Hennessey's *Whitehall* (Secker and Warburg, London, 1988) makes worthwhile and fascinating reading for anyone interested in the governance of Britain.

Of events of the time seen through the eyes of the protagonists, there are remarkably few political memoirs that provide any insights. Only Hugh Dalton's *High Tide and After, Memoirs 1945-1960* (Frederick Muller, London, 1962) offers a little background colour to the passing of the 1949 Act because of his involvement with it as a member of the Lord President's Committee and in the House of Commons. He also offers a brief picture of its working based on his own spell as Minister of Town and Country Planning in succession to Lewis Silkin.

Chapter 5.   The national parks

For the most comprehensive of views of national park management problems in practice, the MacEwen's two books of 1982 and 1987 mentioned in sections 1 and 2 above are highly recommended. But for those who wish to explore in more detail the first couple of years of the working of the Act in relation to the national parks, *Town and Country Planning 1943-1951* (HMSO, London, Cmd. 8204 (Session 1950-51), 1951) is useful. This naturally also provides further background to the run-up to the passing of the Act. For a central administrative view of those early years which gives some emphasis to Hobhouse's intentions in relation to the subsequent task of administering the Act, you should look at the Ministry of Housing and Local Government publication mentioned in section 4 above.

The increasing awareness of administrative shortcomings that had emerged by the mid to late 1960s are recorded in the Longland and Sandford Reports. The official titles of these reports are respectively 'Report on the Administration of National Parks' (contained within *Reform of local government in England and Wales. National Parks Recommendations by the Countryside Commission*) by Sir Jack Longland (Countryside Commission, 1971) and *Report of the National Parks Policies Review Committee* (HMSO, 1974).

The two national park planning boards have each published an Annual Report since 1953 and these contain a reasonably full record of their activities, achievements and frustrations. Where still in print they are obtainable from the Peak District and Lake District Planning Board offices. Both Dartmoor and the North York Moors National Parks have published an Annual Report since 1974/75 and all national parks have published national park plans which are very informative, as well as many other planning documents. Up-to-date publication lists can be obtained from the individual national parks.

The National Parks Commission published Annual Reports from 1949/50 and the Countryside Commission continued such publications from 1968. The Countryside Commission has produced many publications on the national parks as well as on the wider countryside. A full list of these can be obtained from: Countryside Commission Publications, 19/23 Albert Road, Manchester M19 2EQ

An interesting view of current attitudes and concerns of national park administrators, and a suggested new management and grant system coordinating agriculture with national park administration, are contained in a 1988 publication produced by the Association of National Park Officers. Its title is *National Parks — Environmentally Favoured Areas?* and it can be obtained from John Toothill, National Park Officer, Lake District Special Planning Board, Busher Walk, Kendal, Cumbria LA9 4RH.

Chapter 6. Access

The Forbidden Land, The Kinder Trespass and *Freedom to Roam* are classic accounts of how the various interest groups dedicated to free access to the countryside fought their battles as section 2 above makes clear. They are all appropriate to those anxious to understand the 1949 Act and why to many it proved a disappointment from the beginning. Although a newcomer to the field, Tom Stephenson's *Forbidden Land* also looks like joining these accounts having been largely written by one of the doyens of the cause. However, it has the advantage for readers of chapter 6 of this volume of bringing the story up-to-date and adds a little more detail in its introduction to the situation with regard to access in other countries. For those keen to consider the specific recommendations that went forward to government from Hobhouse regarding footpaths and access, the Sub-Committees report *Footpaths and Access to the Countryside: Report of the Special Committee* (England and Wales), (HMSO, London, Cmd. 7207 (Session 1946-47), 1947) is informative.

Whilst the importance of land ownership in the long fight for access is difficult to underestimate, it is useful to gain some further insight into the attitudes of landowners anxious to preserve their exclusive rights, especially for shooting. This may be done from Harry Hopkins' *The Long Affray: the Poaching Wars 1760-1914* (Secker and Warburg, London, 1985). This emphasises clearly the notion that landownership and shooting are the attributes of the powerful and just what some of the pioneers of access were up against. For an analysis of the relationship between landownership and access in the 1980s, this chapter has already quoted from Marion Shoard's *This Land is Our Land: Struggle for Britain's Countryside* (Grafton Books, London, 1987). Although strongly argued and polemic in style, it makes its case in a way that is difficult to ignore.

Once again, for the post 1949 picture regarding access, the MacEwen's offer much that is of value. In their 1987 book (see section 2 above) chapter 8, 'A Walkers' Charter', they not only consider general access questions, but also common lands. It provides an excellent and well-balanced alternative to the story told in chapter 6 of this volume, but also suggests new ways of providing a better deal for the walker in the future. Transport for walkers also receives due attention, regretting what the Transport Act 1985 has done to pioneering public transport schemes in the national parks.

Transport considerations for the walker are also investigated in terms of social equity in a study undertaken by the University of

Manchester. This is reported in *Countryside Recreation; Achieving Access for All?* by D. Groome and C. Tarrant (In Countryside Planning Year Book, Volume 6, Geo. Books, Norwich, 1985). But for those interested in the legal aspects of commons and rights of way, these are given a very full treatment in *Law and the Countryside: the Rights of the Public* by T. Bonyhady (Professional Books, Oxford, 1987).

As for policy, the Countryside Commission has made the opportunities to enjoy rural leisure a clear priority for the late 1980s. In 1987 it produced a consultation paper *Enjoying the Countryside* (CCP 225), as a part of a policy review being undertaken by it. The consulation paper provided a direct input to its recreation policy launch which rested on two main statements, *Enjoying the Countryside: Priorities for Action* (CCP 235, 1987) and *Policies for Enjoying the Countryside* (CCP 234, 1987). The most recent Countryside Commission statement, made in 1989, specifically relating to public rights of way, is *Paths Routes and Trails: Policies and Priorities* (CCP 266) which we refer to directly in the text. These papers are all available from the Countryside Commission (see section 5 above for the address).

Chapter 7. Areas of outstanding natural beauty and the wider countryside

Gordon Cherry's HMSO publication of 1975, and referred to in section 3 above, is again useful in the historical context, as are the reports of Dower (1945) and those of 1947 from Hobhouse and Huxley (see also section 3 above). Both the MacEwen texts of 1982 and 1987 (see section 2 above) allude to the origins of AONBs, but in the latter national parks are seen as experiments in integrated management that could provide useful 'greenprints' for the harmonious management of the wider countryside.

Planning and the Rural Environment by Joan Davidson and Gerald Wibberley (Pergamon, Oxford, 1977) also looks at the wider countryside with particular reference to its use for farming, forestry, leisure and the conservation of wildlife and the landscape. Although now dated in some respects, its particular interest lies in its analysis of a number of early attempts, during the late 1960s and 1970s, at the development of more integrated forms of rural planning. Although a topic of discussion in this chapter, here three of the most important schemes, East Hampshire, Sherwood Forest and the North Pennines are outlined and appraised in more detail.

Amongst the many reports that are germane are those particularly of the Countryside Commission. Apart from the annual general reports which we mentioned above in connection with chapter 5, five of value specifically refer to AONBs. These are *AONBs; A Discussion Paper* (CCP 76, 1974); *AONBs; Report of a Conference, November 1978* (CCP 125, 1979); *AONB; Response to the Countryside Commission's Discussion Paper* (CCP 137, 1980); *A Review of AONBs* (CCP 140, 1981); *AONBs, a Policy Statement* (CCP 141, 1980 and CCP 157, 1983).

Of the rest we may pick out *Countryside Management in the Urban Fringe* (CCP 136, 1981); *New Opportunities for the Countryside* (CCP 224, 1987); *Shaping a New Countryside,* (CCP 243, 1987) and *Planning for Change—Development in a Green Countryside* (CCD 24, 1988). The last three of these refer to the situation after the publication of MAFF's 1987 document *Farming UK* (HMSO, London) and the decision by government to support schemes for farm diversification and set-aside, coupled with a more permissive planning regime in which other forms of new enterprise would be encouraged in the countryside.

Chapter 8. Nature conservation

Not surprisingly we begin with a publication from one of the key figures in events leading to the 1949 Act from a nature conservation point of view, Sir Arthur Tansley. His *Our Heritage of Wild Nature: a Plea for Organised Nature Conservation* (Cambridge University Press, Cambridge, 1945) provides a fascinating insight into the development of many of the ideas that eventually informed much of the thinking of the Huxley Committee and were then endorsed by the Lord President of the Council's Committee. The Wildlife Conservation Special Committee, chaired by Huxley, itself produced *Conservation of Nature in England and Wales* (HMSO, Cmd. 7122 (Session 1946-47), 1947). It and its Scottish equivalent provided the blueprint for nature conservation in Great Britain as we have seen in chapter 8. A reading of Cmd. 7122 offers essential background reading to anyone who wishes to fully understand the 1949 Act as far as nature conservation is concerned.

As a follow-up to this legislation which set up the Nature Conservancy, a detailed description of how the Nature Conservancy was expected to implement the provisions contained therein, can be found in *The Nature Conservancy* (Privy Council on behalf of the Committee of the Privy Council for Agricultural Research and Nature Conservation, 1950). We have already mentioned John Sheail's *Nature in Trust* (see section 1 above), but it is appropriate to point out that this not only deals with the history of nature conservation in Britain prior to the 1949 Act, but also tells something of the story of the Nature Conservancy (Council) thereafter. A splendidly readable volume *The Bird of Time: The Science and Politics of Nature Conservation — a personal account*, by N.W. Moore (Cambridge University Press, Cambridge, 1987) also relates the story of the Conservancy from its beginnings, but has the advantage of being written by one of its former chief advisors who was much involved in establishing the early national nature reserves and SSSIs and only recently retired. However, as the title suggests, his book also has a wider remit.

Although now out of print, *The Environmental Revolution: A Guide for the New Masters of the World* (Penguin, 1972) was written by the second and most influential Director-General of the Nature Conservancy, Max Nicholson. Even though this is a broad review of man's changing relations with nature throughout his history, it offers an interesting comparison of the British experience of developing a framework for nature conservation with that of other nations.

Finally, the Annual Reports of the Nature Conservancy and the Nature Conservancy Council offer a detailed year-by-year picture of how the 1949 Act was implemented and has been acted upon since the early days. These reports are available from the Nature Conservancy Council, Northminster House, Peterborough PE1 1UA.

Chapters 9–11. Conservation, access and the wider countryside, and the future

In this final section we take all three chapters together since our concern throughout has been to see what nine key pressure groups have thought about the workings of the 1949 Act over the past forty years and what needs to be done about the countryside for the future. Since you may wish to keep in touch with one or more of these groups as a way of up-dating your own thinking, we offer brief details of each and how you can most usefully tap into their current concerns. Thus in every instance we give you information on their objectives and their publications which are mainly aimed at their members, with the notable exception of UK 2000. Although they would prefer your membership, all are happy to supply copies of their journals or their other publications to anyone. Some charge will usually be made for these.

The Open Spaces Society has as its current aims the preservation of commons, footpaths and open space, and seeks to promote new footpaths and secure public access to open land. Its membership is about 2,500 and is located at 25a Bell Street, Henley-on-Thames, Oxfordshire RG9 2BA (tel. 0491-573535). Its journal, *Open Space*, appears three times a year.

The Royal Society for the Protection of Birds seeks to encourage the conservation of wild birds, especially rare species, by developing public interest and legal protection and by promoting scientific research. Located at The Lodge, Sandy, Bedfordshire SG19 2DL (tel. 0767-80551), its quarterly publication is called *Birds*. Membership is now 560,000 and rising fast.

The National Trust with more than 1,703,000 members and looking towards 2 million in the immediate future, is far and away the largest of these groups although perhaps the least political. Indeed, its purpose is to acquire and protect places of historic interest and natural beauty. With a strongly developed regional organisation its main publication, *National Trust Magazine*, nevertheless eminates from its headquarters at 36 Queen Anne's Gate, London SW1H 9AS (tel. 01-222-9251). A very glossy product, it is published three times a year.

The Royal Society for Nature Conservation at The Green,

Nettleham, Lincoln LN2 2NR (tel. 0522-752326), has as its objectives the conservation of nature and the education of the public about the need for conservation, although it is keen to promote research and study in this field. *Natural World* appears three times a year and is primarily designed to inform the 250,000 members of this Royal Society.

The Council for the Protection of Rural England, and its counterpart in Wales, keep a watchful eye on all issues relating to the rural environment, seeking to influence the policy making process whenever possible. Although the English organisation lobbies its causes centrally from its headquarters at Warwick House, 25-27 Buckingham Palace Road, London SW1W OPP (tel. 01-976-6433), it has a county structure with some 40,000 members in England. Its magazine is entitled *Countryside Campaigner*. With a membership of 3,000 its Welsh counterpart has a similar organisation. Its magazine is *Rural Wales* and is available from Tŷ Gwyn, 31 High Street, Welshpool, Powys SY21 7JP (tel. 0938-2525). Both publications appear three times a year.

The Ramblers' Association is one of the most specific pressure groups since its aim is the provision of public access to the countryside. Operating from 1-5 Wandsworth Road, London SW8 2XX (tel. 01-582-6878), it is really a federation of more than 300 local ramblers' organisations. Its membership is 70,000 to whom *The Rambler* is sent four times a year. In wider circulation is *The Ramblers' Year book and Accommodation Guide*, a new publishing initiative. It can be purchased from book-sellers.

The Council for National Parks at 45 Shelton Street, London WC2H 9HJ (tel. 01-240-3603), tries to promote public support for and the enjoyment of national parks as well as protecting them. Composed of representatives of thirty constituent organisations concerned with amenity, recreation and wildlife, it is an active lobbyist, but is frequently consulted by government. It publishes *Tarn and Tor*, three times a year for individual members of the public who belong to its associated organisation, Friends of the National Parks.

Friends of the Earth is the first of the two organisations with a different *raison d'être* from the others. The most prominent of the new wave of international environmental groups, it unites the traditional interests of conservation with the more radical global concerns of environmental pollution, the destruction of natural resources and safe energy. With a membership of 105,000 it puts out a quarterly, *Earth Matters*, but also produces from its headquarters at 26-28 Underwood Street, London N1 7JQ (tel. 01-490-1555), a monthly newsletter for its local groups.

Finally, UK 2000 which operates with government funding as well as private sponsorship, nevertheless pursues an independent national environmental campaign to create more and better quality work in the environment, bringing people and organisations together to this end. It produces a quarterly newsletter *UK 2000 News* and publicises its work on individual projects from its offices at Unit 101, Butler's Wharf Business Centre, 45 Curlew Street, London SE1 2ND (tel. 01-378-1847).

Index

nb — page numbers in *italics* refer to maps and illustrations